"This ferociously researched book proves that a fresh set of methods can teach us something new about even this much-studied author. Barchas's innovative evidence base steers a middle course between traditional interest in letters, diaries, and published criticism and the interest in kitsch collectibles and fan fiction that began several decades ago."

—LEAH PRICE, author of *How to Do Things with Books in Victorian Britain*

"Janine Barchas demonstrates that literary works are canonized not by first editions, but by cheap reprints. This is a strikingly innovative approach to the history of reading, which illuminates how popular books become Great Books."

—JONATHAN ROSE, author of *The Intellectual Life of the British Working Classes*

"Before Jane Austen was great, she was popular. Thanks to Barchas's tremendous talents as book historian and book sleuth, we have new tools with which to assess that popularity and a new model of how to write reception history."

—DEIDRE SHAUNA LYNCH, author of *Loving Literature: A Cultural History*

"Janine Barchas's new book makes a fascinating breakthrough in print history, opening up a fresh 'everyday' history of publishing and reading that goes far beyond elite publishers and libraries. A scholarly performance not to be missed."

—JON KLANCHER, author of *Transfiguring the Arts and Sciences: Knowledge and Cultural Institutions in the Romantic Age*

"In this groundbreaking, exquisitely researched, and stunningly illustrated book, Janine Barchas uncovers the unsung and ordinary editions—the 'lost' books— that profoundly shaped Austen's afterlife and evolving literary reputation. It's absolutely delightful to discover, thanks to Barchas, all that we've missed."

—DEVONEY LOOSER, author of *The Making of Jane Austen*

A major new work by Janine Barchas, an outstanding critic both of Jane Austen and of book history. *The Lost Books of Jane Austen* is cogent and persuasive."

—PETER SABOR, editor of *The Cambridge Companion to "Emma"*

The

Lost

Books

of

Jane

Austen

THE
LOST
BOOKS
OF
JANE
AUSTEN

Janine Barchas

Johns Hopkins
University Press
Baltimore

© 2019 Johns Hopkins University Press
All rights reserved. Published 2019
Printed in Canada on acid-free paper
9 8 7 6 5 4 3 2 1

Johns Hopkins University Press
2715 North Charles Street
Baltimore, Maryland 21218-4363
www.press.jhu.edu

Library of Congress Cataloging-in-Publication Data

Names: Barchas, Janine, author.
Title: The lost books of Jane Austen / Janine Barchas.
Description: Baltimore : Johns Hopkins University Press, 2019. | Includes
 bibliographical references and index.
Identifiers: LCCN 2018055373 | ISBN 9781421431598 (hardcover : alk. paper) |
 ISBN 1421431599 (hardcover : alk. paper) | ISBN 9781421431604 (electronic) |
 ISBN 1421431602 (electronic)
Subjects: LCSH: Austen, Jane, 1775–1817—Appreciation. | Austen, Jane,
 1775–1817-Bibliography. | Authors and publishers—Great Britain—History. |
 Literature publishing—Great Britain—History. | Authors and
 readers—Great Britain—History. | Authors and publishers—United States—
 History. | Literature publishing—United States—History. |
 Authors and readers—United States—History.
Classification: LCC PR4037 .B35 2019 | DDC 823/.7—dc23
LC record available at https://lccn.loc.gov/2018055373

A catalog record for this book is available from the British Library.

*Special discounts are available for bulk purchases of this book. For more information,
please contact Special Sales at 410-516-6936 or specialsales@press.jhu.edu.*

Johns Hopkins University Press uses environmentally friendly book materials,
including recycled text paper that is composed of at least 30 percent post-
consumer waste, whenever possible.

For my sister

CONTENTS

PREFACE

Cheap books make authors canonical.

In the latter half of the nineteenth century, cheap and shoddy versions of Jane Austen's novels performed the heavy lifting of bringing her work and reputation before the general public. Inexpensive reprints and early paperbacks of Austen were sold at Victorian railway stations for one or two shillings, traded for soap wrappers, awarded as book prizes in schools, and targeted to Britain's working classes. At just pennies a copy, Austen's novels were also squeezed into tight columns on thin paper. Few of these hard-lived books survive. Yet such scrappy versions of her novels made a substantial difference to Austen's early readership. These were the books bought and read by ordinary people. And these are the books that, owing to their low status and production values, remain uncollected by academic libraries and largely unremarked by scholars. These are the lost books of Jane Austen.

Jane Austen's early reception has effectively been sanitized, creating a falsely decorous sense of how her writerly reputation rose and flourished by the end of the nineteenth century. For once, however, the Victorians are not to blame. The standard view of Austen's reception maintains that the Victorians refashioned her reputation to suit their starched ideal of a proper woman writer. For the so-called Victorianizing of Austen, scholars already blame the biographies by her relatives that promoted the genteel image of "dear Aunt Jane," a public image reinforced by a falsified author portrait from 1870 so influential and ubiquitous that it now circulates on the ten-pound note. In addition, scholars already condemn Victorian sensibilities for prompting Cassandra, who outlived her sister by nearly three decades and became a staunch elderly Victorian lady, to purge letters that might have revealed a freer spirit than the one recorded in the small cache of surviving correspondence. Fingers are even occasionally pointed at nineteenth-century book illustrators who dressed Austen's characters in Victorian-era costumes, repackaging her novels in aesthetics out of step with the Georgian era they depict. I too have airily joined in the academic blame-game of accusing the Victorians for narrowing access to Austen by censoring her biography and remaking her in their own image.

However, a great part of Austen's reputational narrowing is of a much more recent date. Even lamentations about the evil Victorian corseting of Austen's writerly reputation rely upon a contracted set of editions of her work, making them serve as an index of her rising status and public reach. As a result, even the adjusted modern view remains, at best, only a partial picture of Austen's afterlife. History has culled its shelves of the tatty and common Austens produced in heaps by nineteenth-century publishers, leaving only the authoritative and elegant editions granted a scholarly seal of approval. In Britain, the waste-paper drives of both world wars ensured that many cheap editions deemed unimportant were simply pulped. In America, ill-placed concerns about acidic paper resulted in nineteenth-century books being tossed and guillotined by librarians who favored storage on microfilm.[1] In effect, subsequent generations have sanitized, or Victorianized, the shelves of the Victorians, who themselves "bewailed the fearful multiplication of books" and the indecorous manner in which cheap literature was making all manner of reading newly accessible to the hatless masses.[2] When it comes to Austen, it's time to put some of her embarrassingly lowbrow versions back on the shelves so that all of us, scholars and fans alike, can see how her burgeoning literary reputation was not the tidy accretion of polish, status, and starch that we, too, have inadvertently made it out to be.

Let's democratize Jane Austen's reception history by including the cheap versions read by working-class readers, nonscholars, and schoolchildren. These versions were seldom abridged; they offered her stories in their entirety. Yet, in spite of including the same complete stories, in these popular reprints Austen looks different from the novelist of standard accounts that are focused on precious "firsts." First editions of her novels in Britain and America dominate discussions of Austen's early reception, followed closely by the "authoritative" and elegant reprintings safely housed in rare-book libraries. Original, authoritative, and handsome editions in the nineteenth century helped Austen's early visibility, to be sure, but so did the numerous unrecorded reprints at the bottom end of the book market—the latter in messy and startling ways. By literally cheapening Austen, these versions made her an everyday writer whose public appeal differed radically from that of the official canonical author proffered and supported by those fine editions.

In this book, I mix hardcore bibliography with the tactics of the *Antiques Roadshow*. My narrative of "lost books" will probably surprise even the most ardent Janeite collector. Everything here certainly surprised me. How I came to stray from scholarly libraries to eBay and beyond, shifting from bibliographical critic to reluctant hunter of bookish rubbish, is an odd story. It all began in 2010 with a phone call from a distraught teacher at my daughter's all-girl school. The teacher, now my friend, wanted to talk about teaching *Pride and Prejudice* for the first time to her sixth-graders. Knowing her choice was ambitious, she had expected the book to challenge her savvy 11- to 12-year-olds but could not account for their response to Mr. Darcy. "Janine," she said with a hint of despair, "all the girls seem to think he's a vampire. I just don't know where they're getting this idea." After exchanging incredulities, I asked what edition the class was using. A straightforward Teen Edition from HarperCollins had been ordered by the school administrator as suitably inexpensive—one with a floral cover, reasonably large type, and no scholarly footnotes to impede the reading experience. Unfamiliar with the Twilight series, both the administrator and the teacher missed the cover's deliberate mimicry of Stephenie Meyer's vampire romances, with their telltale aesthetic of red, white, and black. The students were reacting to the packaging and not the story.

After a good chuckle, we decided to turn this misapprehension into a teaching moment. I offered to visit the sixth grade armed with other Austen editions from my shelves. What a great lesson this would be for the girls about not judging books by their covers. Seeing that most of my own editions were scholarly and rather austere, I took a trip to two local used bookstores to load up on cheap reading editions with a range of cover designs. I brought my bag of books to the sixth graders, who took my expertise on Austen for granted with the same faith as they assumed my intimate familiarity with the Twilight series. It was a fun session. But after that bag sat around the house for another few weeks, it nagged at me. How aggressively had Austen's early publishers turned covers into alluring marketing canvases? Had far earlier editions of Austen foreshadowed Stephenie-Meyer-style branding? Would I even recognize marketing cues embedded in a cover from long ago? First editions of Austen in the 1810s sold in plain boards or leather bindings, but how had cheap reprints looked to buyers in the nineteenth or early-twentieth centuries? Had cheap versions even existed, early on? Or had Austen mostly been read by the nineteenth-century elite? The standard bibliography showed no cover art and rarely described exteriors. The internet beckoned.

By browsing, I soon found versions absent from the usual inventories. At first, I collected only images, built slideshows, and gave talks about the mercurial appearances of Austen in different book formats and eras. I soon began to hanker after these marvelously lowbrow book dregs, even though my bibliographical training stopped me from granting these volumes interpretive weight or authority. After all, these were not the serious versions quoted by genuine scholars. Ergo, mine was not a serious scholarly Austen project. But thanks to academic tenure, I could indulge my curiosity. As I showed unknown books that cut against the grain of a stable and genteel Austen, my audiences grew in numbers and enthusiasm. Covers proved a popular topic, and I was invited to share some of my finds in a back-pager for the Book Review section of the *New York Times*.

Popularity and scholarship have always been uneasy bedfellows, however. The larger the number of unsung versions turning up on eBay and the like, the more I became aware of an uncomfortable elitism about my own stubborn professional attitude toward these reprints and their packaging. By then my shelves teemed with hundreds of cheap old Austens rarely included in the historical record and never professionally valued. What kinds of people had read them? Before I could determine the impact of these books, I needed to find out more—about original prices, publishing practices, and the history of reading.

Academic libraries collect editions, but people read books. Identifying and safeguarding important editions for posterity is the good work performed by academic libraries. Lending libraries, on the other hand, provide copies for reading, and those books tend to be replaced as soon as they wear out. Scholars know this distinction and have developed a set of tools that privilege the stable holdings of academic libraries. Their resulting bibliographical inventories offer in-depth data about landmark editions but skim over many of the derivative reprints owned by ordinary readers. When scholars talk to one another, they again cite a narrow range of important editions. This is fine for much of the critical work that scholars do, which requires anchoring references in definitive texts that are free from error. Claims about reception history and cultural engagement, however, demand a different approach.

Austen scholars are not alone in ignoring working-class readerships, and historian Jonathan Rose has shown how some of that missing reading history might be recovered from personal diaries, library ledgers, correspondence, and memoirs.[3] Unfortunately, and as Rose observes, although his sources "are quite forthcoming about books and authors read, they only occasionally mention specific editions."[4] And yet those absent specifics matter, because working-class readers did not just borrow from lending libraries but benefited from the proliferation of cheap books at ever-lower prices. In the 1830s, when the first Austen reprints appeared, 57 percent of Bristol's poor families owned Bibles or prayer books, but 27 percent had no books whatsoever. By the early 1930s, however, a survey of a "mainly working-class London neighborhood" found that "only 6 percent of households possessed fewer than six books, while 23 percent had more than a hundred."[5] In other words, book ownership among the British working poor grew rapidly and exponentially during the first century of Austen's afterlife. For example, by 1930 the family of one Soho dustman, living over a secondhand bookstore, had accumulated 750 volumes. Such cheap books, so vitally important to working-class readers, are often absent from the official record. To build a clearer narrative about Austen's reception, I became a champion of those lost editions.

Yet this book is not just about Jane Austen. She is a convenient lens on a much larger set of phenomena. Her inexpensive reprints suggest an inventory of ordinary readers extending well beyond the reception of a single author. Partly owing to timing, Austen's reputation has benefited from every significant modern innovation in the making and marketing of cheap books over the past two centuries. That reception history, starting in earnest with her first reprintings in the 1830s, doubles as the story of the increasingly inexpensive book. Whenever Austen appears in a low-priced publisher's series, she is accompanied by other writers similarly benefiting from innovations. But whereas many of her companions fell in and out of fashion, the sustained public interest in Austen allows her uninterrupted reprintings to narrate how cheaper bindings and new printing practices disseminated popular literature among the working classes. Although my account of unsung books may surprise diehard Janeiacs and collectors the most, I hope it will also speak to those broadly interested in the modern history of reading and publishing.

By championing the cheapest books, I challenge the narrow collecting strategies of academic libraries and scholars. Commonly held assumptions among editorial, analytical, and bibliographical practices continue to filter book-collecting practices by means of elite criteria about "authoritative" editions. Because the technical vocabulary of bibliography does not bother to record all the runs of reprints made from the same stereotype plates, most elite libraries have slighted the derivative trade in cheap repackaged reprints, judging that such books are not proper "editions." But even if my revisionist argument proves convincing, it will be hard to reverse established collecting policies. That is because cheap early reprints have now largely disappeared—pulped in paper drives or read to bits. Even though some of their original runs were in the tens of thousands, and a few over a hundred thousand, many of the "lost" books shown in my illustrations are far more rare today than copies of the tiny runs of Austen's first editions—estimated between five hundred and two thousand—painstakingly safeguarded by collectors and libraries.

Without access to Austen's mass-market reprints, gift books, and so-called school editions, fans and scholars have not grasped the full range of her popular reach. Cheap books adjust the prevailing tale of Austen's rise and reception. Striking differences, for example, between the early marketing of Austen's books in nineteenth-century America and her early presence in Britain remain visible only across inexpensive reprints. Softly cartelized publishing practices made the nineteenth-century American trade in Austen more modest in runs and readers than scholars have speculated. We have overestimated her early American reach while mischaracterizing her readership in nineteenth-century Britain. We looked for similarity where there was difference. Compared to the crowded competition in Britain at a dizzying range of price points, the nineteenth-century American market for Austen was a thin and lackluster affair. Only in Britain did Austen's strong presence among the earliest paperbacks published for working-class readers prove her recruitability for radical and conservative projects alike. Then suddenly, in the second half of the twentieth century, a new generation of cheap paperbacks changed global perceptions about her readership along gendered lines. Thus, Austen's least-studied reprintings expose the true fault lines in her reception history.

In the main chapters of my book, I show how these neglected reprintings track important publishing trends over two centuries: the use of book covers as marketing canvas; the emergence of the popular paperback; books as commercial giveaways; religious-book packaging; and the rise of "chick lit." Along the way, I acknowledge the influence of technical advances such as stereotyping and railway travel on book ownership and show how other factors—from early legislation for universal education to Hollywood films—pushed and pulled Jane Austen's popularity.

Between my wide-angled arguments, I zoom in on "lost" copies of Austen—privately owned, unstudied survivors whose extraordinary ordinariness remains unappreciated by historians or literary scholars. I label these shorter provenance histories or book bios "vignettes," a term derived from the small ornamental "vines" once separating chapters in hand-press books. Each vignette presents a palpable example of subjects expanded on in the thematic chapters. Although I did not intentionally shape my selection to demonstrate the wide range of Austen's audience, these minibiographies of copies and their owners cross boundaries of gender, age, class, nation, and economics. I never expected to find her being read from Hampton Court Palace to the tenements of the working poor, in Scotland and France as well as America, or by aging sea captains as well as school girls—and simultaneously. I simply chose these stray copies for their capacity to humanize my more general arguments about early marketing practices, price points, and technology.

All the copies discussed here deserve a permanent place in Austen's reception history. Only some belong to me, but most are in private hands, and I gratefully acknowledge the many collectors who helped. Admittedly, my book is not an exhaustive inventory of all the hidden Austens that survive, for such a reconstruction will take many more years and more book hunters. Nonetheless, these battered survivors prove that Austen's progress toward canonicity was far more kinetic and colorful than previously assumed. I am now unabashed in my enthusiasm for the shoddy and quirky reprintings of Austen's novels that were previously thought unworthy of critical notice. That is because I believe that Jane Austen's place in the literary canon is now so firmly and deservedly fixed, her reputation so robust, that it can withstand the acknowledgment that before she was great, she was popular.

The

Lost

Books

of

Jane

Austen

V.I.1. Gertrude Wallace's copy of *Sense and Sensibility* in Railway Library series (London: George Routledge and Co., 1851). Original printed boards. Author's collection.

Vignette I
Marianne & Gertrude

Struggles with genteel poverty in *Sense and Sensibility* map onto the ownership history of this modest "One Shilling" reprint from 1851 (figure V.I.1).

The Victorian books that sold in simple printed paper boards were distributed via bookstalls and newspaper vendors in railway stations, anticipating today's airport paperbacks. Published by George Routledge, the Railway Library's brassy tagline read: "The cheapest books ever published." Being cheap, these books were not built to last, so both the paper and the binding of this copy have, understandably, deteriorated. In addition, the title page has been awkwardly sheared on two sides, likely to remove a previous owner's signature, traces of which remain visible. The book has been reinscribed, however, in a clear, educated hand in black ink (figure V.I.2). This time, the signature was placed defiantly in the center, at a strong diagonal, across the title:

Gertrude Wallace
Plymouth

If Gertrude had indeed scissored an earlier owner's name from the title page, she clearly intended that no one should ever do the same with *her* signature. This forceful claim seems out of proportion with the modesty of a one-shilling book.

One person only by the name of Wallace appears in the 1852–53 City Directory for Plymouth, Devon: "Wallace Captain James R.N. 2 Alfred Place."[1] In 1851, the census confirms that this address was also the home of Gertrude Wallace, then 13 years old. At 2 Alfred Place lived James Wallace (62), his aptly named wife Marianne (48), and their three daughters:

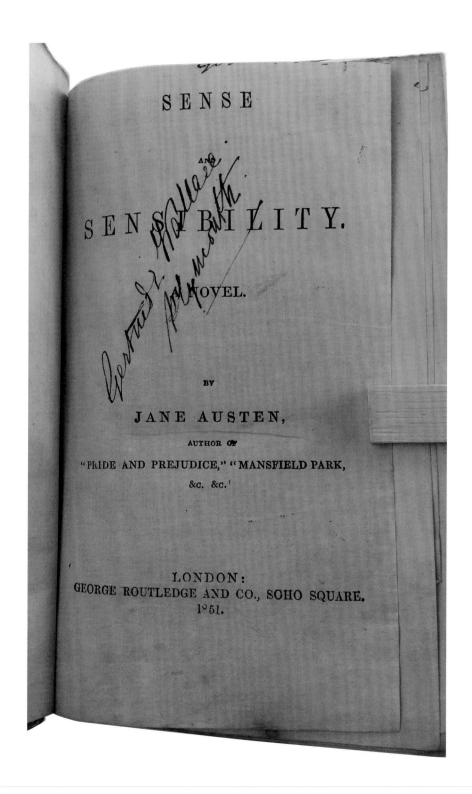

V.I.2. Trimmed title page with inscription "Gertrude Wallace / Plymouth." Author's collection.

Georgina (22), Isabel (16), and Gertrude (13). The census gives James Wallace's correct naval rank as "Com^r R.N.," just short of captain. His salary seems to have allowed for two live-in servants, one who acted as housemaid and another as cook.[2] The discrepancy in records of James's rank may result from the fact that by the time the 1852–53 city directory was produced, James Wallace—who had probably anticipated retiring to the rank of captain—had died, leaving all his property to his "beloved wife Mary Anne," a variant spelling.[3] That the Plymouth directory places the Wallaces among the "Nobility, Gentry and Clergy" rather than among the city's tradesmen may seem mere affectation now, but it remained—as in Austen's time—an important social distinction. The book's physical fragility, however, reflects the precariousness of social position. The four Wallace women were forced to economize and fend off genteel poverty—just like the Dashwood women of Austen's story.

If the Wallaces purchased this book new at the time of publication, and the trimmed title page allows for prior owners outside the family, they lived cautiously even while the commander was alive. The book was not sold at a train station but in a proper Plymouth bookshop. Embossed on the free endpaper is the oval logo of the bookseller: "W.H. Luke / Printer, Bookseller & Stationer / Bedford St. / Plymouth." Since William Henry Luke had his shop at 33 Bedford Street, which Google confirms was a mere three-minute walk from 2 Alfred Place, it was little effort for one of the Wallaces to buy this inexpensive book at the nearby bookseller. W. H. Luke's was definitely stylish, for it advertised in 1853 as a "Book, Stationer, and Printing establishment by special appointment to her Majesty," catering to a varied clientele with a wide-ranging selection of books as well as "plain and fancy stationery."[4] Luke boasted "books of merit" in a choice of binding styles the same day as published in London, and for books not in stock, orders could be had "per return of mail." Whether or not the 1851 title was a special order, the Wallace sisters purchased their Austen not in the Bentley editions then selling for 3s. 6d., nor even in the sensible Routledge cloth binding option at 2s., but in the cheapest possible version—for one shilling in plain printed boards.

Life on the edge of gentility became increasingly tenuous for the Wallace women. Ten years later, in 1861, the census locates Gertrude (24) and her mother, "Mary A. Wallace" (58), in a lodging house run by a Hester Cox in the seaside town of Weston-super-Mare, in Somerset. Georgina and Isabel remain untraced. Other occupants include Charles (27) and Robert Griffith (25), a "Classical Tutor" and "School Master," who reside there with their father.[5] Neither of the scholarly Griffiths appears to have caught the eye of Gertrude, who remained single. A further decade hence, in 1871, Gertrude, now 34, and her mother, Mary Ann, aged 68, still rent rooms from Hester Cox at number 4 Royal Crescent, a good central street where many other such lodgers lived, including an elderly "colonel's widow" with her "companion." By then, the Griffiths have been replaced by another tutor of classics (age 38) and a bachelor banker (24).[6] If Georgina and Isabel did make splendid marriages, their husbands failed to provide lavishly for their mother and spinster sister. No rich cousin came to offer Marianne or Gertrude a commodious Devonshire cottage or pluck them out of lodging-house life. Did Gertrude read and reread *Sense and Sensibility*, hoping for an intervention?

Census descriptions under "Rank, Profession, or Occupation" tend to be thin, especially for women, and in 1871 Mary Ann Wallace remains defined by her husband's death: "naval commander's widow." Gertrude, on the other hand, is no longer described as "daughter" but as "professor of music." In the census, school-age children were routinely termed "scholars" and many types of teachers labeled "professor." That is, the entry may simply mean that Gertrude taught music lessons to paying pupils, or it may indicate that she worked more officially as music instructor at the nearby National School, a college that had operated since 1845 at the corner of Knightstone and Lower Church Roads, a four-minute walk from her lodgings. Perhaps connections made at the boarding house helped her obtain a formal teaching post. Whatever Gertrude's true job description, that self-same spirit who boldly staked her claim across Austen's title page still insisted, twenty years later, upon independent recognition.

Coincidence between fact and fiction invites connections between a book's provenance and its content, especially since a sheet of music holds together the green paper boards of Gertrude's copy. Over time, the loss of the book's spine exposed the scrap of music beneath—which Gertrude herself may not have known was there. This remnant of music may provide a final echo of Gertrude's circumstances. On the outside is a bass line using a standard classical era technique known as the Alberti bass, arpeggiated chords to accompany melodies. Since such notations can be found for the music of Mozart, Haydn, and popular tunes of the mid-nineteenth century, it could be from any number of pieces. On the other side of the remnant, two bars of the melody line remain visible tucked inside the binding. Sadly, not enough notes survive to identify the actual song, but I suspect it is a complex melody.

AUSTEN ON THE CHEAP

It is well known that Jane Austen's reputation lay dormant for fifteen years or so following her death in 1817. The orthodox view is that she reached a wider English audience only after Richard Bentley (1794–1871) revived her work for his Standard Novels reprint series in 1833. But Bentley, although he was a catalyst, is not the true hero of this Sleeping-Beauty story.

His books were also not as cheap and accessible as scholars, taking Bentley's advertisements at their word, have assumed. Bentley emphasized the inexpensive nature of his handsomely produced compact volumes, ornamented with elegant frontispiece illustrations and title-page vignettes: "price only 6s." and "Cheap Edition."[1] He was an early adopter of publisher-issued bindings in cloth, and his prices reflected not only the paper savings of his three-in-one-volume format but also the sudden freedom from traditional leather bindings. Scholars have amply recorded and praised Bentley's reprintings of Austen as "Standard Novels," stressing their authority (that is, he paid for proper copyrights) and importance as Austen's reputational turnkey.[2] As a result of this attention, Bentley's sedate volumes are now highly sought after. However, Bentley's influence upon Austen's reception may be greatly overplayed, for his books were quickly joined by far cheaper versions with a wider impact. The role of these less-princely reprints has been largely ignored in the dominant fairytale version of Austen's reception.

My focus is therefore not on Bentley's well-touted reprints but on the neglected books of his down-market competitors. Bentley's prices and his own claims to cheapness, however, do help to calibrate what came next. In 1811, the first edition of *Sense and Sensibility* had sold in three volumes for fifteen shillings in boards—a proper binding remained extra.[3] In December 1815, advertisements for the first edition of *Emma* raised that price by six shillings to a guinea, or £1.1s., for its three volumes in boards.[4] Hand-press books in Austen's lifetime remained luxury items, and her novels appeared in modest runs—possibly as low as 750 for *Sense and Sensibility* and as high as 2,000 copies for *Emma*.[5] Then, in 1833, Bentley introduced his well-made reprints of Miss Austen in single volumes at six shillings each in durable publisher's bindings of plum-colored linen, or maroon-ribbed cloth, with paper labels.[6] Royal A. Gettmann, the first chronicler of Bentley's Standard Novels series, points out that "the expenditure on advertising was liberal" and costs high enough so that "the break-even point was about 3300 copies," with average runs per title under 4,000.[7] Years later, fellow publisher George Routledge remarked of the early nineteenth century that "in those days an edition of 500 was considered large, and one of 2,000 enormous."[8] Thus, Bentley's runs were ambitious for the time and his six-shilling price tag comparatively low. By means of *stereotyping,* a new method of reprinting that led to cheaper book prices, Bentley periodically continued to reissue identical Austen volumes through 1866; he briefly lowered his price still further in the 1840s. Meanwhile, the cost for an upmarket first edition of a new novel in the three-decker format made popular by Sir Walter Scott stubbornly held at £1. 11s. 6d. until the mid 1890s.[9] No wonder, then, that scholars, comparing Bentley's prices to those for first editions, have hailed him as Austen's reputational Prince Charming.

Bentley's relative bargains certainly pushed Austen into public visibility, but his six-shilling reprints were still not within easy reach for a skilled worker earning twenty shillings per week, let alone an unskilled laborer earning half that wage.[10] Even with books at six shillings, bookselling remained "a peculiarly rotten system of providing only for the select few."[11] In 1846, after the copyright of Austen's first three novels expired and competition by upstart publishers increased, the fastidious Bentley was briefly forced to drop his price to 2s.6d. per volume, adjusted by 1848 to 3s.6d.[12] Surviving Bentley copies of Austen from this period are rare, but those in their original publisher's bindings bear witness on their spines to his momentary drop in price, itself a fraught response to the radical changes in the marketplace wrought by cheaper fare (figure I.1). With his books selling for 2s.6d. and 3s.6d., before climbing safely back to his preferred six-shilling rung, Bentley briefly found himself slumming it—offering Austen at roughly one-twelfth to one-ninth the cost of brand new fiction. Inside, the original endpapers of these rare Bentley survivors claim: "Cheapest Collection of Novels in the English Language." Even so, Bentley's much-hailed "cheap" books remained the purview of well-to-do Victorian clients such as socialite Lady Molesworth of Pencarrow, who owned a complete set of his Austens, dated 1856, in an aftermarket binding of green publisher's cloth prettily stamped with a gilt design.[13] Far cheaper reprintings of Austen in astonishingly large numbers and unprecedented variety were then newly reaching working-class audiences. Fluctuating production values, including paper quality, meant that not all of these other nineteenth-century versions aged well. Few ended up in libraries. And yet these other reprints, dismissed as dubious by all but the occasional antiquarian in favor of the sturdier stuff of authoritative firsts or scholarly editions, nevertheless launched Austen's global celebrity.

By tracking the most popular author since Shakespeare through her least authoritative incarnations, I urge a more inclusive reception history.[14] These urgings occasionally read against the grain of bibliographical values that have deep-rooted prides and prejudices. In 1905, Henry James sneered at Austen's proliferation in "pretty reproduction in every variety of what is called tasteful, and in what seemingly proves to be saleable form."[15] From such a rarefied point of view, bibliography itself goes slumming in my project, for I seek to raise to scholarly visibility the schlockiest of Austen reprints: tawdry shilling or sixpence versions sold at the bookstalls of nineteenth-century railway stations, penny and halfpenny serializations, schmaltzy Victorian gift books, giveaways in advertising campaigns, reprints for coal miners in a religious temperance society, flimsy wartime formats for soldiers, and a plethora of dodgy paperbacks

I.1. Copies of Jane Austen's novels in the Standard Novels and Romances series published by Richard Bentley in 1846. In original publisher's binding, with price "2/6" stamped on spines. Collection of Sandra Clark.

for all manner of readers. The books I discuss practice crude sensationalism and commit fashion errors. Many contain sloppy misprints and some prove deeply misguided in their choice of decoration or embellishment. I overlook these flaws in the search for a more complete picture of the immense range of formats and communities that participated in Jane Austen's literary celebrity over the first two centuries of her literary afterlife.[16] I risk bibliographical misdemeanors in the interest of a fuller and more hands-on reckoning of Austen's popular reception.

Many other scholars have already written articulately about the Cult of Jane.[17] For the most part, however, the author's fame continues to be measured by the published responses from critics, scholars, and fellow writers—usually led by Sir Walter Scott, who famously reviewed *Emma* in 1816—rather than by the manner in which her books were marketed to the general public.[18] In my criticism of the narrowness of Austen studies, I join voices with Devoney Looser, whose recent book *The Making of Jane Austen* brought to light many early Austen influencers unrecognized by the academy. Both she and I remark on the perpetual recruitability of Jane Austen for this or that ideological cause. Similarly, Annika Bautz has let fresh air into the vaults of Austen scholarship with research into sixpenny editions of *Pride and Prejudice,* drawing attention to a neglected working-class format.[19] As James's sneer indicates, the lowbrow reprints of Austen, so popular with reading publics beyond the academy, have long been passed over for treasured first editions. Even so, the history of pearly firsts does not string together into the strong chain of reception history.

Admittedly, important first editions surviving in scholarly libraries may yet tell us more, as Juliette Wells argues in *Reading Austen in America* about the earliest American printings in 1816 and 1832–33.[20] The print runs of these Austen firsts, however, have misled scholars about her American reception. Fluctuations and drops in subsequent demand, including sporadic decades in nineteenth-century America when, to put it bluntly, Jane Austen barely maintained a pulse in the American book market, challenge notions of a presumed "gradual rise of Austen's renown" in America.[21] Her market share in America revived only toward the end of the nineteenth century and by means of iffy and often unrecorded publisher's series, where she played an extra rather than a starring role. And sometimes historians hail the wrong books as "firsts." For example, when it comes to the modern editing of Austen, Kathryn Sutherland claimed that, in 1923, Oxford University Press editor R. W. Chapman forged a crucial "first" that laid down a template for future modern editions.[22] And yet, to grant Chapman's edition that status is to ignore the trailblazing "school edition" of his wife, Katharine Metcalfe.[23] An unrelenting selectivity regarding which books are worthy of study and ownership has made even the best academic discussions and the most detailed historical accounts of Austen's reception history relatively clipped and top-heavy affairs. The exclusionary choices of Austen's established bibliographical record demand revision, because they have painted the wrong picture of Austen's early reputation.

Sir Geoffrey Keynes (1887–1982) and David Gilson (1938–2014), Jane Austen's two most influential bibliographers, shaped the collecting strategies of librarians and individuals who turn to scholarly inventories to find out which editions are worth keeping. Keynes's groundbreaking *Jane Austen: A Bibliography* (1929) and Gilson's more voluminous *A Bibliography of Jane Austen* (1982) are monumental contributions to the study of Jane Austen.[24] Current scholars of Austen, including me, continue to rely upon Gilson, whose bibliography remains an indispensable and oft-cited reference text. Inadvertently, however, Keynes and Gilson constrict current understanding of Austen by narrowing down the versions of her books retained for study. Alberta Hirshheimer Burke (1906–1975), the best-known private collector of Austen, is a case in point. Her habit of heavily annotating with clippings from bookseller catalogs her copy of Keynes's 1929 bibliography reveals that Austen's best-known collector identified important books by using Keynes as a checklist against potential purchases.[25] Tellingly, the greatest diversity among the books in her collection may be found among reprints published between 1930 and her death in 1975, years for which no bibliography yet existed to guide her. Burke's collection, in turn, played a role in shaping Gilson's expanded bibliography, especially after the American bibliophile struck up a lasting friendship with the British scholar.[26] Burke's approach remains typical of most collectors, whether private or institutional, for bibliophiles and library curators alike rely on official scholarly bibliographies to identify what books they should purchase or preserve.[27]

David Gilson's own collection of Austen books, now at King's College, Cambridge, reveals a startlingly different picture from that in his published bibliography. Karen Attar alone notices that "the view of books on the shelves makes immediately clear points about publishing trends which can be gained from a bibliography only by concentrated and focused searching." Attar marvels that "most of the editions in the Gilson collection are, or were at their time of publication, cheap, meant to be accessible for the poorest people."[28] It is therefore not the case that all cheap versions of Austen's stories go unrecorded by Gilson only because his 1982 bibliography, submitted to the press in 1978, did not enjoy the benefit of online catalogs, image databases, or Internet commerce—although that is surely true for some missed copies. Few of his subsequent findings made it into the 1997 reprinting of his bibliography.[29] For books at the bottom end of the market, his technical inventory and bibliographical language also remain quiet about publisher's bindings or print runs. His book carries few images, and those few depict only major firsts. My project is heavily illustrated because seeing the actual books is crucial to understanding both their intended audiences and Austen's changing reputation. Attar, a curator of rare books, recognized only when looking at the physical books that Austen "is most startlingly an author of the people"; she saw that the many "cheap Victorian editions" owned by Gilson give the lie to Brian Southam's assessment that during the Victorian era, "by the public at large, she was forgotten."[30] Gilson and Southam formed part of a scholarly generation keen to cement the literary seriousness of Jane Austen. In his bibliography, Gilson sought to establish Austen's canonicity by singling out certain editions for special notice, especially the well-produced books that conveyed a growing professional respect and investment in Austen: first reprinting, first illustrations, first translations, first luxury edition, and so forth. Other scholars, in turn, chose the editions worth studying or collecting by following his lead. Scholarship has thus underemphasized Austen's presence among the flotsam and jetsam of the nineteenth and twentieth centuries' cheapest books, since being popular among the rabble, as James observed, detracts from an author's importance.

Although Gilson enlarged the inventory of known Austen editions, and the voracious Alberta Burke collected all manner of books postdating Keynes, Gilson's bibliography is still far from an exhaustive record of Austen's iterations in print. The order and discipline that bibliography brought to a chaotic landscape of books have masked Austen's early diversity.

SPECIATION & STEREOTYPING

As Linnaeus knew, categories render the order and meaning of things, but family resemblances among books can be hard to sort. The same stereotype technology that enabled the cheap nineteenth-century book complicates the taxonomy that lies at the heart of bibliography. Both the technology and the taxonomy, therefore, warrant brief explanation in order to understand why so many reprintings of a major author have gone unrecorded.

Many nineteenth-century books claim to be new editions when they are actually older books dressed in the frocks of updated title pages and binding styles. Setting a book anew from loose type was time-consuming and costly and took up much of a printer's stock of type for the production of a single work. But stereotyping, a technology fully adopted by the 1840s, enabled cheap books to flourish by allowing printers to mold and then cast in metal the labor-intensive multipage forms of set type. Publishers could then reorder, from printers who used these flat plates, the same printed text at intervals, whenever existing stock became depleted.[31] Individual print runs could be reduced to several hundred copies instead of thousands, further lowering both the risk of overexposure and the cost of inventory storage. Over time, the stereotype plates wore down, lessening the sharpness of the type in later impressions, but printers nonetheless hailed these slabs of metal for their longevity and capacity to retain their value over decades, given careful handling. Book historian William St. Clair gauges "the long life of stereotypes" in England by tracking one set of Byron plates in a British reprint series from 1868 to 1908. He calculates that it generated between forty and fifty impressions, amounting to more than 170,000 copies across four decades.[32] Whenever a publishing firm thought its own market for a title exhausted, or liquidated assets for other reasons, it could pass on the stereotype plates to another publisher via a private sale or a public trade auction. Publishers of cheap books worked plates to their limits, enthusiastically reprinting and repackaging the same text year after year to make old books look perpetually new.

In addition, publishers often sold copies from the same print run simultaneously in different binding options at different price points—in paper wrappers, in a choice of colored cloths, with or without gilt edges. A bibliographer has traditionally had to disregard such superficial variation, instead identifying and recording textual dissimilarities, distilling significant textual differences, or variants, into an exacting list of proper *editions*. By placing eight bibliographically "identical" versions of *Sense and Sensibility* side by side, however, I offer a starting control, hoping to adjust current bibliographical methods for the wider purposes of reception history (figure I.2). George Routledge of London published all eight of these cheap copies from the same stereotype plates. The earliest copy bears a date of 1851, but all the rest are undated. Whereas the handsome iterations of Bentley's stereotyped reprints of *Sense and Sensibility*, including his "four distinct bindings," receive pages of dedicated explanation that is broken down by year of issue, these eight visually distinct physical objects are reduced in the official bibliographical record to two Routledge editions of *Sense and Sensibility*. Gilson assigns a numbered code to each, E12 or E41: the Railway Library or Ruby series, respectively.

Technical codes aside, bibliographers seize upon similarity rather than difference in describing books, and they often conflate print runs. The bibliographical record for the copy pictured on the far left in green glazed paper boards, dated 1851, neatly matches the Railway Library Series edition that Routledge first published in 1849. Gilson shows that series as reprinted every year between 1850 and 1854 in different binding styles that he does not describe.[33] The bibliographical entry most closely matching the seven remaining copies, all undated, belongs to the Ruby Series of "187_."[34] Only three of the seven remaining copies, however, bear the "Ruby Series" tag, and none match the publisher's imprint in the bibliographical record.[35] Survivors of these cheap books are hard to locate. Gilson himself saw no early examples, declaring outright, "No copy seen."[36] His wording of the imprint dutifully replicates the truncated entry in Keynes rather than quoting, as elsewhere, from the title page of an actual copy. Although he allows that between these two series "there may have been an intermediate Routledge reprinting," it is hard to know whether any of the four Routledge books without either the Railway Library brand or that of the Ruby Series would deserve a separate entry. Gilson admits that he has probably not caught every reprint, but collectors arming themselves with his entries have likewise been unable to locate or envision the full range of Austen's diversity. Once you own one Ruby copy, why would you hunt for another unless you are told to expect variation?

Since bibliographers look beyond the surface, cosmetic differences in

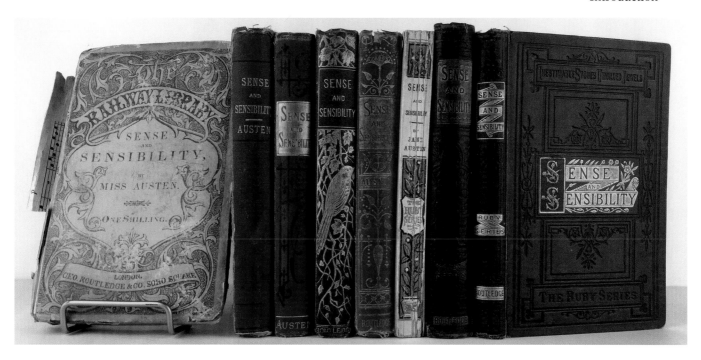

bindings styles go unspecified, being summed up as "paper wrappers or cloth." Similarly, the preliminaries or advertisements bound with texts are used for clues to dating but are not recorded in detail. The key to bibliographical taxonomy turns instead upon the central text, which in all these undated books is identical, printed from the same stereotype plates by the same publisher—with the same words, layout, and page numbers (figure I.3). Then again, although copies of the Railway Library and the Ruby series share that identical text, they get two separate bibliographical entries, because sometime in the 1870s Routledge relaunched Austen as part of a new series. That is to say, Gilson fudges, constructing entries for editions and sometimes, but not always, for a mere reprinting or impression. Technically, these eight books are not separate *editions,* since they contain the same setting of text, but different *impressions* of the same edition, made from the same plates. And there is the bibliographical rub.

The taxonomic category of an *edition* in the age of stereotyping is slippery: "Strictly speaking, an *edition* comprises all copies of a book printed at *any* time or times from one setting-up of type without substantial change."[37]

I.2. Eight bibliographically "identical" cheap copies of *Sense and Sensibility,* published by George Routledge and printed from the same stereotype plates between 1851 and 1883. Collections of Sandra Clark and author.

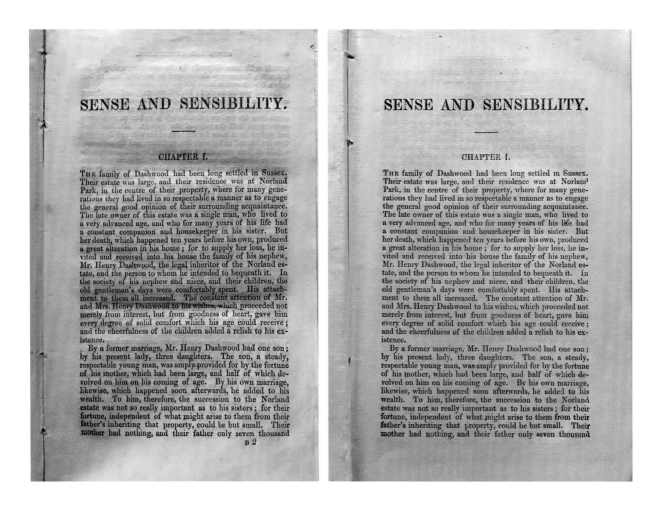

I.3. Opening page of central text of *Sense and Sensibility* in copies from figure I.2 printed decades apart from the same stereotype plate. Author's collection.

An *impression* refers to a printing or reprint run of an *edition* made in one go, without the type or plate being removed from the press. With stereotyping, how much time between print runs by the same publisher from the same plates is enough to warrant a separate bibliographical entry? The bibliographical tipping point for a new entry is subjective. Does the marketing of an old text by Routledge as part of a "new" series, like this switch from Railway Library to Ruby series, truly give rise to a new book? Technically, it should not matter whether a book is marketed in this or that publisher's series or binding style. Cosmetics and prelims are supposed to be ignored in taxonomy. But a change in the imprint wording or address of even the same publisher might require a separate taxonomic number. Of these eight identical—bibliographically speaking—copies of Routledge's *Sense and Sensibility*, most are essentially missing from the official bibliographical record's technical vocabulary and categories (which allows only two entries). More than semantics is at stake here, for these cheap volumes reveal Austen's active participation at the neglected bottom end of the book market, even as they muddy bibliographical waters.

The seven undated versions by Routledge of *Sense and Sensibility*, while bibliographically identical in central text, differ in look, price, and virtue signaling. Their unifying quality, aside from their identical text block, is that they all belong to that class of inexpensive reprints that publisher George Routledge turned into his specialty—from the cheapest at a shilling for the working-class reader to the higher-priced-but-still-sensible versions for two shillings, destined for the home libraries of the middling classes. Publishing houses fanned out according to price. In December 1869, Bentley launched a new premium product in the form of an Author's Edition of Austen, completely reset, "Beautifully Printed," and priced at six shillings per volume—a comfortable return to the firm's original price point of 1833.[38] With this, Bentley's firm abandoned its slide into the Austen down-market, leaving the grubbier trade in the cheaps to publishers such as Routledge and Chapman & Hall, to which it passed on its old 1833 plates of Austen. Thus, in the spring of 1870, Chapman & Hall jumped into the abandoned space with two-shilling versions of all the Austens in picture boards as well as the same books in cloth for half a crown, or 2s.6d., squeezing more life out of Bentley's well-worn plates (figure I.4).[39] Seeing an opportunity to dust off his own Railway Library plates, Routledge quickly announced "Jane Austen's Novels for One Shilling. In fancy cover."[40] The books in figure I.2 suggest that Routledge soon attempted to fill the entire space below Bentley's premium product with a proliferation of cheaper options, at the same time undercutting Chapman & Hall's derivative reprintings. To sort these lowbrow survivors by chronology and potential readerships, I look for the clues that tired copies can still provide about the range of Austen's readers in the Victorian marketplace.

First, let's look at the bindings and inscriptions. Only two out of the seven undated copies of *Sense and Sensibility* sport bindings that are cut, literally, from the same cloth (figure I.5). I suspect that both come from a

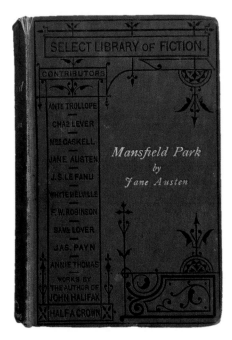

I.4. Copies of *Mansfield Park* made from Bentley's old plates (London: Chapman and Hall, 1870 and 1872). *Left:* In cloth at a half crown, or 2s.6d. Author's collection. *Right:* In picture boards for two shillings. Chester W. Topp collection of Victorian yellowbacks, Stuart A. Rose Manuscript, Archives, and Rare Book Library, Emory University.

five-volume Austen that the *English Catalogue of Books* records as being offered cheaply in 1870, from one shilling per volume in "fancy covers" to a "fine" set at "10s. 6d."[41] It is easy to identify which is the finer of the two survivors in brown cloth, since gilt decoration always cost more. Both styles of binding package *Sense and Sensibility* as part of a potential set, with the plainer, all-purpose casing reading simply "Miss Austen's Novels."[42] The finer copy is stamped with a strong Eastlake design in black, with the title of the specific novel surrounded by bright gilt. On its spine, "AUSTEN" appears where "Routledge" can be found on stand-alone volumes—a telltale mark of a set. The design of this Eastlake binding is tailor-made for an inexpensive publisher's set or series, because each title can be stamped inside the same space on the decorated front board of the cloth casing.[43] In truth, even this copy is not particularly refined, although its frontispiece illustration doubled as a badge of gentility in nineteenth-century books.[44]

The inscription on the finer version shows it to be a gift from a father to

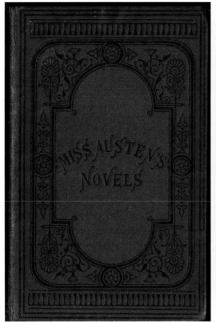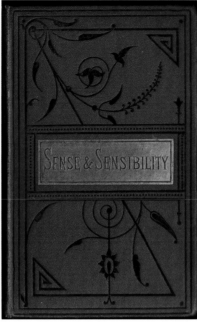

his daughter, providing a concrete date as well as an example of the consumer who bought at the top end of the modest Routledge range:

> *Sybil Daniell*
> *from Father*
> *Bournemouth*
> *Oct: 5th 1870—*

Financier John Henry Daniell (1821–1893) became one of the signatories establishing the Corporation of Foreign Bondholders, formed in 1873 to quell rumors of fraudulent foreign investment schemes by moralizing foreign finance.[45] This formal inscription to his daughter Sybil, who had an October birthday, with the inclusion of her full name, their location, and exact date, reads like a deed of gift and a teaching moment. Here the financier, frugally choosing a fairly inexpensive book, demonstrates to his eldest daughter just how property should be transferred. Did he respond to the opening rhetoric of *Sense and Sensibility*, with its talk about bequests, entails, and moieties, when selecting his gift?

The Daniell family was large and appears to have traveled extensively; this may explain how Sybil's *Sense and Sensibility* became separated from its shelf mates. Daniell, after all, could afford to buy his daughter the full set. The 1871 census places the large and prosperous Daniell family, including 16-year-old Sybil, in the central London parish of St. George's Hanover Square—attended by a nurse, a governess, a "House Keeper & Cook," a butler, two lady's maids, three housemaids, a nursery maid, a kitchen maid, a scullery maid, and two footmen—plus a groom and a married coachman living next door with his wife. Heading this busy household is John Henry, age 49, identified as a "Member of Stock Exchange," and his wife Katharine, age 42. The Daniell children, Henry, Arthur, Sybil, Maud, and John, range in age from 22 to 5. Arthur is an undergraduate at Oxford. At 16, Sybil is listed as "scholar" rather than "single," suggesting that she, too, still pursued her studies.[46] The names Sybil and Maud for the Daniell girls already imply a well-read household—the latter reflecting the popularity of Tennyson. Twenty years later, both Sybil and Maud remain at their old address, presumably running things for their aging father and bachelor brother Arthur, now a barrister.[47] With eleven remaining servants, however, they must have had plenty of time for reading. Sybil Mary Katharine Daniell (1854–1931) likely read a lot of books during her long and well-supplied life, probably even all of Austen. She never married, and at age 77 was buried, in April 1931, at St. Leonard's Church, Chelsham, Surrey, in the same family plot as her father.

In the quest to understand an author's popular reception, every clue about her books is helpful, even when the owners are not scholars and the versions they read editorially insignificant. Thin bibliographical descriptions never intended to conjure up the lives of real readers or the homes into which they brought their copies of Austen. Bibliography exists to compare one book to another. Only recently has the technology become widely available to allow a researcher to locate a name spotted in a book among census, birth, or marriage records without leaving their desk. This ease of access changes the cost-benefit analysis of provenance research for unimportant copies. Remarkably, all eight examples of Routledge's *Sense and Sensibility* survive with names of former owners, though not all provide palpable hits when searched. Victorian readers were proud of their books and keen to protect their property, even when a book's price was relatively low. Demotic reprints may contain data yet unmined, contextual information that anthropologists and sociologists term "thick" description. No matter how bibliographically correct, "thin" descriptions and codes such as "E41" are unsatisfactory tools for reception history. Bibliographers deftly identify textual variants, but they cannot reveal the varied audiences for the different formats of seemingly the same book. Neglected reprints, in their manifold repackagings, need to come back into view. It is fitting that Oxford philosopher Gilbert Ryle (1900–1976) coined the phrase "thick description." When asked if he ever read any novels, Ryle famously replied, "Yes—all six, every year."[48]

Chronologically, the *Sense and Sensibility* in blue cloth bearing the colorful oval illustration on the front comes next, for the name of its owner points to a probable date of 1871 or 1872 (figure I.6). Packaged as a gift book for a juvenile middle-class audience, this copy boasts a gilded bird on the spine and an interlocking border design in black stamped on the front board, with an oval paper onlay that shows a mother and daughter at prayer—behind them a table with a teapot and other dishes. The image implies that Austen is educative and moral reading for young girls within a Christian context. The copy contains a handlist of Routledge's other juvenile series and is carefully inscribed:

> Marion Eddels
> A Birthday present
> from her aff.te
> Friend Alice Halcombe.[49]

The census of 1881 locates one "Marion Eddels," by then 23 years old, living at the elegant address of 5 Campden House Road, Kensington, London, with her mother Anne Eddels, widow and home owner, and one live-in servant. The target age for juvenile gift books was 13 or 14, Marion's ages in 1871 and 1872.[50]

The three volumes emblazoned with the phrase "The Ruby Series" seized upon by Gilson may be dated to at least 1875, when *Sense and Sensibility* first joined that new series as No. 47 (figures I.7 and I.8; see also figure I.2, *far right*). It could be purchased for one shilling "in fancy covers," a stan-

1.6. Gift edition of *Sense and Sensibility* (London and New York: George Routledge and Sons, n.d.) in blue publisher's cloth, with paper onlay. Collection of Sandra Clark.

dard euphemism for decorated paper wrappers.[51] Routledge marketed this series of popular titles by means of a line taken from Richard III: "Inestimable Stones, Unvalued Jewels." By implying as late as 1875 that Austen remained "unvalued," Routledge thumbed its nose at Bentley's editions of Austen among the long-running Standard Novels series, recently recycled by competitor Chapman & Hall. The back cover of this one-shilling paperback includes advertisements of other Ruby titles together with handlists of additional juvenile and Railway books. Roughly sewn, the cheap Ruby paperback was never intended to last. Nevertheless, this paperback jewel was valued by Jeanie Holdsworth, who carefully penned her name at the top of the first free endpaper, already crowded with advertisements for other Routledge publications.

According to the large advertisement on the back of Jeanie's copy, the titles in the new Ruby Series were available for one shilling in paper wrappers, for 1s. 6d. in "cloth, gilt," and for 2s. in "cloth gilt edges." Bling, that is, was extra. Both of the Ruby copies in blue cloth are elaborately stamped in black with titles in gilt. The one with a leafy cannabis-like design also has all its edges gilded and seems inappropriately tricked out for an affordable book at two shillings. Inscribed

Louisa Hernshaw
Minton Sunday School
Dec 31st 1881

it must have made a flashy Sunday school prize. Both of the cloth Ruby copies are bound with the frontispiece illustration reused from the "fine" set of 1870. With a list of "Juvenile Books" at the back

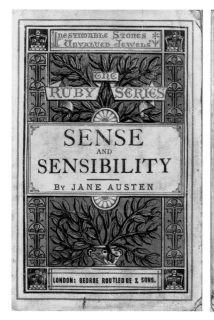
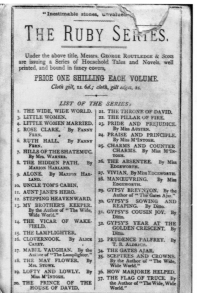
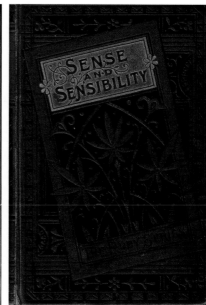

in one and "New Books" from Routledge in the other, both versions typify school reward series (see chapter 3). The cannabis cover design is later in date than the other Ruby series binding style, which belongs to the series launch in 1875.[52] Although the date of the Sunday school inscription does not preclude its having been printed earlier, book prizes tended to be current, edging the example with the cannabis cover to 1880.

The last copy of *Sense and Sensibility* printed by Routledge is a downmarket version in red cloth containing at least one advertisement dating it to the early 1880s, that is, into the next decade (figure I.9, *top*). Production values are low, and the flatly stamped black ironwork pattern is almost completely worn off the front cover. Inside, commercial advertisements hawk medicines, soap, matches, cocoa, watches, and even bank loans—including one for the Birkbeck Building Society's investment schemes whose language resembles similar advertisements in books with definitive dates of 1882 and 1883. These crass ads would have further lowered the printing costs of this shoddily bound book. But none of this prevented J. Owen Woodward from proudly claiming ownership on the title page, underlining his name with an elegant flourish, just opposite the full-page announcement for "Bennett's

I.7. Early paperback of *Sense and Sensibility* in the Ruby Series (London and New York: George Routledge and Sons, n.d.). Collection of Sandra Clark.

I.8. *Sense and Sensibility* in blue publisher cloth of the Ruby Series (London and New York: George Routledge and Sons, n.d.). School book prize inscription dated December 31, 1881. Author's collection.

I.9. *Sense and Sensibility* in stamped red publisher's cloth, bound with original advertisements (London and New York: George Routledge and Sons, n.d.). Author's collection.

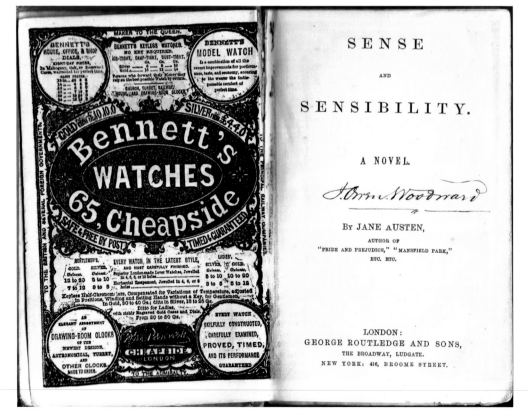

Watches" at "65, Cheapside" (figure I.9, *bottom*). Bibliographers routinely scan advertisements for clues to dating, but Gilson lacked the benefit of seeing any copies of these undated Routledge reprints, let alone seven. Book history becomes a chicken-or-the-egg dilemma when scholars cannot study or record copies unknown to libraries or major collectors.

One incomplete bibliographical entry for seven undated books, all ostensibly the same, is problematic, for each copy may tell a different story. I suggest that the time has come to redefine the genus and species of books by means of a deeper assessment of the cheap stuff—not just the fine edition, but the dodgy reprint that was read and bought by ordinary people, real people with names rather than generic readers conjured up as abstractions. Bibliography, newly augmented with digital tools and search engines, can act as a servant, not an overbearing master, to reception and social history.

MARK TWAIN & THE THAYER SISTERS

The fact that I highlight neglected, lowbrow versions of Austen's books does not mean that the knowledge gained from such copies applies only to obscure readers whose names, even when recorded, are unheard of. Although publishers of books today talk a mean game about "niche audiences" and "market segmentation," grouping readers by price is an old trick that has never been an exact science. When books pass through communities as physical objects over time, the barrier between high and low culture proves permeable, because these inexpensive, ordinary, error-filled Austen reprints reached extraordinary and influential readers as well as many now unknown. Some of Austen's most important critics and fellow writers encountered her in workmanlike copies. After all, everyone likes a bargain. Those who claim special expertise do not necessarily own the most accurate or elegant edition available. Quality or cost is not an index of an owner's fandom or insight, and yet the battle scars of books do tell stories.[53]

Sisters Essie Charlotte Thayer (1868–1953) and Josephine B. Thayer (1871–1961) shared a home, an education at Wellesley College in the classes of 1889 and of 1892, and, after a lifetime together, a grave in Milford, Massachusetts.[54] They also shared a pretty-but-ordinary Routledge reprint of Jane Austen's *Mansfield Park*, undated and bound in a modestly gilded publisher's binding stamped with a decorative design of shell and feathers (figure I.10).[55] Pasted on the inside cover is the bookplate of the two sisters,

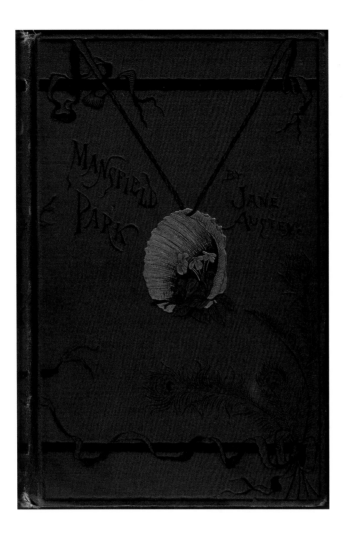

I.10. Copy of *Mansfield Park* (London, Glasgow, Manchester, and New York: George Routledge and Sons, n.d. [circa 1890]), with ex libris of Essie C. and Josephine Thayer. Author's collection.

while on the first blank leaf an inked stamp of their mother's name, Mrs. Thomas B. Thayer, and Josephine's written signature stake additional claims. "Woodfall & Kinder, Printers. 70 to 76 Long Acre, London, W.C." produced the book from the stereotype plates of the 1883 edition. An advertisement section stating the prices of other Routledge books in pence narrows the date to 1890.[56] If the copy arrived in Milford, Massachusetts, via Routledge's New York office, rather than being purchased abroad, then the advertisements suggest that it was imported already bound. Although it lacks an introduction and editorial matter, this reprint boasts a frontispiece of Fanny accepting from Edmund a gold chain for William's cross, an unsigned image also recycled from the edition of 1883.[57] That Essie and Josephine pasted their bookplate into this run-of-the-mill reprint, and that family members added their names, proclaim two things: they liked *Mansfield Park* well enough to keep it, and they were wealthy and bibliophilic enough to own personalized ex libris. Fancy bookplates are uncommon in surviving reprints of truly ordinary Austens like this. Thayer is a fine New England name, and this copy belonged to a well-established, highly educated, mercantile family. Regrettably, the Thayer sisters of Milford left no annotations to record their views on Jane Austen in their unremarkable Routledge reprint.

At just about this time, another American reader was more definitive: Samuel Clemens (1835–1910), better known as Mark Twain. On his shelves in Hartford, Connecticut, sat a copy of *Northanger Abbey–Persuasion* in a Routledge series binding identical to the one owned by the

Thayer sisters. Like their copy, it was printed from the 1883 plates and produced circa 1890. Twain's reprint was purchased locally, for it still retains the bookseller ticket of "Brown & Gross Booksellers, Hartford, CT." on the rear pastedown (figure I.11), increasing the likelihood that the Thayer sisters purchased theirs in the same manner. In 1908 Twain moved to a large new mansion near Redding, known as Stormfield, and there his book remained until his death, when it was donated in 1910, along with the bulk of his personal library, to the nearby Mark Twain Library that he helped to found.[58] Through to the 1930s, his *Northanger Abbey–Persuasion* circulated as part of the library's public collection. Today, thankfully, it remains among the library's noncirculating treasured copies owned by Samuel Clemens.

I.11. Bookseller's ticket inside Mark Twain's copy of *Northanger Abbey-Persuasion*. Courtesy of the Mark Twain Library, Redding, CT.

Both privately and under his famous pen name, Twain turned into one of Austen's fiercest critics. Before 1895, he never once even mentioned her, but during the last fifteen years of his life, he expressed a harsh contempt for her work. Twain directed his ire not just at a novelistic style he judged as outmoded, or "Thoroughly artificial," but at the sudden public enthusiasm for Austen in the 1890s that he thought unwarranted. Twain's description of a ship's library in his travelogue *Following the Equator* (1897) anticipates James's objection about the omnipresence of her novels: "Jane Austen's books, too, are absent from this library. Just that one omission alone would make a fairly good library out of a library that hadn't a book in it." As with Henry James, it is not Austen's old-fashioned content but her modern proliferation and popularity that makes the blood of the fellow novelist boil. His most-quoted barb occurs in a letter of September 13, 1898, written to his best friend, Joseph Twichell: "I haven't any right to criticise books, and I don't do it except when I hate them. I often want to criticise Jane Austen, but her books madden me so that I can't conceal my frenzy from the reader; and therefore I have to stop every time I begin. Every time I read 'Pride and Prejudice' I want to dig her up and beat her over the skull with her own shin-bone."[59] Some Austen critics have tried to read his "every time" as if a clandestine admission of fandom, but such an interpretation surely amounts to special pleading. Given these strong opinions, it's

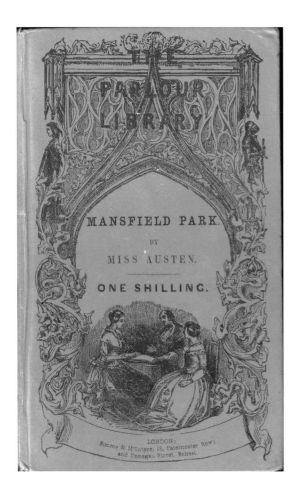

I.12. Ellen Horwood's one-shilling copy, in green boards, of *Mansfield Park* in the Parlour Library series (London and Belfast: Simms and M'Intyre, 1851). Collection of Sandra Clark.

no wonder that Twain declines to invest in an elaborately produced set of her novels in fancy bindings.

For all his posturing and lambasting, Twain's home library held multiple Austen titles. According to his bibliographer, and on the basis of evidence in letters and notebooks, he also owned *Pride and Prejudice* and *Sense and Sensibility*. The specific editions of these two novels are unknown, however, and the copies lost. He owned *Mansfield Park* in a cheap Bernhard Tauchnitz reprint dated 1867.[60] Since Tauchnitz reprints were unavailable in America, Twain probably acquired it on his European travels. That means that he, or a family member, bothered to bring Austen home. Poor production values need not be a barometer of the buyer's literary opinion, however, nor does owning a cheap Tauchnitz reprint rather than a more permanent, fancier edition necessarily mark dismissal. When James Joyce, a man always low on cash, lived in Trieste, his library contained dozens of scruffy Tauchnitz copies of fellow novelists, poets, and playwrights: Sir Walter Scott, George Eliot, H. G. Wells, Joseph Conrad, Oscar Wilde, Oliver Goldsmith, George Bernard Shaw, Edgar Allan Poe, and many Shakespeares. Indeed, the coffee and wine stains on Joyce's Tauchnitz paperback of *As You Like It* might mark his closeness to the Bard, to the point of eating and drinking with him.[61] Depending on the buyer's financial situation, even the cheapest edition may constitute a luxury or heartfelt literary investment. I suspect, however, that this was probably not the case with Twain's inexpensive Austens—even if the Thayers treasured an identically bound version of *Mansfield Park*.

VIRGINIA WOOLF & THE MEAT-SELLER

For the book historian, the physical condition of surviving copies reflects upon owners and authors alike. The green, glazed paper boards of *Mansfield Park* in one copy of the Parlour Library reprint of 1851 by publisher Simms and M'Intyre seem as bright as the day they were issued (figure I.12).[62] The firm's Parlour Library of popular works, mostly novels, bound in the radically innovative format of colorful waxed paper boards and initially sold for the unprecedented low price of two shillings, later just one, helped revolutionize nineteenth-century publishing. This humble reprint is the type of throwaway book, a forerunner of the modern paperback, sold by the first generation of W. H. Smith newsagents at Victorian railway stations and book vendors. The signature "Ellen Martha Horwood," written neatly with a thin

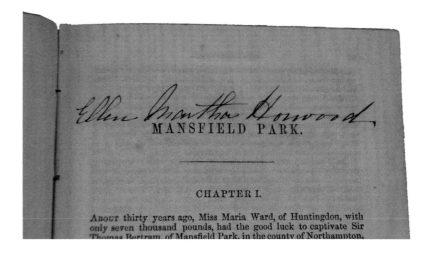

pen, runs across the top of the novel's opening page (figure I.13). Perhaps she was unable to afford the cloth version for a further sixpence and had no notion of her reprint's transience, but she was certainly determined to keep it, for she also wrote "Miss Ellen Horwood" on the series title page in the same confident hand—to further protect her modest literary property.

I.13. Ownership signature of Ellen Martha Horwood (b. 1825) on opening page of *Mansfield Park*. Collection of Sandra Clark.

Names in inscriptions are rarely complete or unique enough to trace. In this lucky instance, however, a chancery suit of 1855 preserves Ellen Martha Horwood's name. She was a defendant in a legal dispute with a meat salesman called John Kennedy, who claimed to be a creditor of the estate of "Martha Capurn Horwood late of 11 Warwick Lane, Newgate Market, London, widow and meat sales woman," and Ellen was her mother's executrix.[63] Armed with name and address, I found that Ellen was baptized on January 12, 1825, and married, at age 29, to a "butcher" like her father, widower Thomas Nicklinson.[64] In January 1852, when her *Mansfield Park* remained brand new, Ellen turned 27.

This random copy reveals that one Victorian reader of *Mansfield Park* was a woman born into the wholesale meat trade, a daughter of butchers working in Newgate Market, a large open-air meat market near St. Paul's. As a contemporary Victorian guidebook explains, at Newgate "are sold pigs and poultry killed in the country, together with hog-meat, game, fresh butter, eggs, &e. to an astonishing amount."[65] The tagline "The Parlour Library" and the stock image of two well-dressed Victorian ladies and

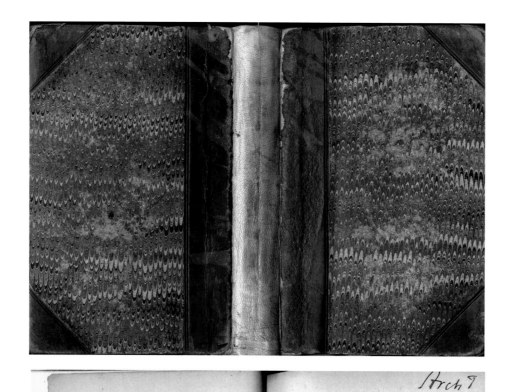

PRIDE

AND

PREJUDICE.

A NOVEL.

By JANE AUSTEN,

AUTHOR OF

"SENSE AND SENSIBILITY," "MANSFIELD PARK,"

ETC. ETC.

LONDON:

GEORGE ROUTLEDGE AND SONS,

THE BROADWAY, LUDGATE.

NEW YORK: 416, BROOME STREET.

a gentleman poring over a large book must have impressed Ellen with a distant elegance, even on mere paper boards. I like to imagine Ellen, after a no-nonsense day of selling hind quarters of pork and freshly killed chickens in the noise and stench of the busy marketplace, sitting down to read the rags-to-riches story of Fanny Price. Her copy remains too pristine for her to have taken it to work or exposed it to sunlight. And yet the double signature vehemently denies the disinterest that might otherwise be suspected from a pristine book. There is nothing here to suggest it has not been carefully read—no uncut pages to bear witness against the owner. Instead, the forensic evidence suggests the book has been treated, in Ellen's lifetime and for generations thereafter, as a treasured possession.

Only three miles from Newgate Market, but more than half a century later, Leonard and Virginia Woolf also owned a shilling reprint of Austen. Living in the well-to-do squares of Tavistock and Mecklenburgh, the Woolfs possessed a cheap secondhand copy of *Pride and Prejudice*, dated 1870 by an early owner, that was part of the same revival of old Railway Library plates as the versions of *Sense and Sensibility* printed by Routledge in figure I.2. The Woolfs' Routledge reprint survives not in its original publisher's binding but in upgraded marbled boards with leather reinforcements on the corners and spine, known as quarter calf (figure I.14). Leonard, a committed socialist and advocate for workers' rights, acquired his working-class edition secondhand in 1903, while still a bachelor. It cannot be known whether the erstwhile binding, which lost its strip of leather along the spine, was in better shape at the time of purchase or reflects his own effort at rebinding. Even in its current damaged condition, the book would not have stood out among the many other, and more up-to-date, copies by and about Austen assembled by the couple after their marriage in 1910, for their library books—inherited, bought, and received—were not of a piece. Like Twain's hodgepodge of Austen copies, the Woolfs assembled a modern working library. Theirs was not a collection with matching spines and elegant bindings arranged in neat rows, but an assembly of thousands of mismatched books and well-worn editions—old, rare, new, commonplace, many of them in bad shape.

The Woolfs owned at least a baker's dozen of Austen's publications: novels, juvenilia, letters, memoirs, and a facsimile edition of the canceled chapter of *Persuasion*.[66] One of their copies of *Pride and Prejudice* was a

I.14. *Pride and Prejudice* (London: George Routledge and Sons, n.d.). Former owner's signature is dated 1870, but this copy is also inscribed "L. Sidney Woolf Oct 1903." The Library of Leonard and Virginia Woolf collection at MASC, Washington State University.

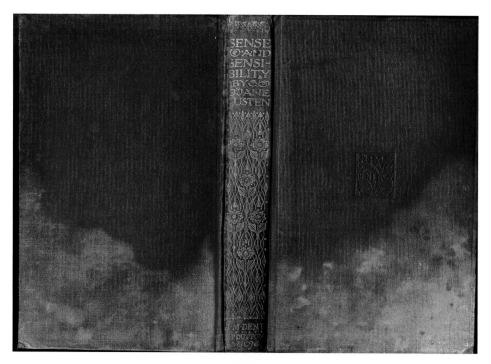

A TALE WHICH HOLDETH CHILDREN FROM PLAY & OLD MEN FROM THE CHIMNEY CORNER

SIR PHILIP SIDNEY

SENSE & SENSIBILITY BY JANE AUSTEN

LONDON: PUBLISHED by J. M. DENT. & CO AND IN NEW YORK BY E. P. DUTTON & CO

run-of-the-mill Everyman's Library edition of 1906 in red publisher's cloth, the other a rare and valuable edition of 1817—printed by Thomas Egerton, Austen's first publisher. The latter was given to Virginia by economist John Maynard Keynes, the elder brother of Austen's bibliographer Geoffrey Keynes and a close friend.[67] The Woolfs also owned an all-in-one edition of Austen, *The Complete Novels* (1928), with an introduction by J. C. Squire, a man described by Virginia in 1919 as "more repulsive than words can express, and malignant into the bargain."[68] Two further copies came from the cheap 1906 Everyman's Library, *Sense and Sensibility* and *Emma*, again in unassuming red publisher's cloth.[69] These copies kept company with a Thomas Nelson edition of *Mansfield Park*, also in red cloth, with the same democratizing purpose as the Everyman's Library, but not quite identical in size. Thus, the Woolfs seem to have gathered Austen titles over many years without bothering to match sets or fussily curate their books. When they founded the Hogarth Press, Virginia bound and repaired books herself, yet the Woolfs were not careful book owners in any literal sense. To judge from the down-at-the-heels bindings, bleached spines, damaged covers, and water stains on their Austen books, I surmise that while they read they also bathed, ate, smoked, drank, and used their books as household trays or shuttlecocks.[70] Some stains are so severe that I can only assume that on warm rainy days they propped open the windows of 52 Tavistock Square with Austen and her shelf mates (figure I.15).

I cannot even guess when the hardest-wearing moments in the lives of these books occurred, since their next London residence at 37 Mecklenburgh Square was damaged by World War II bombs. Perhaps these books were casualties of war, not carelessness. Even so, to compare the damaged Austens associated with the scholarly Woolfs to the pristine shilling reprint owned by meat-seller Ellen Horwood in the 1850s is to contemplate how the condition of a book projects respect for an author. After all, this is the reason that libraries do not preserve ill-made reprints on bad paper. In the case of the Woolfs, a well-worn book could suggest a well-read or even a well-loved author. In her own novel *Orlando* (1928), Woolf invokes the essential humanity of damaged books when Orlando detects "a brownish stain" on the velvet prayer book "held by Mary Queen of Scots on the scaffold" and finds inside "also a lock of hair and a crumb of pastry," to which she adds "a flake of tobacco" while reading and smoking with "a reverent air."[71] In light of

I.15. Virginia and Leonard Woolf's copy of *Sense and Sensibility* in Everyman's Library series (London and New York: Dent and Dutton, 1906). The Library of Leonard and Virginia Woolf collection at MASC, Washington State University.

the heavily stained library of the Woolfs, this passage confirms an attitude toward books as intellectual territories necessarily marked by the readers who pass through them. For Woolf, damage to a book is not defilement but palpable evidence of intellectual engagement, a bookish version of Joyce's modernist motto "Dirty cleans." Yet Ellen's impeccable care of her shilling *Mansfield Park*, twice claimed by her neat signature and carefully protected against the elements, surely reflects an equally fervent, if differently expressed, respect for Austen and her work.

Virginia Woolf's professional respect for Austen as a fellow novelist is beyond doubt, however badly she treated her actual books. In 1925 Woolf publicly praised Austen's genius, writing, "The balance of her gifts was singularly perfect. Among her finished novels there are no failures."[72] Privately, too, she reread and marveled as late as 1940: "S&S. all scenes. very sharp. Surprises. masterly. . . . Very dramatic. Plot from the 18th Century. Mistressly in her winding up. No flagging. . . . And the love so intense, so poignant. . . . Elinor I suppose Cassandra: Marianne Jane, edited."[73] I assume that Woolf read her own Everyman's Library copy of *Sense and Sensibility*, and yet she stresses the heritage of Austen's style as "from the 18th Century" even while reading an edition dated 1906. She recognized an exceptional author even in that unexceptional—and possibly heavily stained—form. These copies prove that Woolf could bypass the faux medievalism of J. M. Dent's laboriously ornamented title pages to enter Austen's Georgian world, undistracted by the flimflam of modish printing. Woolf's own copies animate and enrich her literary criticism, not because her interpretations turn upon a typographical misprint or a variant, but because her actual physical books humanize the seemingly detached critic.

ASSOCIATION COPIES & UNKNOWNS

Even ordinary or damaged copies can thus be made extraordinary by the people who owned them. Indeed, previous ownership by the likes of Twain or Woolf has hitherto been the only way that the occasional lowbrow edition of Austen slipped into major libraries. For example, although the Harry Ransom Center (HRC) never set out to own Austen in any deep way, it houses—in addition to an impressive collection of first editions—a haphazard assortment of copies acquired as part of the books and papers of other famous writers and artists: e. e. cummings (1894–1962), Sir Arthur Conan

Doyle (1859–1930), literary scholar Stuart Gilbert (1883–1969), Scottish writer Sir Compton Mackenzie (1883–1972), American poet-journalist Christopher Morley (1890–1957), H. G. Wells (1866–1946), T. H. White (1906–1964), and playwright Stark Young (1881–1963). The mystique of a famous author as lowly reader provides a rare incentive to preserve the occasional workmanlike edition of Austen as an "association copy." In the case of H. G. Wells's copy of *Northanger Abbey–Persuasion*, private family dynamics are made visible in the inscription to his young wife, "*A. C. Wells,*" on February 25, 1899: "*Prize for Good Conduct.*"[74] The HRC is atypical in its detailed record-keeping of author libraries and provenance, for many older institutions either absorbed extra books silently into their collection or tossed what they considered duplicates. Regardless, the academy makes way for a lowbrow edition of Austen only if it rested for years, like a fine wine, on the shelves of some lofty personage.

Even copies secured for posterity by accident rather than design, now safely tucked away in rare-book libraries, are not my central concern, although I promise to shamelessly namedrop owners from time to time. I now abandon authoritative firsts and even the unremarkable versions read by famous writers to focus on copies that, for practical and professional reasons, have neither been collected by libraries nor studied by scholars. The bulk of my examples, derived from private collections, are reprints with little monetary value—like the copies once owned by Gertrude Wallace, Sybil Daniell, Ellen Horwood, and the Thayer sisters. Bibliographers proudly reserve the technical term *association copy* for a copy associated closely with the book's own author, because it is annotated or inscribed. Only recently has the term come to loosely refer to any book owned by a famous person. Either way, the posh term does not fit the bedraggled copies of unknown devotees of Austen. I shall argue, however, that the unsung copies of ordinary people are remarkable material objects in the history of the printed book—as clues about actual readers and as evidence for Austen's messy and animated reception history.

V.II.1. Emma Morris's copy of *Emma* in Railway Library series (London and New York: G. Routledge and Co., 1857). Original printed boards with price "eighteen pence." Author's collection.

Vignette II
Emma at the Seaside

Published in 1857, this copy of *Emma* was, like Gertrude Wallace's earlier *Sense and Sensibility*, part of Routledge's Railway Library series (figure V.II.1).[1] The young owner of this reprint at eighteen pence in picture boards could not have known that a story set in a remote English village, so far from her familiar Scottish surroundings by the sea, would warn of circumstances important to her own short life.

The red printed cover of this *Emma* is now badly torn at the spine, where the lower half is missing, but the illustrated front board showing the picnic scene remains remarkably bright. When fresh, the book's allure must have been vivid indeed. A yellow stub, tipped in or glued to the usual hurly-burly of publisher's advertisements on the crowded endpapers at the front, advertises one further title by Routledge, *Harry Ogilvie, Or the Black Dragoons*, a historical swashbuckler by Scottish writer James Grant (1822–1887). The blurb on yellow paper stresses that this "new" novel is "connected with a most exciting period of Scottish history" (figure V.II.2). Routledge, it seems, customized book advertisements even in its cheapest reprints, taking the trouble to insert this extra ad into a simple eighteen-penny Railway Edition because it was intended for distribution in Scotland. The owner's signature confirms its Scottish destination.

In fact, the owner has perfectly imitated Routledge's professionally tipped-in stub with an announcement of her own, carefully glued in just the same manner to the book's next leaf. Fastened to lie perfectly over the printed "EMMA"

V.II.2. Extra advertisement on yellow paper, tipped into Emma Morris's copy at first free end-paper. Author's collection.

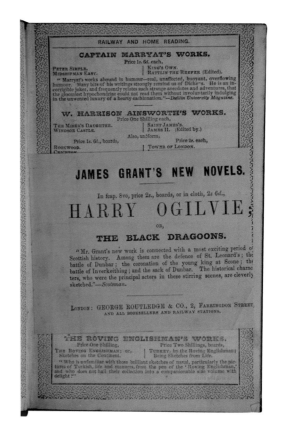

of the half title, a fragment of blue writing paper neatly announces the owner's name—also Emma—and address (figure V.II.3):

Miss Emma Morris
Major Morris
Moorburn
Largs

Margaret Emma Morris (May 4, 1837–May 25, 1863) was the youngest daughter of Major Robert Morris (1788–1862), of Moorburn Manor in the town of Largs in Ayrshire, Scotland.[2] She seems to have preferred her middle name, or perhaps she stressed it here to signal a special affinity with Austen's heroine. Emma grew up with her nine older siblings in a busy and popular seaside resort; Largs already boasted public baths, hotels, and a pier built in 1834. Her father, Robert Morris, served as justice of the peace from Moorburn Manor.[3] In 1855, an ordinance survey reveals a small stream on this manor running to the sea, a cottage, a main house, and "a plantation."[4] Emma's home must have been sizable, for its "shallow pond" was listed in the local directory as the regular meeting place of the town's established curling club, proudly dubbed the Noddle Curling Club by residents of Largs.

Emma did not need to own a copy in order to read Jane Austen, for in addition to two midwives, an M.D., and a surgeon, the town of Largs could lay claim to a substantial lending library, with "upwards of 400 volumes of well-selected books in various departments of literature."[5] Located at 30 Bath Street, and open daily from eleven to dusk, the library was not free: initial "entry money" was one guinea, and an annual subscription cost 10s.6d. Although visitors could subscribe for a week, a month, three months, or a half year, the initial membership fee plus a yearly subscription amounted to laying out the combined price of twenty-one such Railway editions. While Emma probably had access to other reading materials at home, including possibly a library subscription shared with her siblings, her carefully placed signature and address suggests that she was proud to claim a book of her very own.

Emma was 20 when the book was printed in 1857, and it must have seemed strange to read about a rich English heroine of her age who had never seen the sea. Like Austen's fictional heroine, Emma was motherless,

Mary Morris having died in 1851, when her daughter was just 14. Judging from his portrait, Robert, her father, was a serious but unassuming man, with fashionable sideburns and a fondness for dogs. A print of *Major Morris, Moorburn, Largs* in the British Museum shows a disarming, tweedy, country gentleman, seated on a wooden chair as he casually holds a top hat by the rim between his knees.[6] His right elbow rests unceremoniously on the low back of the chair, as a trim greyhound leans familiarly over his knee. He is dressed not in uniform but in a dark suit with a pale waistcoat. Because the father resembles a Victorian version of a kindly Mr. Woodhouse, perhaps life at Moorburn Manor also contained very little to distress or vex this Emma.

But even if her life was happy, it was not long. Soon after reading *Emma*, and still at age 20, Emma Morris married James Barclay Murdoch of nearby Glasgow. After giving birth to two sons and a daughter in quick succession, she died within weeks of her twenty-fifth birthday. I found no record of the cause of her death, or indeed any further trace of Emma Morris other than this book, but the odds that she suffered childbirth complications are high. Two years later, her widower husband remarried. The scantiness of these biographical facts makes it especially poignant that *Emma* opens with the celebration of a second marriage and reveals a world with missing mothers and stepparents. Jane Fairfax, Emma Woodhouse, Frank Churchill, and Harriet Smith are all motherless. *Emma* is filled with references to ailments and medical advice—from Mr. Perry, Highbury's omnipresent apothecary, to Mr. Wingfield, the London physician who attends John Knightley's family in Brunswick Square. The dangerous specter of childbirth looms over the newly married Mrs. Weston and even over Emma herself at the end of the novel—a danger reinforced by Highbury's history of missing mothers. In the case of Emma Morris, one can echo Mr. Woodhouse and "sink into 'poor Emma.'"

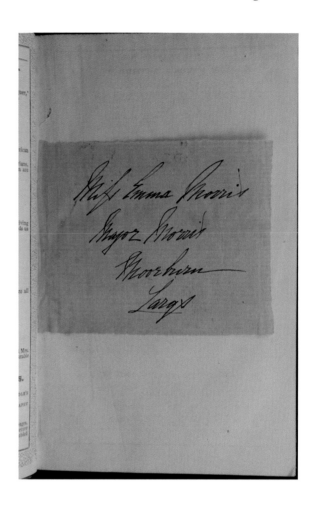

V.II.3. Ownership inscription, glued neatly at the gutter in imitation of the way the previous publisher's advertisement was attached. Author's collection.

CHAPTER 1

PAPERBACK FIGHTER
Austen for the People

The proliferation of Jane Austen's work and reputation owes much to the early forerunners of the modern paperback. This is because mass-market paperbacks were by no means the mid-twentieth-century phenomenon celebrated in the ballads of our popular culture. As early as 1847, Austen's works began to appear in Britain as paperbound books in the form of reprints at a fraction of the cost of new fiction. The first-generation paperbacks of her books, in waxed paper boards or buff paper wrappers, sold cheaply for one to two shillings in Victorian railway stations. Subsequent iterations of the paperback format were even cheaper—soon available for mere pennies each. These versions, which made her books increasingly affordable to the working classes, have largely disappeared from view, a result of their inevitable fragility, shoddy production values, and intolerable cheapness. As these lowbrow formats disappeared, some of Austen's earliest public appearances became invisible, in effect sanitizing her ebullient and disordered progress into the literary canon.

Serious collectors do not aim at Austen in paperback. As a result, and as book historian William St. Clair points out, "a vast amount of cheap books never made it into libraries and therefore into lists of titles" that are the inventories reckoned by scholars and bibliophiles.[1] The scarcity today of examples of the nineteenth- and early-twentieth-century reprints of her books that came in picture boards or buff paper wrappers is remarkable, considering how many were produced. The exact first print runs of *Sense and Sensibility* and *Pride and Prejudice* in 1811 and 1813 are not known, but bibliographers optimistically estimate 750 and 1,500 copies, respectively.[2] Far harder to locate now than precious survivors of those first editions, the earliest paperbacked versions of Austen's novels were run off in the tens of thousands—and over the lifetime of even a single set of stereotype plates, possibly up to several hundred thousand. While bibliographers such as Gilson are quick off the mark when estimating runs of Austen's landmark firsts, her cheapest reprints often go uncounted. As a publishing rule of thumb, the cheaper the book, the larger the likely print run and potential readership. The book historian's corollary to this rule is that the lower a book's original price, the harder it will be to relocate a century or more later.

Not only was Jane Austen present among the earliest experiments in mass-market paperbacks, but these lowly books prove how her entrance into the literary canon occurred in a much cruder fashion than most of her fans today imagine. At one or two shillings in waxed paper boards, many of Austen's novels were fronted by sensational illustrations that resembled the packaging of popular crime stories known as Penny Dreadfuls. By the early 1880s, several of her novels could also be owned for a mere sixpence, or half a shilling, as dual-columned floppy booklets. Next, they could be had in weekly installments that looked more like magazines, again with striking contemporary illustrations. For half a penny per number, a reader might enjoy two of her novels in weekly parts, mixed in with bits of *Uncle Tom's Cabin*, *The Scarlet Letter*, and *Handy Andy*. In the late 1890s, *Sense and Sensibility* could be purchased, in its entirety, for only two pennies as a skeletal cramped paperback, in twin weekly parts, and a distilled *Pride and Prejudice* could be had for a mere penny. In America, Austen became publishing fodder for dime novels packaged as periodicals. These unprecedented prices were made possible by the falling cost of paper, by technical advances such as steam presses and stereotyping, and, above all, by the distribution networks enabled by the new railroad system. Book innovation does not occur in a political vacuum, and the push for universal education with, in Britain, legislation such as the Elementary Education Act of 1870 also expanded the late-century market for cheap books by increasing readership at the bottom end. But all this is not merely about Austen in larger numbers and at lower prices. These "lost" Austen versions affected not only her readership but also her public persona. The Victorian sensationalism as well as the schmaltz used to market these cheaper reprints introduced the public to a Miss Austen who was an author of the everyday and the commonplace rather than a would-be member of the literary elite. These lowbrow versions created, to Henry James's chagrin, the People's Jane.

By means of cheap paperbacks seldom found in institutional libraries, this chapter tracks Jane Austen as a writer who, in the first century of her literary afterlife, finds herself at the center of escalating rhetoric about getting worthy books into the hands of the working classes. In *The Intellectual Life of the British Working Classes*, Jonathan Rose points to the fierce belief in the "emancipatory power of literature."[3] At every turn of the publishing industry to accommodate that emancipatory power, Austen comes into contact with those who make history with innovative paperbacks sold at increasingly lower prices—from cheap to cheaper to cheapest. Long before university professors added explanatory introductions and endnotes to today's scholarly paperbacks, a phrase that surely began as an oxymoron, Austen was edited by investigative journalists and campaigners for social improvement who intended, surprisingly, to use her to educate the young and the working poor. As mass-market paperbacks, Austen entered railway depots and newspaper stands. While the individual copies featured in my vignettes show how one inexpensive Jane Austen might reach a particular reader, the paperback format may be what allowed her reputation to spread furthest—but at the dubiously low end of the marketplace. These early paperbacks document Austen's ascendance by means of her plebeian proliferation.

YELLOWBACK JANE

In 1846 Simms & M'Intyre forever changed the face of fiction reading and book buying with their reprints priced at one or two shillings. From the start, Jane Austen was present at this innovation. Originally from Belfast but soon with offices in London, Simms & M'Intyre began their cheap Parlour Library by refashioning titles from their established Parlor Novelist series, which was then an elegant middle-class product on a par with Bentley's Standard Novels. Bentley responded to the competition by dropping his own reprint prices to 2s.6d. in 1846, adjusted to 3s.6d. in 1848. At first, Simms & M'Intyre simply repackaged their existing series so that they could sell their books more cheaply than those available in publisher's cloth, creating a new type of book that was both sold and read in sturdy paper boards. Initial sales at the two-shilling price were encouraging enough to prompt them to soon reset their Parlour Library texts more tightly to save on paper, removing all internal ornamentation and typographical extras.[4] For example, the modest leather binding of Captain Baird's copy of *Mansfield Park* typifies an original Parlor Novelist exemplar in 1846, while Ellen Horwood's copy in green glazed boards of the same Simms & M'Intyre title by 1851 (reset

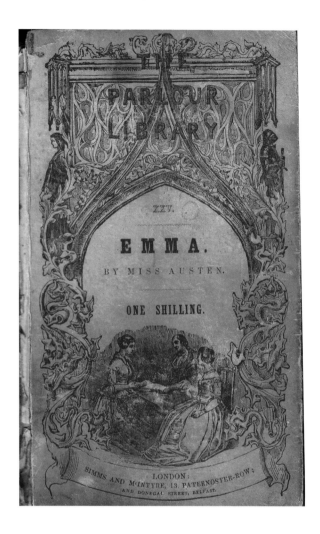

1.1. One-shilling *Emma* in green printed boards for the Parlour Library series (London and Belfast: Simms and M'Intyre, 1849). Collection of Sandra Clark.

and reprinted for the Parlour Library) shows the new style of cheaper book (compare the copy shown in vignette III to figure I.12).

Sized to fit into a greatcoat pocket, and bound in paper boards of (at first) green or white designs, these new Simms & M'Intyre volumes differed from their ancestors. Sold for one to two shillings, and sometimes for the jaw-dropping price of sixpence, these cheap reads had no pretentions to become part of a lending library or even the family collections of the middle classes. These no-nonsense volumes in waxed paper covers were a new species of book: ephemeral pleasure reads. The kind of throwaway-fiction reading that had been the purview of serials in newspapers and popular miscellanies could now be experienced in one satisfying go at a price far lower than a standard reprint of a novel in publisher's cloth. In 1847 *Mansfield Park*, its copyright having expired in 1842, was almost immediately included in the Parlour Library series at No. 4. In early 1849, in defiance of copyright and good manners, *Emma*, to which Bentley officially enjoyed exclusivity through to 1857, joined the cheap seats at Simms & M'Intyre at No. 25 for one shilling (figure 1.1).[5] And the combo of *Northanger Abbey* and *Persuasion*, whose copyrights officially belonged to Bentley through 1860, joined this same series in 1850, at No. 47—also selling individually at sixpence in the paperbound Books for the People series (figure 1.2).[6] These paperbound books flew in the face of professional niceties such as copyright, fussy bindings, and pricing norms. These new rebels of the book market embraced Jane Austen as one of their own.

By not just dropping the market price but also changing the location where books might be purchased, this fiction format quickly altered the way consumers thought of the very act of reading. These paperback novels promised to entertain the new generation of travelers who suddenly found themselves with many hours to fill while enjoying relatively smooth stretches of track, but they also utilized the distribution chains of news agents at railway stations to reach a different type of customer from the traditional browser of dedicated bookshops in urban areas. The books circulated via the W. H. Smith outlets and stalls that began in 1848. Nearly a century later, Pocket Books in America and Penguin Books in England successfully pursued similar product relocation strategies with their own generation of paperbacks. The busy advertisements on the endpapers and back boards of these cheap Victorian books helped to offset production costs, allowing the further step down in price to one shilling. The accompanying ads made the books look less like the elite and genteel tomes of yore and more like the commonplace commodities of soap and cocoa powder shown on their back covers and endpapers. These nonchalantly priced volumes made the reading of a whole book an ordinary act of consumption rather than the intellectual activity of a privileged toff. The standout ads on the back, dominantly printed on yellow paper, became over time such a hallmark of these cheap books that the whole genre, regardless of the color of their earliest paper boards,

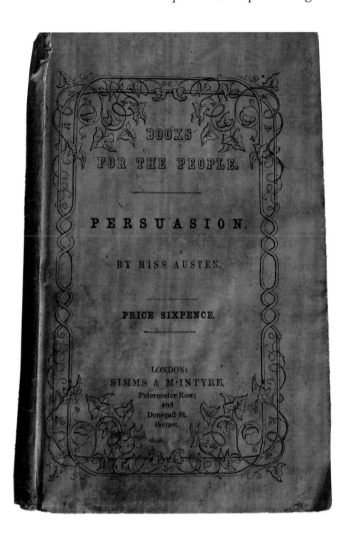

1.2. Sixpence *Persuasion* in printed paper boards for Books for the People series (London and Belfast: Simms & M'Intyre, 1852). The John Spiers Collection of Victorian and Edwardian Fiction.

took the name "yellowback." Because of their extremely low production values, yellowbacks were not of interest to collectors or scholars until John Carter and Michael Sadleir urged their historical consequence in 1934.[7] By then, most copies had been read to bits and thrown out.

The yellowback phenomenon shook up the publishing world, stimulating many imitators.[8] When it came to Austen, George Routledge, in particular, enthusiastically copied the innovation, in some cases by cheekily setting his printed text of her works directly from Simms & M'Intyre's tightly printed copies.[9] Starting in 1849, Routledge's participatory weight forced the bottom price down to one shilling as their Railway Library steamed ahead under the banner "The cheapest books ever published." Austen's *Sense and Sensibility* and *Pride and Prejudice* became numbers 8 and 10, respectively, in the Railway Library, while the boards remained green and white (see vignette I). These early not-yet-yellow yellowbacks tend to be the most fragile, because they were often held together with printer's waste, as seen in the example of Gertrude Wallace's copy. Soon, publishers like Routledge reinforced their yellowbacks with jute along the spine, as in Emma Morris's 1857 copy of *Emma* at eighteen pence (see vignette II).

Eventually, other houses made yellowbacks (again, not always yellow) of Austen's novels too, including Chapman & Hall, Ward & Lock, and Cassell & Company. In this crowded market, book stalls and news vendors such as W. H. Smith displayed an array of cheap Austens in paper boards costing from one shilling to two for the remainder of the century. For a further sixpence or shilling in any bookstore, the same reprints might be had in sedate blind-stamped publisher's cloth, without the sensational top-board illustrations that often mimicked the tawdry hallmark stylings of the Penny Dreadful, a genre that courted a juvenile and working-class readership with stories of criminals and vice. Perhaps the most outrageous packaging in this vein is Chapman & Hall's yellowback edition of *Pride and Prejudice* in 1870, printed from Bentley's old 1833 plates. It tantalized buyers with a lurid picture of Lydia among the soldiers in the camp at Brighton, a scene so risqué it occurs off-page in the novel itself (figure 1.3).[10] Chapman & Hall, and later Ward & Lock, when they took over these Jane Austen plates, put out yellowbacks of *Sense and Sensibility* in "picture boards" showing a slouched Marianne penning letters, presumably to Willoughby, on her knees (figure 1.4). The *Northanger Abbey–Persuasion* yellowback similarly mixed a dash of melodrama with Gothic lettering (figure 1.5). The picture board of the yellowback *Mansfield Park* intimates a struggle between angels and demons with an image of Mary Crawford playing the harp for a broody Edmund Bertram, whose dark silhouette bodes ill, while just behind Mary another woman—Fanny, perhaps—reads a newspaper whose pointed shape bestows upon the female rake a false set of angelic wings (see introduction, figure I.4). The very first picture boards for *Mansfield Park* were those of the 1857 Railway Library edition by Routledge—depicting a seemingly innocent outdoor scene in bright red, with Edmund, Fanny, and Mary sitting on a bench in the gardens of Sotherton. And yet this scene, as Jill Heydt-Stevenson explains, holds erotic humor.[11] Not all of the yellowback illustrations had shock value; the sedate cover image of Mr. Collins proposing to a composed Elizabeth may have helped steer one 1883 yellowback of *Pride and Prejudice* toward the Bodleian Library.[12] In 1887, Cassell & Company reluctantly gave in to this new format with a monthly series that included Austen in red paper over cardboard, stubbornly fronted by an image of the same series, the Red Library, in cloth on a bookshelf (figure 1.6). The cloth version was then priced at 2s., while the paper one was just 1s. The lofty language of the back advertisements on paperback for "rich" tea and "luxury" coffee remained, like their totemic cover image, slightly at odds with the yellowback's jubilant embrace of all that was showy and affordable.

On the outside, none of these lowbrow, even garish, paper Austens resembled the elegant Richard Bentley reprints, with their genteel frontispieces, that preceded them in understated publisher's cloth, although some were printed directly from his old plates. Nonetheless, the yellowback phenomenon affected Bentley's business. By 1856 yellowbacks had altered the publishing landscape of popular fiction so much that Bentley temporarily opted out of the increasingly chaotic reprint frenzy, auctioning off his remaining stocks of the Standard Novels, along with all his stereotyped and steel plates—including those for his Austens.[13] But in 1866 he experienced a change of heart about Austen specifically and, after a decade's absence, stepped back into her reprint traffic with, unexpectedly, his familiar Austens still offered at the stubbornly pricey thirty shillings for a set of five volumes. Soon reduced to 21s. for the set, these Bentley volumes were mere reprints from his familiar 1833 plates, which he had either slyly retained at the auction or retrieved afterward.[14] Not until 1869, as mentioned previously, did Bentley permanently abandon the field of the inexpensive reprint, passing on his old plates to Chapman & Hall, a firm that then immediately tarted Austen up with sensational yellowback cover art. Instead, Bentley's firm climbed to higher ground with a brand new edition stiffly priced at, once again, six shillings per reset volume, still stubbornly accompanied by the steel-plate frontispieces retained since 1833. For her nineteenth-century British readers, the yellowback phenomenon split Jane Austen's reputational personalities: at local bookstores she was dressed as the epitome of literary gentility for anywhere from two and a half to six shillings, which is

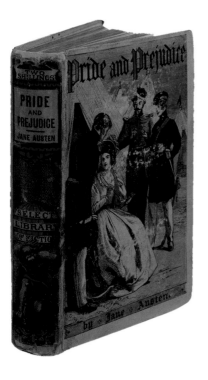

1.3. *Pride and Prejudice* in picture boards (London: Chapman and Hall, 1872). Chester W. Topp collection of Victorian yellowbacks, Stuart A. Rose Manuscript, Archives, and Rare Book Library, Emory University.

1.4. *Sense and Sensibility* in picture boards. *Left:* (London: Chapman and Hall, 1872). *Right:* (London: Ward, Lock, and Co., n.d.). The John Spiers Collection of Victorian and Edwardian Fiction.

the way scholars have studied her, while at a busy train station she might be spotted dressed in the guise of a brassy yellowback with a sensational cover illustration for one shilling or less. And with so much recycling of plates and shared features, these public personae surely overlapped. By cheapening identical texts, literally and figuratively, yellowbacks eroded traditional signals of value.

Not only did yellowbacks occupy a formidable-if-chaotic space in publishing, but the loud top-board illustrations disturbed what has been termed Bentley's "visual monopoly" on Austen by those who politely assumed that his hold on her copyright was an insuperable barrier to competition.[15] The ten monochromatic, Victorianized frontispieces and title-page images in the long-lived Bentley editions may be aesthetically superior, but they simply cannot match what in modern advertising parlance is termed the "sticking power" of a yellowback's cover art. As early as the 1850s, yellowbacks abandoned stock images and transferred attendant illustrations from inside

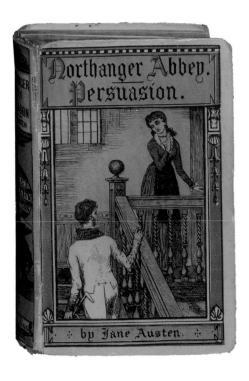

a book to its top board. From that point onward, Austen risks becoming certifiably lowbrow at a passing glance. Because so many yellowbacks were lost, some cover images remain untraced, but survivors showed to passersby of book displays at railway stations a flirty Lydia making a spectacle of herself at Brighton, a minxy Mary Crawford—ever the harpy—seducing Edmund with her playing, and an indecorous Marianne whose body language conveys private despair to augment a moody mise en scène. Overall, however, what guides a reader's sense of value may not be the specifics of the yellowback's cover art so much as its resemblance to Penny Dreadfuls. As is true for all illustrations of Austen until the 1890s, the costumes worn by her characters in these images tend to shift the stories closer to the time of a reprint's sale. Starting in the 1850s, the mass-market yellowback editions of Austen have all the hallmarks of a pop-culture Jane who shadows the official author on her way into the literary canon.

As individual copies, yellowbacks were not built to last, and yet their for-

1.5. *Northanger Abbey-Persuasion* in picture boards. London: Chapman and Hall, 1872. Monash University Library Rare Books Collection.

1.6. Early paperback of *Sense and Sensibility* in Cassell's Red Library series (London, Paris, New York, and Melbourne: Cassell & Company, Limited, n.d. [circa 1885]). The John Spiers Collection of Victorian and Edwardian Fiction.

1.7. Reprint of *Sense and Sensibility* as vol. 735 in the Tauchnitz Collection of British and American Authors series, in 1930s wrappers (Leipzig: Bernhard Tauchnitz, 1864). Author's collection.

mat survived—along with their implied non-chalance toward Austen's stories and status.

TAUCHNITZ PAPERBACKS

In 1864, under the aegis of the Tauchnitz brand, Jane Austen joined the thriving market in paperback reprints of English-language books on the European continent. Christian Bernhard Tauchnitz (1816–1895) was a German pirate-turned-megapublisher of English language books. After apprenticing with an uncle who introduced stereotyping into Germany, young Bernhard decided to specialize in printing books by this new method, choosing titles in foreign languages, particularly English, to circumvent copyright restrictions. To be fair, when his series was first launched in 1842, no recognized international copyright convention existed, and it was common for English-language books to be published in Europe without payment to an author or previous publisher. In other words, nearly everyone who printed contemporary English books on the Continent was a pirate. The series called Tauchnitz Collection of British Authors, which soon included American authors, was aimed at tourists and general readers with a knowledge of English. It began modestly in the 1840s and, over a century, grew to more than fifty-three hundred titles in standard paper wrappers.[16] In 1943 the series came to an end after an allied bombing raid, but by then Tauchnitz had been almost entirely absorbed into Albatross Books.[17]

Although Bernhard Tauchnitz started by reprinting English books already widely available in Germany, with no authorization from authors, he soon saw profit in plain dealing, realizing that explicit authorization from authors in return for payment might increase his profits if it gave him exclusive early access to the latest successes in English. In the summer of 1843, Tauchnitz approached a handful of popular living authors, including Dickens and Disraeli, offering them a fee in return for exclusive authorization to publish on the Continent. Such contemporary works appeared in the Tauchnitz series as original editions "sanctioned by the author" over the next three years. The core of his business, however, remained reprintings. The reprints carried a warning on their covers that they were not intended for resale in Britain or the United States, where copyright restrictions were in effect.

For reasons that remain unclear, Tauchnitz was slow to take on Jane Austen, even after she ran out of copyright, and slower still to include all of her novels:

Sense and Sensibility (Tauchnitz, 1864)
Mansfield Park (Tauchnitz, 1867)
Pride and Prejudice (Tauchnitz, 1870)
Northanger Abbey–Persuasion (Tauchnitz, 1871)
Emma (Tauchnitz, 1877)

By then, Austen had become attractive enough to be translated into French, German, Swedish, and Danish.[18] In addition, and because of Richard Bentley's initial relationship with the Paris-based firm of Galignani in 1833, a small number of Bentley's earliest Austen reprints must have still survived on the Continent as a way to measure interest. As the Tauchnitz reprint dates indicate, however, Austen cannot have been a runaway bestseller on the Continent in her original language, because it took Tauchnitz thirteen years to allocate five spots to her novels among, at that point, his roomy list of more than sixteen hundred titles.[19]

Today, Tauchnitz copies remain a conundrum for collectors, because early printings are almost impossible to identify, adding to the sense of confusion about dates and influences. He famously did not alter the initial publication date on his title pages, even on reissues of the identical reprint decades later. For example, I own a battered Tauchnitz copy of *Sense and Sensibility* in original 1930s paper wrappers, and yet it reads 1864 on its title page (figure 1.7). This dating quirk was part of Tauchnitz's unique set of business practices—as if, in their initial reprinting of a book, its text was reborn and the Tauchnitz birthdate should trump all. As a result, Tauchnitz copies play by different rules. Reprints with radically different dates on their title pages can, in the case of Tauchnitz copies, have been printed or purchased as new at the same time, and decades after the date stated on a title page.

Like most of Tauchnitz's editions, his Austens were originally published and sold as paperbacks, but very few copies remain in their original wrappers, owing to another publishing habit. That is, Tauchnitz paperbacks sold in their unreinforced paper wrappers for half a thaler, which was reckoned as equivalent to 2 franks or 1s.6d. at that time.[20] In comparison to the one-shilling yellowbacks in their sturdy waxed boards in England and the many sixpenny paperbacks that soon accompanied them, this price remained at the high end of cheap for a completely unreinforced book. The price of Tauchnitz paperbacks reflected their good-quality paper, allowing these particular paperbacks to be privately bound and integrated into permanent home libraries. Unlike the boarded yellowbacks, the paper wrappers on a Tauchnitz were intended as ephemeral, whereas the quality of the paper and the printed text block was fairly high. Although Tauchnitz also offered many of his books in his own publisher's bindings, many consumers choose to bind after purchase, perhaps after an initial reading in mere wrappers to judge whether the book was worth the extra expense or likely to be reread. This proved an ideal format for travelers, who bought books on the cheap and carted home only those they wished to keep, without the bulk or upfront expense of a binding that could be placed on the innards later.

Admittedly, English-speaking travelers on the Continent were, by definition, not the masses. Although Tauchnitz print runs were healthy and his prices low, he was not a publisher intending to educate the common people or Europe's working poor. The shilling editions of Austen that sold at newsagents in Britain (with multiple print runs spanning decades), as well as the sixpenny, threepenny, and penny versions that followed, come far closer to doling out Jane to the hoi polloi. Instead, Tauchnitz reprints aimed at middle-class travelers like Heman Burr, the 23-year-old Harvard law student who binge read all six of Jane Austen's novels in Tauchnitz editions during his summer holiday in Paris in 1879 (see vignette V). These same reprints also reached the privileged Eveline Harriet Hamlyn Fane (1854–1909), who acquired a complete set of Tauchnitz's Austens on her visit to Rome in 1885 before returning to England, where the Fanes had occupied Fulbeck Hall, in Lincolnshire, since 1632. Eveline, however, did not bring her copies back unbound. Her Austen set remains in the pretty leather binding that she chose in Italy—with its telltale vellum trim, decorative gilt tooling, and comely endpapers of Italian design.[21] Owned by one American lawyer and one member of the British landed gentry, Heman's and Eveline's Tauchnitz sets are the his-and-hers versions of Austen for the prosperous tourist. Nonetheless, these cheap reprintings increased Austen's visibility outside of England, adding to the sense of her popularity, which was not yet the same as a sense of her canonicity.

It was probably the Tauchnitz editions in which Lady Charlotte Schreiber (1812–1895)—scholar, socialite, and collector of antiques—first read Austen, while traveling through Europe. From Brussels, Lady Charlotte writes in her diary on July 1, 1876, that she has "been studiously reading four of Miss Austen's novels, incited thereto by Macaulay's praise, Pride and Prejudice Northanger Abbey, Persuasion, Mansfield Park. I like the first least of all; I think I like the last the best, but I cannot quite make up my mind to whether I am alive to their very great merit. For the epoch at which they appeared, some sixty years ago, they are very remarkable."[22] "Macaulay's praise," of course, refers to his *Edinburgh Review* of 1843, which famously likened Austen to Shakespeare.[23] Perhaps Lady Charlotte stumbled upon the old review while traveling, prompting her to locate copies of Austen while in Brussels. Tellingly, she does not mention *Emma,* which was not available as a Tauchnitz paperback until the following year. Lady Charlotte remains somewhat nonplussed, and her experience does not instantly convert her into a committed Austenista. Still, if not for readily available Tauchnitz reprints, such chance encounters with Austen on the Continent in the author's own language might not have occurred.

SIXPENNY & DIME NOVELS

In the 1880s and 1890s, as one-shilling yellowbacks still sold at British newsstands and Tauchnitz continued to furnish travelers with inexpensive paperbacks abroad, cheaper versions of Austen's novels emerged in London at the low price of sixpence—just as she became newly available in this format in

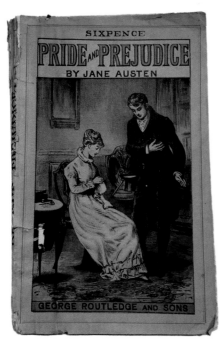 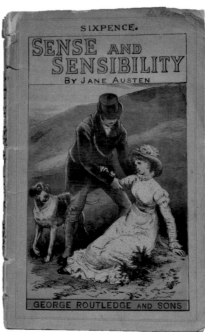 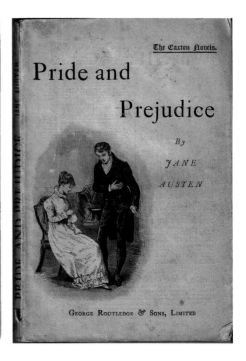

1.8. *Left and center:* Sixpence versions of *Pride and Prejudice* and *Sense and Sensibility* (London and New York: George Routledge and Sons, n.d. [circa 1883-84]). *Left:* Collection of Elizabeth Steele. *Right:* Photo courtesy of George Bayntun, Bookseller, Bath.

1.9. *Right:* Sixpence *Pride and Prejudice* sold as part of the Caxton Novels series (London, Manchester, and New York: George Routledge & Sons, Limited, n.d.). Author's collection.

America too, for a dime or 15 cents. At half the cost of a shilling railway edition, sixpenny Austens were printed in tight double columns, in tiny type, on flimsy paper, making for thin floppy volumes about half the size of today's standard 8 × 11 sheet of printer paper. Like their shilling cousins, the sixpenny editions, often with covers of slightly stiffened paper but by no means as durable as the waxed boards of the yellowbacks, contained eye-catching graphics and were packaged with mundane advertisements for soaps, flannels, patent medicines, and even "flat furnishers" who offered customers an "instalment plan." The intrepid Annika Bautz has combed through the old Routledge ledgers to compare the number of sixpenny paperbacks of *Pride and Prejudice* to the firm's runs of one-shilling and two-shilling editions. She calculates that "from 1881–1901, Routledge printed 7500 copies at 2s., 11,000 at 1s., and 20,000 at 6d."[24] Although the popularity of sixpenny editions was relatively short-lived, spurring fewer publishers to join in, these numbers are highly suggestive of the impact of this neglected format at the end of the century. Sixpenny paperbacks constitute yet another working-class Austen

1.10. Sixpence reprints of *Pride and Prejudice* and *Sense and Sensibility* (London: George Routledge & Sons, L^D., n.d.). Collection of Sandra Clark.

absent from dominant discussions of her "chocolate-box" illustrations or "the nineteenth century's first attempt at a luxury edition."[25]

In defiance of their extraordinary rarity today, images of five Austen paperback survivors from Routledge's sixpenny range are reproduced in this section (figures 1.8, 1.9, and 1.10). These paperbacks are all undated, but their accompanying cover graphics help to sort them. The colored covers of the earlier Routledge sixpennies modify the images that had, starting in 1883, appeared as monochrome frontispieces in cloth versions and as colored illustrations on the boards of yellowbacks. Some sixpenny versions for Routledge bear woodcuts signed "F. C. Tilney," likely Frederick Colin Tilney (1870–1951), who would supply the architectural "ornaments" to the dainty ten-volume Dent edition of the complete works of Jane Austen in 1892.[26] In recording Routledge's rare sixpenny editions, Gilson admits to "some confusion" with the firm's versions in waxed paper boards, and he writes, "No copy found," for *Pride and Prejudice*.[27] To add to category confusion, all three sixpence Routledge issues of *Pride and Prejudice* pictured here were printed from the same stereotype plates of their 150-page text, probably years apart.[28] The firm's 121-page sixpenny versions of *Sense and Sensibility* were similarly produced from identical plates. Although the text and the price remain the same, self-presentation sends a different message, with later versions replacing neatly balanced packaging with rougher woodcuts by F. C. Tilney. His woodcut for *Sense and Sensibility,* which shows Marianne on her sickbed, is particularly crude, printed carelessly askew on this surviving copy. Adhering to the commonsense rule that a retailer leads with their best product, the sleeker sixpennies came first, followed by more slapdash reprints at the same price.

The sixpenny novel was a format pushed by John Thomas Dicks (c. 1818–1881), a newspaper publisher whose firm, armed with one hundred employees and more than a dozen steam presses, was able to print quickly in such large numbers that he could afford to radically lower the unit price.[29] Dicks was constantly stirring up publishing practices by reformulating reprints in unique formats at mere pennies each. He rose to prominence by means of a long-term partnership with the volatile and enigmatic George W. M. Reynolds (1814–1879), a writer and publisher of sensational fiction more widely read than his contemporaries Dickens or Thackeray but now all but forgotten. Their firm grew during the latter half of the century into "one of the largest and busiest printing and publishing offices in England."[30] In 1866 Dicks launched his game-changing series Dicks' Shakespeare, offering individual plays for a penny, and thirty-seven plays in one volume for a shilling. A mere two years later, the firm could boast that it had sold upwards of 150,000 copies of their weekly penny Shakespeares and 700,000 of the one-shilling Shakespeare in sturdy wrappers.[31] Even if the well-established celebrity of William Shakespeare made him an outlier, such sales still attest to the immense reach of cheaply printed versions. Dicks's bold pricing structure—that is, print so many that you can price them at a penny—launched experimental reprints of authors who, like Austen, were out of copyright, in formats not previously tried.

Dicks's sixpenny editions of *Sense and Sensibility* and *Pride and Prejudice,* first published in March 1887, boast cover images that bear telltale marks of his publishing firm, where illustrations were a prominent selling point (figures 1.11 and 1.12). Copies of these ephemeral productions are so scarce that Gilson records only one Dicks sixpenny version of *Pride and Prejudice,*

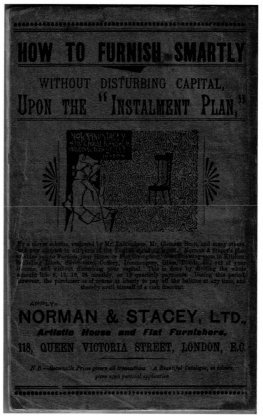

and from a copy missing its wrappers.[32] The pictured copy of *Sense and Sensibility* was reprinted in 1901, as proved by the curious language of the furniture advertisement on the back cover.[33] Published unabridged in 114 and 120 pages of cramped type in double columns, these slim Dicks paperbacks make room for a large number of full-page illustrations on the inside. The Routledge editions at sixpence, in contrast, contain no illustrations except on the wrapper. Harry Evans's illustration of a dancing couple for *Pride and Prejudice* is relatively tame, but his cover image for *Sense and Sensibility* is as sensationalistic as anything that screenwriter Andrew Davies, dubbed "king of the heaving bosom and glimpsed buttock" by London's *Evening Standard*, ever conceived for his adaptations of Austen's novels.[34] Evans's dramatic woodcut depicts an off-page duel between Colonel Brandon and

1.11. Sixpence *Sense and Sensibility* (London: John Dicks, n.d.; 1901 reissue of 1887 version). Collection of Sandra Clark.

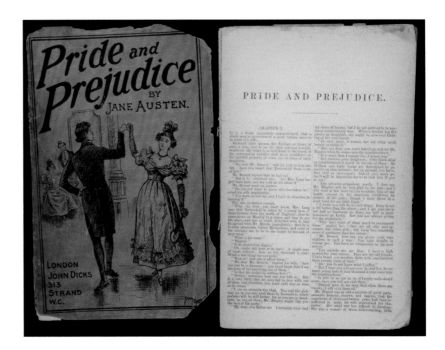

1.12. Sixpence *Pride and Prejudice* (London: John Dicks, n.d.; 1901 reissue of 1887 version). Goucher College Special Collections.

Willoughby at the moment when both men, arms extended, point their dueling pistols at each other. Two men in top hats, presumably the men's seconds, look sternly on from the background. This action scene, which would be fairly unremarkable if attached to one of the Sherlock Holmes stories that Dicks also published, is startling as a piece of cover art for Austen. Tonally at odds with the text, the packaging boldly shows a confrontation only euphemistically hinted at in the novel. Evans's other six internal illustrations, emphasized on the title page as "press etchings," redirect the focus of the book entirely to the love triangle between Willoughby, Marianne, and Brandon.[35] If a buyer judged this story by the accompanying pictures—and visual signals are hard to ignore—Elinor becomes a mere cipher in the melodrama surrounding Marianne, even though the accompanying text is complete and unchanged. Here we see classic Victorian sales tactics at work. Dicks promised the masses melodrama when he fed them Austen's novels at sixpence each.

The flipside of Victorian sensationalism is Victorian schmaltz, and Austen seems to have solicited that in spades too—even at the sixpenny rung. Although the dominant publishers in the sixpennny format were George

Routledge and John Dicks, one late-stage follower was S. W. Partridge & Co., with offices at 8 and 9 Paternoster Row, who announced on June 4, 1896, that a brand new sixpenny trio called the Marigold Series would commence with *Pride and Prejudice* at 130 pages in "stiff paper covers" in "imperial 8vo," the octavo format (one-eighth of a printing sheet) that most sixpennies were already using. The top cover shows an engraving of Mr. and Mrs. Bennet in what Partridge's handlists are quick to point out were "eight colours" (figure 1.13). The image, which is repeated as a half-tone frontispiece inside, mimics the toothache-worthy sweetness of Charles E. Brock, who in the previous year had illustrated the clothbound edition of *Pride and Prejudice* published by Macmillan, a firm that had taken its cues directly from the success of George Allen's edition of *Pride and Prejudice* in 1894, which was copiously and memorably illustrated by Hugh Thomson and known as the Peacock Edition (see figure 2.4, chapter 2). Partridge's sixpenny edition, which cuts corners by being stapled rather than sewn, promises a tiny taste of the sweet indulgence of the fad for lavishly illustrated books. The lure worked, for this Austen title continues to appear under the 6d. listings in Partridge catalogs through at least 1906.

Austen appears on the Partridge list among temperance books, missionary biographies, and juvenile literature. This, then, is a lowbrow Austen with a hint of the religious (see chapter 3). Samuel William Partridge (1810–1903), author of several books of poetry and hymns, including the dazzlingly popular memento-mori-in-verse *Upward and Onward: A Thought Book for the Threshold of Active Life* (1858), regretfully warned in his own writings of ill choices made in an unguided youth. Even under previous ownership, the established firm already enjoyed a reputation as a conservative Christian bookstore, active in the temperance movement and keen to promote reading among the poor, with wholesome picture books for children. The sixpenny model thus served publishers of various stripes. Austen kept company with all manner of Grub Street figures—page churners, jobbing illustrators, and schmaltz-peddlers.

John Dicks's high-volume experiments in cheap Austens extended beyond the sixpenny format to mass-market serialization in weekly installments for a halfpenny each. In 1885 and 1886, *Mansfield Park* and *Sense and Sensibility* appeared in *Dicks' English Library of Standard Works*, a periodical reprint project that consisted of the serial reissue of popular novels

SIXPENCE NETT

PRIDE AND PREJUDICE

THE MARIGOLD SERIES

By Jane Austen

S. W. PARTRIDGE & Cº.
8 & 9, PATERNOSTER ROW, LONDON.

in weekly numbers, each made up of sixteen pages and priced at a half-penny. In typical Dicks style, the firm prominently included sentimental and sensational illustrations in each weekly number, which shuffled parts of at least three books into a randomized order like a deck of cards.[36] The weekly numbers were twice the size of sixpenny editions, or roughly as tall as a standard piece of modern American paper (11 inches, or 28 centimeters), and printed in small type in three tight columns. Continuous pagination of the weeklies encouraged subsequent sales of bundles as a monthly in a format costing three pennies, which facilitated binding into large twice-yearly volumes made up of twenty-six weeklies, amounting to 416 pages each, plus title and frontispiece, for the bargain price of 1s.6d.[37] The serial of *Mansfield Park* appeared across twelve weeklies, dated March 4 to May 20, 1885, interrupted by installments of Lamb's *Tales from Shakspere* and *Uncle Tom's Cabin*, while the shorter *Sense and Sensibility* appeared in four weekly numbers, from February 3 to 24, 1886, mixed with sections from *The Scarlet Letter* and *Handy Andy. A Tale of Irish Life* (figure 1.14).

Rare copies of these serials survive as bound numbers among the larger half-annuals of *Dicks' English Library of Standard Works*. Trying to read these chopped texts as a bound book is chaotic, since any reading of the complete story of *Sense and Sensibility,* for example, means that, just as soon as the Dashwood women have settled "with tolerable comfort" at Barton and Sir John is asked whether he knows "any gentleman of the name of Willoughby at Allenham," the reader must skip over a scaffold showing Pearl and Hester Prynne supporting the limp body of Arthur Dimmesdale, ignore further comical shenanigans of Furlong hiding behind a bed curtain, and overlook something about a man on a horse, only to find the talk of Willoughby resuming in the next number, along with an illustration of the man himself, sporting an enormous handlebar mustache, as he cuts off "a long lock" of Marianne's hair (figure 1.15). Avoiding curious cross readings is like avoiding downtown traffic at rush hour. This is not just Austen on the cheap, but a literary smashup. There is little dignity in an issue of Dicks, just a bit of sport and modest profit. Even so, Austen's presence in this format boosted her public profile. The serializations tend to remake Austen in the popular mold of Charles Dickens, and indeed many of the stops and starts create ingenious approximation of cliffhangers.

Above all, part publication allowed consumers to spread out cost. *Mans-*

1.13. Sixpence *Pride and Prejudice* (London: S. W. Partridge & Co., n.d.; circa 1896). Courtesy of Robert Frew Ltd., Antiquarian Books, London.

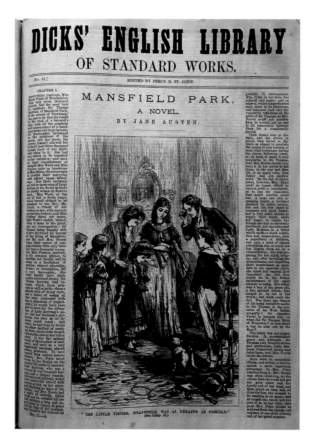

1.14. Half-penny installments of *Mansfield Park* and *Sense and Sensibility* in *Dicks' English Library of Standard Works* (London: John Dicks, 1885 and 1886). Collections of Devoney Looser and author.

field Park in parts would still have cost a total of sixpence, but in this format the reader need not part with the sum all at once. A buyer of Dicks's *Sense and Sensibility* in parts, spending a halfpenny a week on just the targeted issues of the shorter novel, paid only two pennies for the whole text, with bits of *The Scarlet Letter* and *Handy Andy* tossed into the bargain. Such schemes made the most sense for young readers and workers of the lower classes. Given the track record of John Dicks's firm, there may have been further creative experiments with Austen's other novels that went unrecorded. *The Dictionary of National Biography* warns that "survival in libraries of books that bear the Dicks imprint is haphazard and his several series of cheap reprints of English classics are almost everywhere incomplete." Because the firm constantly issued and reissued publications, the dates of some series

1.15. A page from a half-penny installment of *Sense and Sensibility* in *Dicks' English Library of Standard Works* (London: John Dicks, 1886). Author's collection.

also remain uncertain. "But his achievement is clear: he was one of the most important forces in the increase of cheap reading material for the masses."[38] As his obituary indicated, his publishing concern was "a marvel in cheap and good literature."[39] Jane Austen took part in that chaotic marvel.

In America, and as early as 1845, the firm of Carey and Hart of Philadelphia briefly trialed cheap, dual-columned paperbacks of at least two Austen

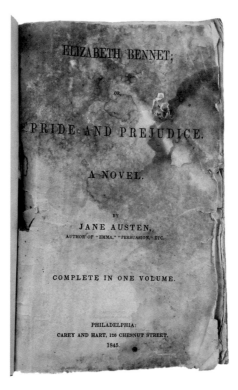
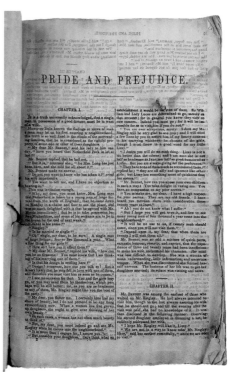

1.16. Title page and opening text from 25-cent *Elizabeth Bennet; or Pride and Prejudice* (Philadelphia: Carey and Hart, 1845). Collection of Sandra Clark.

novels, produced in small type on thin paper and sold in blue printed wrappers—forerunners of the dime novels. It is hard to know what impact these extremely early American paperbacks had on Austen's reputation, as only a handful now survive, and none with their original printed wrappers completely intact (figure 1.16). On the basis of an advertisement bound with a surviving copy at Jane Austen's House Museum of the paperback version of *Elizabeth Bennet; or Pride and Prejudice*, Gilson assumes the existence of all six novels in this cheap format, yet only two titles have ever been confirmed, the other being *Mansfield Park*.[40] The advertisement for all six announces "PRICE 25 CENTS EACH."[41] In 1833, when these titles were last published individually by the same Philadelphia firm, the lowest recorded retail price was 83 cents for each novel as two slim volumes in boards.[42] Production values on the few survivors from 1845 confirm that the paperback versions were made cheaply for the bottom end of the market. Even if Carey and

Hart's 1845 innovation remained limited to only two novels, their low-priced paperback experiment was truly ahead of its time and perhaps failed to find the necessary distribution network to make a profit.

Decades later, the handful of dime novels of Austen bear a marked resemblance to the part-publications of *Dicks' English Library of Standard Works*, although less chaotic because unshuffled. Dime novels looked like magazines, complete with mastheads at the start of a number, allowing American publishers to exploit the low second-class postal rates that applied to periodical subscriptions but not to books. Printed in crammed type in multiple columns per page, these American reprints were novels thinly disguised in the costumes of weekly magazines. Some readers of dime novels were middling householders who paid for subscriptions to a series of stories suitable for the whole family, rather than selecting individual issues. But many more would have purchased them opportunistically from newsstands. The format of these voracious freestanding weeklies needed constant fueling with a variety of copy, so much so that these early paperback versions of Austen in America look like indiscriminate publishing fodder rather than a considered pedagogical choice or a reliable index of popular taste. Nothing like the fierce competition over Austen in Victorian England, as shown by the crowded yellowback and sixpenny market shares, appears to have taken place across the Atlantic. In 1880, both Harper & Brothers and George Munro of New York did include Jane Austen in their dime novel series of popular fiction, but almost as if part of a late-date awakening to her presence in America (see chapter 4). *Pride and Prejudice*, cramped and unillustrated, joined the Franklin Square Library series published by Harper & Brothers as number 135 (figure 1.17). George Munro reached for every Austen novel except *Persuasion* to toss into his cheap Seaside Library series in 1880 and 1881. In 1882 his series even bundled the little-known *Lady Susan* with the even lesser-known *The Watsons* as number 1313 (figure 1.18).[43] Munro's American Austens were priced at 15 cents for sixty pages, or 20 cents for double numbers, with their text squeezed into three

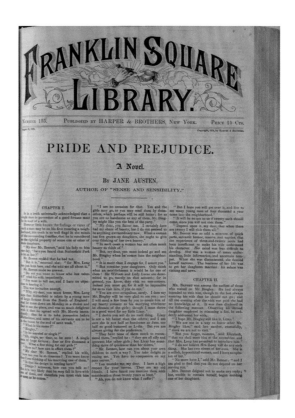

1.17. American dime-novel reprint of *Pride and Prejudice*, priced at 15 cents (New York: Harper & Brothers, 1880). Harry Ransom Center, University of Texas at Austin.

1.18. American dime-novel reprint of *Lady Susan and The Watsons* as number 1313 in the Seaside Library series, "price 10 cents" (New York: George Munro, 1882). John G. White Special Collections, Cleveland Public Library Digital Gallery.

tightly printed columns.[44] Just like their British cousins, the cheap magazine-style reprints of Austen in America, originally churned out in the tens of thousands, are now also far scarcer than her first editions.[45]

Perhaps the rarest of the ghost paperbacks is a British threepenny version of *Sense and Sensibility* published in September 1892. With establishments in London and Manchester, W. H. White & Co. broke through the sixpenny floor with its sensational Manchester Library series. *Sense and Sensibility* squeezed itself by means of small type and tight double columns into ninety-seven pages to become the series's eighteenth title. Hailed as "marvels of cheapness," the Manchester Library titles sold for only three pennies in paper wrappers and in cloth for sixpence.[46] Even the cramped paperbacks allowed room for eye-catching, if crude and disjointed, illustrations. *Sense and Sensibility* contains not only a gratuitous frontispiece labeled "Elinor Perceives Willoughby" but also a title-page woodcut of Willoughby's rescue of Marianne that might be mistaken for a hackneyed bridal cake topper (figure 1.19). Although there are no copies of White's *Sense and Sensibility* recorded in the composite catalog of the world's major scholarly libraries, known as WorldCat (Online Computer Library Center [OCLC]), I located three survivors—none of which, sadly, remain in their original paper wrappers. Instead, the extant copies are bound in publisher's cloth along with other Manchester Library volumes, which seem to have totaled nineteen titles over as many months. Two of these copies survive in bound volumes that bundle Austen with Charlotte Brontë's *Jane Eyre*, Gaskell's *Mary Barton*, and Carlyle's *Past and Present*.[47] The third survivor (pictured) substitutes *Jane Eyre* with Poe's *Tales of Mystery*, the last recorded title in the series. Advertisements for White's Manchester Library promised that the threepenny paperbacks, produced at monthly intervals, would "bring the vast store of Standard English Literature within the reach of the general mass of

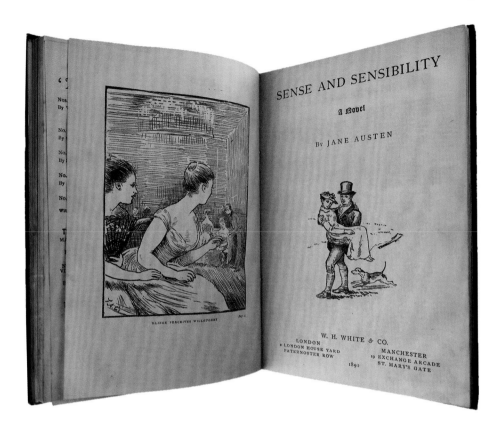

SENSE AND SENSIBILITY

a Novel

BY JANE AUSTEN

W. H. WHITE & CO.
LONDON
8 LONDON HOUSE YARD
PATERNOSTER ROW

MANCHESTER
19 EXCHANGE ARCADE
ST. MARY'S GATE

1892

ELINOR PERCEIVES WILLOUGHBY

the reading public."[48] The existence of many testimonials from newspapers suggests that the low-priced series, which ran from 1891 to 1893, made quite a splash before it came to a halt, although depressingly little evidence of that impact survives.

"PENNY DELIGHTFUL"

In 1896 two radical publishers, George Newnes and W. T. Stead, working in cooperation and guided by similar goals for social justice, produced ultracheap editions of Austen for a mere penny—to give the poor access to better books (figures 1.20 and 1.21). Physically, these little penny editions were ugly ducklings. Roughly stapled and glued, each unillustrated text is barely larger than a small modern paperback and a lot thinner. If you look closely, you can locate the staples through their meager covers. In this penny format, George Newnes Limited produced a complete edition of *Sense and*

1.19. Thruppence *Sense and Sensibility* (London and Manchester: W. H. White & Co., 1892). Bound in original green cloth with the Manchester Library's threepenny versions of Carlyle's *Past and Present*, Gaskell's *Mary Barton,* and Poe's *Tales of Mystery.* Collection of Sandra Clark.

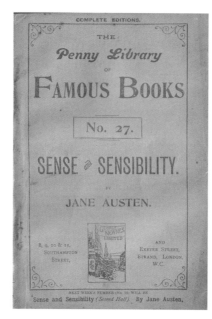
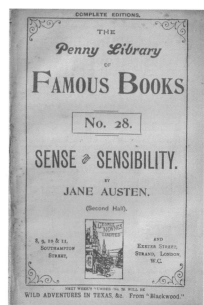

1.20. *Sense and Sensibility* as numbers 27 and 28 in the Penny Library of Famous Books (London: George Newnes Limited, n.d. [1896]). Author's collection.

Sensibility in two parts, each under one hundred pages in tiny but clear type, under the rubric Penny Library of Famous Books, touted as "a shelf-load of Entertaining volumes for every Working Man, Woman and Youth in the Kingdom."[49] As numbers 27 and 28 in this weekly series, each half of *Sense and Sensibility* could be had for a penny, anarchically followed by *Wild Adventures in Texas, and Other Tales* at number 29. So, for one-third the cost of the cheap sixpence versions, and less than even White's great bargains, one might still read and possess the complete Austen novel, albeit in an even more ephemeral format. Almost simultaneously, the Review of Reviews Office produced a boiled-down version of *Pride and Prejudice,* abridged to fifty-eight tightly printed pages, as number 16 among their Penny Popular Novels. Nearly all the books discussed so far came without any introductory matter, but this cheapest and shortest of them all contains a miniature "Preface" that follows an ad for a patent medicine. In this wee threshold to the book, the editor emphasizes how Miss Austen writes about "the ordinary middle-class society of her day," insisting that "her characters are every-day characters and her incidents every-day incidents." For the two men behind these penny-book projects, Austen served a far-reaching social agenda for universal education and reform. They thought it crucial that Austen, talent aside, present herself as an accessible recorder of the commonplace and not as a distant member of the landed gentry or a novitiate of the rarefied class of literati.

A publishing empire with the goal of turning the newest working-class generation of magazine readers into lovers of books and learning was one of the forces transforming Austen into a penny novel. George Newnes (1851–1910) was a towering figure in publishing during the Victorian and Edwardian eras and is considered a founder of modern journalism.[50] In 1881 he started a news weekly called *Tit-Bits* that responded directly to the Elementary Education Act of 1870, introducing universal education for ages 5 to 12 in England and Wales and creating a new generation able to read. *Tit-Bits*, which was squarely aimed at the lower middle classes and reached a staggering circulation of seven hundred thousand by the end of the century, provided—just as its name implies—light extracts and juicy snippets of news and informative literature in an easy-to-read manner. In its selections and range of topics, the magazine advocated eloquently for universal education. Newnes may be best known for publishing the *Strand* magazine, begun in 1891, which offered many of Arthur Conan Doyle's stories about Sherlock Holmes. In 1897, George Newnes Ltd. restructured and started publishing books.

In January 1896, ahead of publishing proper books, Newnes launched a mashup of magazine printing and book publishing, called the Penny Library of Famous Books, to displace the "pernicious literature" known generically as the Penny Dreadful. These lurid tales, Newnes argued, were so widely associated with criminal behavior—"having passed from the domain of opinion on to that of indisputable demonstration"—that there was talk of "strenuous prosecution of the chief offenders." In a full-page advertisement in *The Bookseller*, Newnes rejects the "application of the law," urging that prosecution of distributors would only backfire. Instead, he suggests that the industry put "a 'Penny Delightful' in vigorous competition with the justly

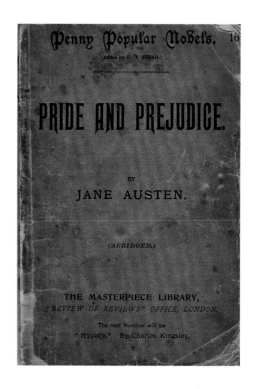

1.21. Penny digest of *Pride and Prejudice,* abridged by W. T. Stead, for Penny Popular Novels series (London: Review of Reviews Office, n.d. [1896]). Author's collection.

reprobated 'Penny Dreadful.'" Newnes prefers carrot over stick, laughter over sermon, and proposes "works which have given immeasurable enjoyment to readers in the past." He promises that "the conductors of The Penny Library of Famous Books will demonstrate to the buyers of penny publications that there is a world of delightful reading which may be brought within the compass of their means of expenditure—which run through the whole gamut of emotion, now thrilling the reader with healthy excitement, now irresistibly compelling his laughter or tears."[51]

Given his placement of the advertisement, Newnes implies that fellow booksellers and publishers should solve this self-made dilemma before the government interferes in their profession. Newnes claims that he has cast small new type "expressly for the purpose" and announces his first four titles: *The Vicar of Wakefield*, by Oliver Goldsmith; *Tales of Adventure, Mystery & Imagination*, by Edgar Allan Poe; *Suil Dhuv, the Coiner*, by Gerald Griffin; and *Feats on the Fiord*, by Harriet Martineau. This cheap format, then, was not about selling generic reprints in ever-larger numbers for profit, but about offering literature as a tool for critical thinking and social improvement to England's working poor. Austen's inclusion is less about the canon formation that might interest scholars than about co-opting her plots for moral instruction. Writers of merit might somehow help the poor avoid a life of crime and gain an education. These penny editions were not mere moneymaking schemes as much as optimistic social-welfare projects, within the bounds of Victorian mores.

William Thomas Stead (1849–1912), Newnes's business partner on *The Review of Reviews* and the abridger of the parallel *Pride and Prejudice* at one penny, was an English newspaper editor who pioneered a daring style of investigative journalism with reportage on child welfare, social legislation, and criminal codes. Some of his tactics were decidedly unsavory, but Stead stressed that journalists could help govern by changing public opinion and by disclosing formerly ignored facts. In 1885, a decade before he boiled Austen down, Stead became famous for a series of articles in the *Pall Mall Gazette* in support of a bill, eventually termed "the Stead Act," that would raise the age of consent from 13 to 16. His shocking articles alleged the prevalence of child prostitution in Victorian London and the need for immediate legislative reforms.[52] As part of his investigations for this series of sexually explicit articles, Stead contracted to "purchase" Eliza Armstrong, the 13-year-old daughter of an alcoholic mother who was willing to sell her for £5. Although he handed Eliza over to others who whisked her to safety in France with a Salvationist family, Stead was jailed for three months on the technical charge of kidnapping—but only after his newspaper actually ran out of paper printing extra copies of the story. Stead demonstrated that sensational journalism could sell papers while also doing some good.

In December 1895, in the wake of the massive success of his Penny Poets series, Stead announced the launch of Penny Prose-Classics, offering a list of fifty-two proposed novels to be distilled into 30,000 to 40,000 words; *Pride and Prejudice* was planned as number 30 but moved up to 16. He launched the series with "a first edition of 250,000 copies" of Rider Haggard's *She.*[53] Coordinating with similar efforts by Newnes, Stead hoped that his Penny Prose-Classics would enable a "reading revival."[54] Reasoning that "as long as books cost a day's wage, or even a quarter of a day's wage, it was ridiculous to expect that many books would be bought by the poorer millions," Stead soon congratulates himself that the recent "experiment" has set "other publishers to work, with the result that penny editions are the order of the day."[55] He recommends the penny books to "teachers, and those who have an opportunity of suggesting reading to young men and young women." With an anecdote from his own youth, he compares the thrill a teenager could gain from reading a good book to "the intoxication produced by champagne."[56] He directs his double-barreled rhetoric not just at those who would deny all but practical training to girls but also at the astringent type of reformer who couples advocacy of universal education with temperance policies or religious restrictions.

Stead quotes at length from other correspondents, possibly invented, including a teacher who laments that "public money may not be employed for the furnishing of school libraries." This, then, is why Newnes and Stead, two newspapermen and social reformers, are printing and editing classics, including Austen, at a penny apiece. A quarter century after the hard-won right to universal education for children ages 5 to 12, the government blames crime on the proliferation of the cheap Penny Dreadful but does not see fit to fund school libraries with alternative reading. Outraged, Stead asks his readers, especially teachers, "for a list of the fifty best books that they would like to have reproduced for a penny, for the purpose of a school library."[57] He cautions that any such list should take into account that copyright lasts, even after an author's death, for forty-two years after a book's publication. The Penny Novels were published in ninety weekly numbers for eighteen months, amounting, reckons one historian, to "approximately 9 million" copies of abridgements.[58] Of Austen's share, which comes to roughly one hundred thousand copies of a fifty-eight-page digest of *Pride and Prejudice,* fewer than a handful are recorded as surviving in libraries.[59]

SCHOOLING WITH JANE

Fired by the passions of educational reformers even before the twentieth century begins, Jane Austen in paperback becomes a go-to author for those with big educational ambitions and small budgets. Nevertheless, the impression that paperbacks, as opposed to clothbound books, were merely for the poor or the schoolroom lingered on for decades, as did the idea that paperbacks were paltry substitutes for genuine hardback books. During the 1910s, 1920s, and 1930s, the dutiful paperbacks that fulfilled an educational function looked bland and utilitarian. Gone were the colorful picture boards of those railway editions in the nineteenth century and the visual sensationalism of reprints by John Dicks. In the early decades of the twentieth century, paperbacks lost their sense of fun. In exchange, they gained a modicum of status as an educational tool. Admittedly, most school editions of canonical authors remained hardback books, increasingly with explanatory introductions aimed at teachers and students. In 1923, of course, Oxford University Press published the complete works of Jane Austen, edited by R. W. Chapman, a landmark moment. Austen also ghosted the schoolroom as book prizes (see chapter 3). These prizes, gift books, and school editions all tended to be hardbacks. The reigning prejudice appears to have been that floppy and flimsy paperbacks failed to convey the gravity of literature or the importance of rigorous canonical reading.

When publishing firms such as Blackie & Son did produce inexpensive paperbacks as set texts, they were lackluster affairs—compact and sometimes reinforced with oilcloth to make a "limp" binding, and duly approved by the Board of Education. In October 1904, Blackie announced their New English Texts series, edited by "W. H. D. Rouse, Litt. D.," as fulfilling the "new Syllabus for Secondary Schools."[60] Each paperback edition of a famous work contained a brief introduction but "no notes," since such textbook features were thought off-putting to younger readers. The series thrived in secondary schools for decades, as attested by a 1921 edition of *Emma*, priced at one shilling, in the long-running Blackie's English Texts series (figure 1.22).[61] The abridgement model instigated by W. T. Stead persisted, for Rouse's 128-page extract reprints only the first chapters of the novel, "down to Emma's first disillusionment." The diminutive volume ends with Emma's return to Hartfield after her claustrophobic carriage ride with Mr. Elton. Such schoolroom paperbacks were intended as a kind of teaser: "I hope it will send readers to the whole book, where they will see what happens to Mr. Elton, Harriet, and Emma herself."[62] By "the whole book," Rouse gestures to a hardback version now presumed available outside of school or in a local library. An old school stamp found in my own copy of Blackie's *Emma* dramatically brings home the potential inaccessibility of the remainder of the story to a reader studying an oilcloth-reinforced paperback in a rural school: "Tresco School, Isles of Scilly." Tresco, an island in the archipelago off the Cornish coast, had a population of 217 permanent residents in 1921, the year this copy of *Emma* was printed. Today the population is not much higher. With few books on the island in the 1920s and 1930s, students who were assigned this shilling copy of *Emma* at the remote island school of Tresco likely never found out how the story ended.

William Henry Denham Rouse (1863–1950), the editor of the Blackie's series, is identified in advertisements and book lists as "Headmaster of the Perse School, Cambridge." By implication, therefore, this paperback is not merely, in the tradition of Newnes's magazine, a tidbit of prose by Jane Austen, but a way of accessing a high-profile educator from Cambridge—regardless of the location of the pupil. Rouse was an expert in Latin and Greek with a reputation for

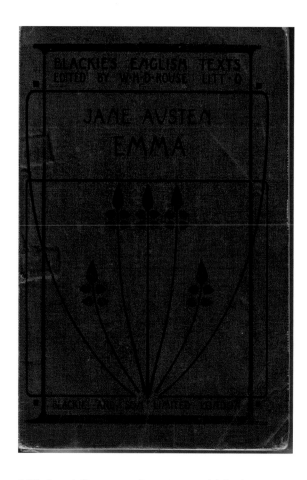

1.22. One-shilling extract from *Emma,* published as one of Blackie's English Texts for schools and edited by W. H. D. Rouse (London, Glasgow, and Bombay: Blackie & Son Limited, 1921). Author's collection.

1.23. In order to show relative size, here is a selection of the publications discussed in this chapter. The blue booklet is *What Great Women Have Said About Men* (Girard, Kansas: Haldeman-Julius Company, n.d. [1922]). Author's collection.

modern classroom methods. As a linguist and a founding member of the Loeb Classics series, he emphasized accessibility in his classrooms, teaching even ancient languages as if they were vibrant spoken tongues. In his published translations of Homer, which remain in print today, Rouse stressed the playful colloquial nature of the poet's expressions. Although Austen needs no translation, Rouse similarly points not just to the author's timeless account of human character but also to her "urbane humour . . . not without a spice of mischief, enough to cause a delightful tingling, but never cruel or bitter."[63] More's the pity that a Tresco student could not see *Emma*'s humor through to the end.

Meanwhile, in America, socialist entrepreneur Emanuel Haldeman-Julius (1889–1951) tried out a more relaxed approach to paperback publishing that, by playing fast and loose with editorial standards, perpetuated the lowbrow status of the paperback even as it helped educate the masses. Known as "the Barnum of Books," Haldeman-Julius published millions of tiny pamphlet versions of classic literature out of Girard, Kansas.[64] His extracts and reprints soon sold for 10 or 5 cents to the working classes in the form of thin, 3½-by-5-inch, stapled miniaturized books in no-frills printed wrappers. Since his firm radically doctored and reduced many of the classics, to the point of inventing lurid new titles to increase sales, the fact that the several thousand titles in his Pocket Series, better known as "Little Blue Books," did not include any Jane Austen novel may have been for the best. In 1922, snippets of Austen's work nonetheless found their way into his anthology *What Great Women Have Said About Men*, part of his Ten-Cent Pocket Series (No. 304), in which Austen was allowed to take the lead among "Great Women"[65] (see figure 1.23). The sixty-page pamphlet opens with five and a half pages of quips from Austen about menfolk, including the opening sentence of *Pride and Prejudice* and nuggets such as "Men of sense do not want silly wives." Removed from their robust context and thus cleansed of irony, the quotes make for an anemic inventory of Austen's literary contributions, as if chosen "to offer those little delicate compliments which," Mr. Collins urges, "are always acceptable to ladies."[66]

Then in 1939, a North American firm briefly explored the potential pedagogical role of cheap paperbacks in the working-class home—as self-help tools for adults outside the college classroom. During the Depression, and with up to 20 percent unemployment in the United States, the cautious and conservative decade of the 1930s witnessed an uptick in the genre of the self-improvement book, in anthologies such as *Reader's Digest*, and in subscriptions to book clubs.[67] Organizations such as the Book-of-the-Month Club and the Literary Guild thrived, exerting real influence upon the publishing industry. Although these subscription book clubs widened general readership, catching flak for lowering standards of tastes and homogenizing literature, they inadvertently increased the fetishization of the hardback and required fees

1.24. Set Number 1 of the University Classics educational paperbacks in original box (lid not shown), containing dime reprint of *Sense and Sensibility* (Greenwich, CT: Appleby & Company, n.d. [1939]). Author's collection.

that were not within everyone's reach.[68] To Appleby & Company of Connecticut and Toronto, paperbacks seemed an ideal tool for readers eager to better themselves through education but who had missed out on a traditional college classroom and could not afford hardbacks or club fees. Appleby briefly produced self-study paperback sets of "the most powerful books ever written," sold under the series title of University Classics. When bought as a set, they promised a university education in a box for around a dollar (figure 1.24).[69]

The first set of University Classics consisted of eight paperback titles, listed here in the order they appear on the paper label of the unadorned, cardboard box—with lid—in which they originally sold:

House of Seven Gables—Hawthorne
Sense and Sensibility—Austen
Fathers and Sons—Turgeniev
Scarlet Letter—Hawthorne
Madame Bovary—Flaubert
Green Mansions—Hudson
Manon Lescaut—Prevost
Sapho—Daudet

Here, Austen—the standout sole representative of British literature—keeps company with an impressive set of worldly men. Appleby also published *Pride and Prejudice,* available by itself and as part of another set. Since I can confirm only twenty-five total Appleby titles, the perceived importance of Austen to a college reading curriculum was, by 1939, truly significant.[70] In this series, only *Short Stories* by Fiodor Dostoievski, as Appleby spelled it, was ever noted by *Publishers' Weekly,* which lists the price as a miraculous 10 cents.[71] Production values fail to meet even the low bar of the utilitarian schoolbooks, but for what amounts to $1.75 per volume in today's currency, that must be overlooked. Although the print is clear and easy to read, the paper is rough to the touch and quick to brown. With the exception of an endearingly childlike label printed on the first leaf to encourage the owner to write their name in the book, the volumes are devoid of graphic flourishes and glued into covers of dark grey thick paper, embossed rather than printed, with raised text that can be read only in good light. The books look quite drab and serious.[72] The message is clear: in this box you will find a no-frills education whose quality lies in the wisdom of the texts themselves. The books have no editorial interventions—no notes and no explanatory introductions. Authors, suggests the box, are their own best teachers.

At the front of every copy, the Appleby management offers a rationale for their publishing approach: "The University Classics are so named because they are the books most colleges urge, and frequently require their students to read; and because, by reading them, anyone will acquire much of the essence of a college education." After a redundant mention of low costs and a selection process that allegedly took into account recommendations by the National Council of Teachers of English, the explanatory blurb concludes with a quotation from a famous lecture by Thomas Carlyle on May 19, 1840: "The true university of these days is a Collection of Books."[73] A century earlier, Carlyle had praised the Victorian proliferation of cheaply available books, criticizing the role of the traditional university as increasingly elitist, complacent, and intellectually aloof. Speaking to a middle-class audience, Carlyle rejected the medieval vision of universities as robed scholars speaking from on high. He urged instead that all people avail themselves of libraries and the new generation of cheap books to read the great thinkers for themselves. The quote pulled by Appleby is famous enough to have been carved in stone on the Library of Congress and the San Francisco Library (now the Asian Art Museum). Carlyle's declaration became the implied slogan of all autodidacts.

In other words, Appleby paperbacks were, in spite of their dull appearance, still ablaze with social idealism and democratization. Austen burned brightly among these ambitious books. Yet the Appleby project was short-lived and left little trace.[74] After producing a few dozen titles as mass-market paperbacks and in boxed sets in 1939, Appleby & Company quietly disappeared. Their sudden exit from the field was doubtless due to the introduction, that same year, of the colorful 25-cent paperback by Pocket Books, which so utterly changed the face of reading in America that it made a project like Appleby's dull boxed-up educational matter obsolete. Since our modern eyes are used to seeing well-designed, even overdesigned, paperbacks, it is only in contrast with the staunchness of Appleby's University Classics paperbacks that the next set of paperback innovations by Penguin and Pocket Books can be truly appreciated.

1.25. *Northanger Abbey* and *Persuasion* in distinctive orange striped covers (Harmondsworth, UK: Penguin Books, 1943). Author's collection.

PENGUINS & POCKETS

A few years before Appleby's experiment, the paperbacks of a new company called Penguin Books had begun to rock the publishing world in England. The origin story of Penguin Books, started by Allen Lane in 1935, often credits Lane with *inventing* the mass-market paperback, but, as Austen's cheapest versions show, such inflationary rhetoric is false. Ironically, company legend has it that Lane got his initial idea for Penguin Books at a train station—the birthplace of the original shilling yellowback. As he waited for a train home to London after a weekend as the guest of writer Agatha Christie, Lane allegedly could not find anything worthwhile to read among the meager offerings at the station. This epiphany generated Penguin Books, whose first ten authors fittingly included Christie. Lane reasoned that a good read should not cost more than a package of cigarettes, so his paperbacks were initially priced at 6d. (just like the sixpenny paperbacks of the 1890s, although with inflation the true cost was effectively halved). Lane's actual innovation was neither the format nor the price, but the method of display. He is credited with designing, for his books, upright wire racks that could be added to nearly any existing retail space. In these freestanding racks, books could be sold not just in bookstores and train stations (as had the yellowbacks), but also in pharmacies and cigarette shops—brand new venues for the sale of whole books.

Lane's big break came when the British branch of Woolworths, which after expansion to England as a "penny and sixpence store" in 1909 had more than six hundred stores, placed a starting order for a whopping sixty-three thousand books. Ten months in, Penguin had printed 1 million books and soon became famous for selling cheap paperbacks color-coded by genre—with green for mystery, orange for fiction, blue for biography, and so on.

Penguin's long-lasting contribution to the standardization of book covers also proved their great marketing advantage. Two solid bands of color sandwiching a band of white became a way of announcing the genre or nature of a Penguin book long before a browser stood close enough to read the specific title. Until the 1960s, when Penguin modified the look, their color-coded books were instantly recognizable. Even when adjusted and remodified into the Penguin "grid," the uniformity of their designs was a matter of pride and a hallmark of their brand. The power of the Penguin branding style may be even more evident today, as mugs, T-shirts, postcards, wrapping paper, and all manner of nostalgia revives for nonbook use the telltale covers that Penguin stopped producing more than a half century ago.

1.26. Wartime advertisements that appeared on the backs of *Northanger Abbey* and *Persuasion* (Harmondsworth, UK: Penguin Books, 1943) (figure 1.23). Author's collection.

Jane Austen naturally appeared among her orange brethren in the fiction section, just as soon as Penguin started printing fiction "classics" in 1938. Then, *Pride and Prejudice* was first among the ten literary greats chosen for Penguin's brief flirtation with illustrative woodcuts (discussed in chapter 4). With texts apparently set from the Everyman's Library edition in hardback, *Northanger Abbey* and *Persuasion* eventually joined the ranks of the distinctive orange books in 1943 (figure 1.25).[75] Printed in accordance with wartime paper restrictions, these Austens had to adhere to the Book Production War Economy Agreement regulations. Penguin consequently eliminated dust jackets, trimmed margins, and replaced sewn bindings with metal staples. These wartime paperbacks, of slightly lesser quality than their later reprintings, also contain subsidizing advertisements for Mars bars, light bulbs, dog food, cigarettes, and toothpaste—reminiscent of the popular yellowbacks that preceded them (figure 1.26). The wartime ads, warning of "sweet rationing" and promising "brighter times," neatly, if unintentionally, echo

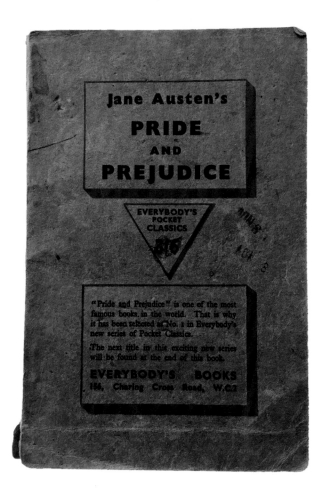

1.27. Everybody's Pocket Classics reprint of *Pride and Prejudice* (London: Everybody's Books, 1946). Author's collection.

Persuasion's own wartime setting, but they may distract a reader trying to cross the threshold of *Northanger Abbey*. In slightly amended uniforms of orange and purple, the two wartime Austens were immediately enlisted into the Penguin Forces Club series, a select group of titles sent to British soldiers on active duty during World War II (discussed in chapter 5). In sum, Austen enjoyed her fair share of the iconic Penguin experience, even if her hard-earned status as a "classic" delayed her inclusion and wartime circumstances cut corners with her production values, yet again.

During wartime inflation and paper scarcities, these Penguin paperbacks remained coveted commodities that retained their retail value as secondhand books. In 1946 Everybody's Bookstore in London advertised they would buy back "paper-covered fiction such as Penguin, Cherry Tree, Crime Club, etc." at 4d. each—with "bound fiction" fetching "Up to 5s." Traders in secondhand books were responding to paper rationing: "Nearly every house in the country contains books which will never be read again. Sell them to us now. Every book that does its job twice is helping the vital 'Save Paper' campaign." This same bookstore chain briefly published their own series of paperbacks, named Everybody's Pocket Classics, roughly stapled and glued in printed paper wrappers made from low-grade recycled paper. *Pride and Prejudice* led the experiment at No. 1, because, as the cover explained, it "is one of the most famous books in the world" (figure 1.27).[76] In times of scarcity, Austen remained popular as a no-nonsense paperback at three and a half shillings, and as hand-me-downs.

Back in 1939, America was suffering an unemployment rate of nearly 18 percent. A packet of cigarettes in New York, to use Allen Lane's measurement, cost 15 cents—although a quarter might buy you two packs at once. The E. P. Dutton edition of *Pride and Prejudice* in cloth, however, would set you back $2.00. The latest bestsellers, such as *Gone with the Wind* or *The Grapes of Wrath*, cost even more—at least $2.75 in hardback. Macmillan advertised a limited edition of Margaret Mitchell's book for sale in Atlanta, timed to coincide with the movie premiere in December. It cost $7.50 for two volumes bound in "grey and butternut-colored cloth, trimmed in gold, with a reproduction of the Confederate flag on the front."[77] Books were out of sync with—and out of the reach of—the common American reader, and this was why Appleby started publishing those no-frills minilibraries in cardboard boxes.

On June 19, 1939, Robert de Graff changed all of this with 25-cent paperbacks that were a mixture of new and classic titles. That day he brazenly took out a full-page advertisement in the *New York Times:* "Out Today—The New Pocket Books That May Transform New York's Reading Habits." Dubbing the launch of the 25-cent paperback "the most important literary coming-out party," the advertisement included celebrity endorsements from "Leaders of America," pictures of the first ten titles, a coupon for ordering by mail, and a money-back guarantee.[78] American publishers had noticed the success of Penguin Books, but most were skeptical about whether such a flimsy and down-market format would appeal to the American mainstream reader. With the heads of Simon & Schuster as minority partners, de Graff proved them wrong, for his initial run of one hundred thousand copies of a modest ten titles, in a launch modeled after Penguin's with one mystery by Christie, sold out within a week.[79]

With only twenty-eight hundred bookstores in the United States, the established distribution network for traditional books could not move enough copies at 25 cents retail to make a profit. De Graff had to find a way to sell paperbacks in the volume usually reserved for newspapers and magazines. But in the 17,000 newsstands, the 18,000 cigar stores, and the tens of thousands of lunch counters, drugstores, and train or bus stations already displaying magazines, de Graff saw a ready-made distribution network, not dissimilar to the ones that Simms & M'Intyre in 1847 and Lane in 1935 had also spotted.[80] Pocket Books first sold at subway stations, newspaper stands, and cigar stores in and around New York, placing cheap books within reach of suburban commuters. Expansion into the Northeast corridor was quick and definitive, and after eight weeks de Graff had sold 325,000 copies. When it came to packaging his paperbacks, however, De Graff went in a new, untried direction with splashes of color so brassy and with artworks so over-the-top that even the most hardened reader of sensational yellowbacks might have raised an eyebrow. Where Penguin used color to sort neatly by genre, de Graff deliberately mixed old and new titles, high with low, in a higgledy-piggledy manner as liberating as it was unnerving. Where the covers of the European color-coded Penguins were reassuringly tidy, straight-edged, and relatively understated, de Graff promoted a cacophony of mismatched covers, with each shouting its presence more loudly than the last, tossing aside any notions of symmetry or consistency of typographical choices. De Graff's mass-market covers had little discipline and much swagger. Hail, the birth of pulp![81]

Pride and Prejudice joined Pocket Books as number 63, its first cover typical of the lowbrow, colorful look of all Pocket Books—complete with stained page edges (figure 1.28). Two hands exchanging a wedding band as they float in a sea of pink promise readers a romance, the difference in skin color neatly translating the social distinctions between Elizabeth Bennet and Fitzwilliam Darcy as equivalent to a modern racial divide. The back blurb calls the book a classic but makes no mention of Austen's Englishness or period setting, explaining only that this is a story "about the gradual union of two people, one held back by unconquerable pride, the other by prejudice." Readers who did not yet know of Jane Austen might conclude that she wrote an important American novel about conquering racial prejudice.[82] The next paragraph nods to the upcoming movie starring Laurence Olivier, in case the lure of cinematic commitment to the story might be a better consumer trigger. John Dicks himself could not have done better.

One curious feature of Pocket Book's first printing of *Pride and Prejudice* is its concession to the view that paperbacks are merely a starter book and not the real deal. The page following the ending contains a notice that asks "Did you like this Book?" This notice is worth reproducing in full, because it offers readers a 25-cent credit on their investment in the paperback if they now upgrade to a hardback:

> THE publishers hope that you have enjoyed this book, enjoyed it so much that you may wish to own it in a more permanent edition than is made possible by *Pocket* BOOKS.
>
> *Pride and Prejudice* is also available in many other editions, substantially bound in durable cloth. Two of them are:
>
> Grosset & Dunlap Universal Library edition $1.00
> E. P. Dutton edition (illustrated) $2.00

If you wish to own one of these editions of *Pride and Prejudice* to add permanently to your library, you may secure it in the following way: Return to the publishers, Pocket Books, Inc., 1230 Sixth Avenue, Rockefeller Center, New York City, this book which will comprise a 25¢ part payment against the price of the edition you want. Thus, for instance, should you want the edition selling for $1.00, mail us this book and 75¢, and we will send you a brand-new copy of that edition. The book returned to us will be given to a worthy charity.

Whatever arrangement Pocket Books made with these publishers, it did not last long, for the invitation to upgrade soon disappears from further reprintings. After the confident, let's-break-all-the-rules cover art, there is something disarmingly self-deprecating about this statement of a paperback as ephemeral and inferior. In 1939, home libraries were still deemed legit only if made up of hardback books in "durable cloth." For all of its strutting and unabashed loudness, this paperback humbly offers itself up to the reader as merely a Starter Jane.

Ephemeral or not, the new generation of paperbacks proved to be big business. Penguin opened an American office two months after the launch of Pocket Books, and other publishing houses quickly jumped in to compete for market share: Avon launched in 1941, Popular Library in 1942, and Dell in 1943. The war slowed the surge, but once peace arrived, a half dozen other American houses sprang up, including Bantam in 1945; New American Library, which published fiction under the Signet imprint, in 1948; and Airmont in 1951. A full century after the introduction of the yellowback in Britain's railway stations, America was finally ready for its own era of pulp fiction, a topic revisited in chapter 5. By then, Jane Austen had been part of cheap paperback reading for over a hundred years and yet the format managed to reinvent itself.

1.28. A 25-cent Pocket Books reprint of *Pride and Prejudice* (New York: Pocket Books, Inc., 1940). Author's collection.

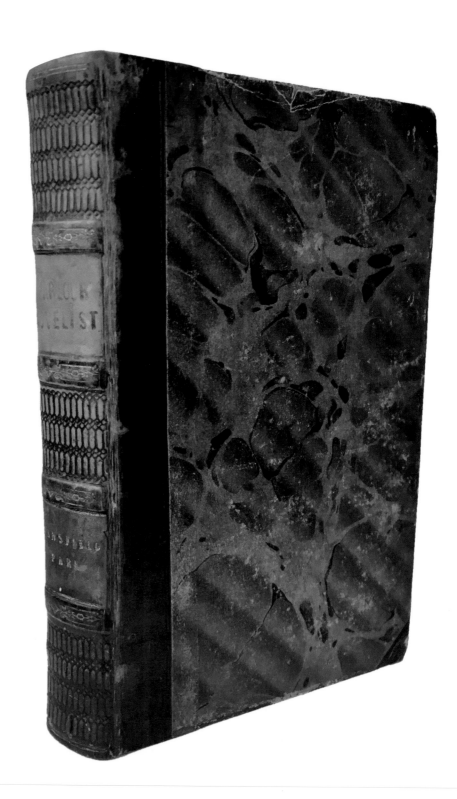

V.III.1. Captain Andrew Baird's copy of *Mansfield Park* in the Parlour Novelist series (Belfast and London: Simms & M'Intyre and W.S. Orr & Co., 1846). Collection of Sandra Clark.

Vignette III
The Old Sea Captain & William Price

In 1846, Simms & M'Intyre of Belfast and W.S. Orr & Company of London published this reprint of *Mansfield Park* as Number 4 in the Parlour Novelist series (figure V.III.1). With this series began the radical experimentation with ultracheap reprints in paper boards that soon revolutionized the book trade. In paper boards, a text like *Mansfield Park* sold for two shillings, while a further sixpence bought a version in decorated publisher's cloth. This copy, however, survives in a contemporary binding of rubbed marbled boards, neatly reinforced with green leather corners and a tooled leather strip along the spine—an option that, while still modest, would have raised the total expense.

Remnants of three early signatures attest to a journey through multiple nineteenth-century households. One muddied signature on the top right-hand corner of the heavily decorated series title page may read *K. Thomas./ 64.* At the head of the formal title page, another signature has been cut away, perhaps by its namesake when the book was sold or passed on, or by a subsequent owner who did not want another person's name on their secondhand book. Finally, beneath the words "Mansfield Park" on that crudely lopped title page, is the inscription (figure V.III.2), penned a bit shakily with black ink:

Capt Andrew Baird R N
1871

By 1871 this twenty-five-year-old reprint was far from new but apparently still worth claiming. The location of the inscription, forced by other owners having already occupied the more obvious spaces, suggests that Captain Andrew Baird of the Royal Navy was, at the very least, the book's third

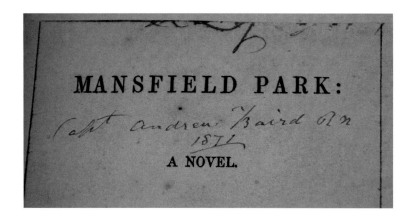

V.III.2. Cropped title page with ownership inscription "Capᵗ Andrew Baird R N / 1871." Collection of Sandra Clark.

owner. Did he mark it as his property because he was sharing accommodation? Even modest volumes were still considered prized possessions, carefully passed from hand to hand among the working classes with a palpable consciousness that privately owned books signaled ambition and status.

The National Archives record only one naval officer by this name living at this date. Andrew Baird (d. 1881) joined the navy during the Napoleonic War. Beginning as a "young gentleman" mustered variously as a midshipman, an able-bodied seaman, and a master's mate, he rose steadily to lieutenant and then commander. But there he stalled. Only as a man of 60-odd was Baird raised to the rank of captain, after lean decades on half pay. Baird's long and lackluster career history may be typical for an officer without connections or extraordinary luck in combat. Only his longevity seems unusual, for he may have lived into his 90s.

His naval experiences likely influenced his reading of Austen. Baird's date of birth goes unrecorded, but he appears in one source as an able-bodied seaman in "1807 or 08" on the *Quebec*, a 32-gun fifth-rate frigate.[1] From 1809 to 1812, he remained with the *Quebec*, which saw action near the river Scheldt. In September 1812 he appears as a master's mate on the *Pique*, a 36-gun ship of the fifth rate, en route to the West India Station.[2] On Valentine's Day 1815, he joined the *Venerable* as a midshipman, although some sources call him a mere master's mate. Only after accumulating enough sea time, six years with at least two as a midshipman or master's mate, could he have stood for the lieutenant's exam that he passed on May 28, 1815. The very next month, the Battle of Waterloo ended the war, and peace likely slowed his progress, since passing the exam qualified a candidate for promotion but did not guarantee a place. Not until September 19, 1816, was Baird officially promoted; or, as Austen would have said, he was "made."[3] Without a ship, however, he was probably stuck on half pay onshore until 1818, when all accounts agree that he finally became a lieutenant on the lowly *Sappho*, a 16- or 18-gun brig-sloop, or unrated ship. Then in 1820 he was invalided from St. Helena, where the *Sappho* was presumably ensuring that Napoleon didn't escape again. By then, probably in his late 20s, Baird returned to active duty, traveling to South America as a lieutenant on the *Fly*, then to the East Indies on the *Boadicea*, and finally given command of the *Arachne* sloop in 1825. He sailed her to Rangoon during the Burmese War and rose to commander in 1826. The accounts end in 1842 with him still as inspecting-commander of the Coast Guard on half pay. Promoted to post-captain in 1856, as part of a mass promotion to remove from the navy's books, in Victorian peacetime, the balloon of aging active officers on half pay, he accepted terminal promotion to captain, which would have raised his retirement pay a little, allowing him to buy this modest secondhand copy of *Mansfield Park*. He lived until 1881. No obituary survives except the appearance of his name among deceased captains in the navy list of 1881.

I give a detailed account of Baird's naval career not because his time on certain ships overlapped with that of Francis Austen (1774–1865) or of Charles Austen (1779–1852).[4] That would be too neat. I cannot even be sure that Captain Baird was aware that the Jane Austen on his book's title page was the sister of two admirals under whom he had served. Possibly. He certainly would have known of Admiral of the Fleet Sir Francis Austen and of Rear-Admiral Charles Austen, whether or not they ever crossed planks. Is name recognition the reason he bought the novel? In any case, Baird lived within the years of Austen's setting for *Mansfield Park* and might well have taken special notice of the Portsmouth scenes describing the narrow economics of a naval officer's struggles to support a family on half pay. By 1815, Baird had sailed to the West Indies, and in 1871 he would have readily picked up the references to Antigua throughout the novel. As an old man in his 70s, perhaps Baird saw himself in young William Price, a deserving midshipman who at 19 is desperate to make lieutenant. Baird was just about the same age when, like William Price, he had passed his lieutenant's exam but was waiting for a promotion. No well-connected Mr. Crawford interceded on his behalf; unlike William, poor Baird waited in limbo for two and a half years to be posted as lieutenant aboard the *Sappho* and get a raise in pay. The circumstances that delayed Baird's own promotion might have made William's dilemma more credible or colored Fanny's reaction to Crawford as insufficiently grateful.

Baird's *Sappho* exactly resembled William Price's *Thrush*, a relatively new 16- or 18-gun brig-sloop. Although smallish and unrated, for a ship needed a minimum of 20 guns to be rated, these sloops were hot little numbers, and their crews liked to imagine them bigger and tougher than they were. A proud Mr. Price says, "If ever there was a perfect beauty afloat, she is one; and there she lays at Spithead, and anybody in England would take her for an eight-and-twenty"—that is, a coveted 28-gun sixth-rate frigate.[5] Austen knows all about naval pride and ambition when she designs William's fictional ship, for Frank Austen's *Peterel* had been a 16-gun ship-sloop, rigged with three masts, when his capture of the *La Ligurienne* 16 in 1800 gained him promotion to post-captain. That had been Frank's magic moment. It was the shared dream of every sailor to be an officer on—or better yet in command of—a fast little sloop that takes a significant prize and gets noticed by the Navy List and the admiralty.[6] The poster child for this exciting feat is Frederick Wentworth, who singlehandedly takes a French frigate while commanding the leaky old sloop *The Asp*. Jane Austen knew all about sloops, and so did Baird, who served on or commanded three 16-gun brig-sloops: the *Sappho*, the *Fly*, and the *Arachne*. In many ways, old Captain Baird was Austen's ideal reader, someone in a position to spot every naval nuance and understand William's hopes.

CHAPTER 2

SENSE, SENSIBILITY, AND SOAP

Lever Promotions in the 1890s

It is a little-known fact that soap manufacturer Lever Brothers published editions of *Sense and Sensibility* and *Pride and Prejudice* during the 1890s as part of a unique marketing campaign for Sunlight soap. The first English company to combine massive product giveaways with large-scale advertising, Lever Brothers offered a range of prizes in "Sunlight Soap Monthly Competitions" to "young folks" (contestants could not be older than 17) who sent in the largest number of soap wrappers. The Sunlight advertising blitz, targeted to working- and lower-middle-class consumers, proved such a boon to sales that Lever Brothers ran the competition for a full seven years, annually escalating the giveaways. Prizes included cash, bicycles, silver key chains, gold watches, and—for the largest number of winners—clothbound books. For this purpose, Lever Brothers published and distributed its own selection of fiction titles by "Popular Authors" and "Standard Authors," including clothbound editions of *Sense and Sensibility* and *Pride and Prejudice*. By 1897, the year the competition closed, Lever Brothers had awarded well over a million volumes.

Lever's Sunlight Library editions were published at a time when advertisements for soap, by corporate giants such as Lever Brothers and Pears Ltd., provided "an immense stimulus to popular literature," underwriting the national thirst for fiction to the tune of hundreds of thousands of pounds per year.[1] In 1901 W. T. Stead, the same man who had abridged Austen for a penny, reported in the *Review of Reviews* that Pears alone had recently spent £126,000 on advertising in a single year, surmising that much "of this a goodly sum must have found its way into the pockets of publishers."[2] Business historians calculate that Lever spent a princely £2 million on advertising between 1885 and 1905, "far more than any of his competitors."[3] Lever and Pears also owned their own publishing outlets, generating annuals, miscel-

lanies, and bits of commissioned fiction. Ad copy employed literary allusions, as in a common newspaper ad in 1886 that praised the "BEAUTIFUL COMPLEXION" achieved with Pears' Soap with snippets from Shakespeare and Pope: "Thou hast the sweetest face I ever looked on" and "If to her share some female errors fall, Look on her face and you'll forget them all." The soap industry's influence on literary taste and print culture innovations in general, and Austen in particular, may be more significant than yet acknowledged.

The soap industry's particular subsidy of Austen came to light during research spurred by a worn, stray copy of the Lever edition of *Sense and Sensibility* (figure 2.1). The book is a revealing piece of social history and, considering its original production values, a remarkable survivor of yet another unrecorded lowbrow Austen. While giveaways may not equate with ephemera, the

2.1. *Sense and Sensibility* in red cloth (Port Sunlight: Lever Brothers Limited, n.d.). Front cover and spine. Author's collection.

Lever edition—printed on cheap paper and bound in decorated cloth—was not printed to last. Modestly attractive on the outside, the book is bound in boards covered in no-nonsense ungrained red cloth. The binding is split-fountain stamped with a floral design, boasting "Lever Bros. Ltd" in faded gilt at the bottom of the spine. The title *Sense and Sensibility* is stamped on the decorated front cover, while Jane Austen's name appears only on the book's internal title page. But for the binding's florals, there are no extras or internal illustrations, although ornamental initial letters and typical head- and tailpieces mark the chapters (figure 2.2). While the central text remains serviceable, if brittle, for reading, the original mix of papers must have been of very low quality, causing the edges of this well-worn copy to stripe as different gatherings browned at different rates over time. The margins, too, are mismatched, with many of the book's 379 pages barely spared loss of text by the binder's cuts. The inking of what look to have been well-worn plates is uneven and sloppy, so that haphazard words retain an accidental bold look while other sections of text appear gaunt and pale.

The tired look of this copy's pages was partly due to the Lever edition's having been printed from secondhand stereotype plates, in this case the ones Routledge commissioned for their Austen novels in 1883 (figure 2.3). With those plates Routledge had produced Austen in picture boards and various cloth casings and binding styles from 1883 to about 1890, offered at a range of price points.[4] Internally, then, the Lever edition text, although devoid of the Routledge frontispiece and equipped with a new title page, matches that of Routledge's earlier editions. The same proved true for the Lever edition of *Pride and Prejudice*, which was also printed from plates first used by Routledge in 1883. Lever, it seems, enlisted some of Routledge's former stereotype plates in the service of promoting soaps. In fact, these same Austen plates fell into the hands of a further three publishers to print at least five more editions of Jane Austen in succession—all of which go similarly unrecorded.

In staking a claim for yet another unsung copy's significance as a historical object, I want to emphasize, ironically, its low production values. Only when compared to the waxed paper boards of the late-nineteenth-century yellowback does the Lever edition's cloth binding appear to take a step toward gentility with its stamped multicolored design, including a hint of gilt on the spine. Nonetheless, the binding's simple and sappy florals (a bunch of daisies?) still mark it as an inexpensive working-class book meant to be enjoyed as a commodity rather than fetishized as an important tome. For calibration, imagine the Lever copy of Austen's novel beside a loftier and now

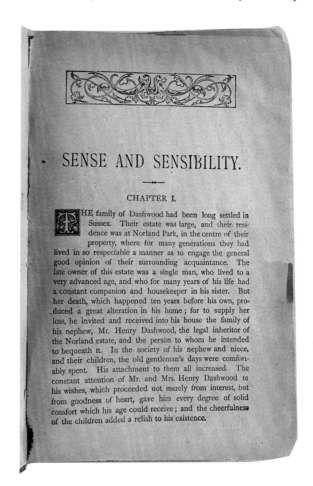

2.2. First page of central text of Lever edition of *Sense and Sensibility.* Author's collection.

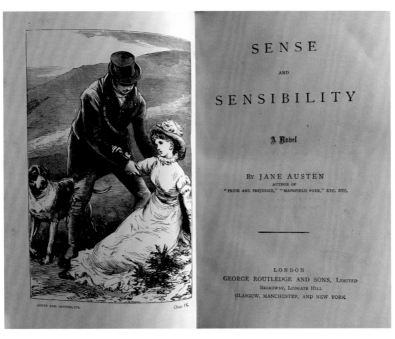

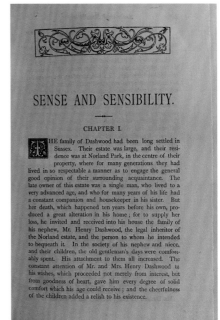

2.3. Pages from Routledge edition of *Sense and Sensibility* (London, Glasgow, Manchester, and New York: George Routledge and Sons, Limited, n.d.) printed from 1883 plates. Author's collection.

much-collected contemporary in another type of publisher's cloth binding: the famous 1894 Peacock Edition of *Pride and Prejudice*, which sold for six shillings with gilded front cover design, lavish line drawings, and full-page illustrations by Hugh Thomson (figure 2.4). The yellowback, Lever, and Peacock editions already give tangible proof of the broad market spectrum for Austen's works at the end of the nineteenth century in Britain, but it is the splendid ordinariness of the surviving Lever copy that offers a unique window into her reception at that time.

Although I have not discovered any early soap ads that actually quote her novels, the Lever edition was not the first (or last) interjection of Austen into the soap business. Novels of manners such as *Sense and Sensibility* and *Pride and Prejudice* seem to have been deemed particularly suitable by both Lever and Pears as vehicles for promoting soap to the working and middle classes. Viewed in conjunction with advertisements for its Sunlight and Swan Soaps, Lever's publication of Jane Austen also partakes of a pervasive nostalgia that mixes with contemporary commercial culture. Obviously, Jane Austen was made an unwitting pawn in the profit-making schemes of Pears and Lever. Nonetheless, reading Austen within early commodity culture yields surprising juxtapositions and insights into how readers of cheap editions may have approached her work under the influence of this edition's peculiar commercial packaging. The fact that such copies seldom make it into scholarly libraries, where collections tend to focus on important firsts or on association copies, should not prevent us from studying them as historical objects.

The Lever Brothers edition of *Sense and Sensibility* bears no date and is not recorded in the bibliography of David Gilson. In the absence of any such record, and with no introduction to help situate or explain the copy's existence, I only came to understand this book's identity as a contest giveaway and late-Victorian marketing tool after scratching away at the history of Lever Brothers, a company about which I knew absolutely nothing at the start. In this chapter I narrate my findings roughly in the order in which the facts revealed themselves, because understanding the process of historical research about a visual object makes plain just how

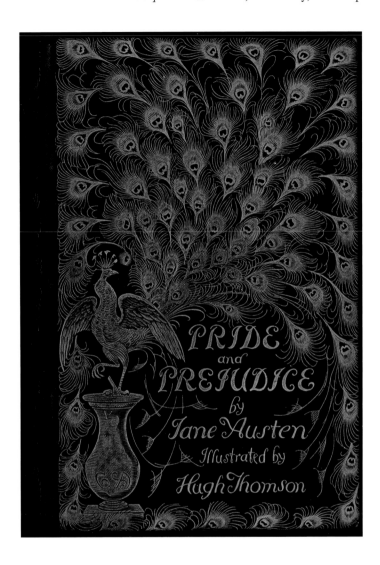

2.4. *Pride and Prejudice* (London: G. Allen, 1894). Copy formerly owned by Evelyn Waugh. Harry Ransom Center, University of Texas at Austin.

such information might be derived for other books, similarly undated. The image-rich databases of open nonlibrary websites can assist in such recovery, when standard bibliographical resources do not account for books produced outside of traditional norms. Cheap cloth bindings, especially series bindings, are rarely the concern of the descriptive bibliographer, whose focus is on the publication process and the authority of the evolving printed text.[5] Even unstable commercial sites where content constantly changes, including eBay and AbeBooks, can therefore supplement the latest scholarly resources in surprising and meaningful ways.

DATING DILEMMAS

At first, a precise dating of and explanation for my Lever Brothers copy of *Sense and Sensibility* seemed, without Gilson's usual aid and no ownership signature, virtually impossible.[6] To make matters worse, WorldCat lists no known extant library copies. The imprint at the bottom of the title page simply reads, "Port Sunlight: Lever Brothers, Limited." As the benevolent despot of his company town, William Hesketh Lever (1851–1925) built homes for his workers and specified the size and use of gardens needed for healthy living. He encouraged organizations at Port Sunlight that promoted art, literature, science, and music, and he "insisted that all his junior staff devoted a portion of their time to education: they were given evening classes in languages, English literature, accountancy, basic science and engineering, all paid for by the company."[7] I started, therefore, to imagine Lever stocking the Port Sunlight library with edifying and entertaining books, including *Sense and Sensibility*. While Lever's manifold social schemes allowed the possibility of in-house publishing merely for the education of his Sunlighters, there were—as we have seen—plenty of inexpensive editions of *Sense and Sensibility* in circulation by 1890. In other words, if Lever needed only a dozen or so copies for a community library, publishing his own would not have been cost-effective. A mandate that all Sunlight employees be equipped with their own copy of Jane Austen seemed, even in view of Lever's panoptic paternalism, unlikely. I therefore searched for another explanation.

The *Oxford Dictionary of National Biography* entry for William Hesketh Lever gave me a starting point, 1889, the year production commenced at Port Sunlight. I next compared the copy's cover art to that of other English books from roughly this era, using eBay as a surprisingly effective, if spotty and uneven, tool. Searching for books by dates, I located and scanned hundreds of images of bindings from the period in a matter of minutes. AbeBooks, a commercial bookseller site with more consistently reliable metadata, provided further images within specific date ranges. The style of the decorated cloth binding quickly and definitively dated the Lever edition to the 1890s, positioning it alongside several other series employing the late-Victorian idiom of symbolic flowers.

Specifically, the decorative art of the Lever binding resembled inexpensive contemporary cloth editions in publishers' series from that decade, including a copy of *Emma* published around 1892 in the Lily Series by Ward, Lock, and Company of London (figure 2.5). For less than $20, I purchased a copy of the Lily *Emma* with advertisement pages at the back. The advertisements revealed that Ward & Lock promoted the hundred-plus titles in their Lily Series as "GIFT BOOKS AT EIGHTEENPENCE EACH," although they offered them in three formats and price points: "Very attractively bound in cloth, with design in gold and silver, price *1s.6d.*; also in cloth gilt, beveled boards, gilt edges, *2s.*; or ornamental wrapper, *1s.*"[8] If bought without gilt edges (my *Emma* had none), the attractive clothbound gift books, in a limited range of colors, were about as expensive as some low-market yellowbacks in picture boards. Since the Lever *Sense and Sensibility* resembles the Lily Series at "*1s.6d.*" in externals (inside, Ward & Lock's *Emma* looked of higher quality), the overall impression of the Lever edition proved even more modest than my anachronistic eye, swayed by the book's age and Victorian aesthetics, had initially gauged. Interestingly, the Lily Series was deemed particularly suitable for school prizes ("Forming admirable Volumes for School Prizes and Presents to Young Ladies"), confirming that pretty-but-inexpensive gift books comprised a familiar genre in the early 1890s. The same title could be had in different colors (*Emma* came in green and red cloth, and possibly other colors), so as to better tailor its look for the intended recipient.

Suggestive of scholarly dismissal of this whole category of cheap books was that Ward & Lock's *Emma* in the Lily Series also fails to secure mention in Gilson's *Bibliography*.[9] A standout exception is Chester W. Topp, who codified his enthusiasm for yellowbacks into the nine volumes of *Victorian Yellowbacks and Paperbacks, 1849–1905*, an inventory that devotes an entire volume to the cheapest of Ward & Lock publications.[10] Armed with Topp's inventory, augmented by old publisher's catalogs on GoogleBooks and the Hathi Trust Digital Library website, it was easy to confirm that this publisher specialized in niche marketing to the working classes through inexpensively packaged books, including a Pansy Series (aimed at young readers and sporting covers decorated with pansies) as well as the Laddie Series (targeted especially to boys) (figure 2.6). The practice of marketing serviceable series of clothbound books named for sunshine and flowers to

2.5. *Emma* in the Lily Series in green cloth (London and New York: Ward, Lock, and Co., n.d.). Author's collection.

the literate working classes was transparently ubiquitous in the 1890s, with the Religious Tract Society (RTS) publishing a Sunshine Series and a Buttercup & Daisy Series, as well as its Golden Sunbeam and May Blossom books. In fact, the RTS announced its mission as offering "Cheap Books for Children" for use as "Gifts and Rewards" in print advertisements that showed children washing their hands and faces. In other words, books were deemed suitable rewards for good personal hygiene too. Given the Sunlight brand of soap for which Lever had become famous, along with what I took to be iconic daisies on the cover of its *Sense and Sensibility*, the Lever edition seemed to want to align itself, and by extension Jane Austen, with the mission of the RTS. These aesthetic clues were in keeping with Lever's paternalistic vision for Port Sunlight and its community of workers, which he ruled like "a benign puppet-master."[11]

A WorldCat search for titles published by Lever Brothers between 1890 and 1900 confirmed that its in-house books and pamphlets were largely concerned with the running of the firm and the advertising and packaging of soap, even when those publications exhibited a literary bent. Much energy seems to have been devoted to the *Sunlight Year Book*, a multipurpose annual filled with household advice and sundry information, including world maps, train tables, fashion plates, and even instructions about pet care. Released annually around Christmas, their encyclopedia–address book–atlas–minipeerage swiftly became "the standard reference work for the schools to which it was given away free." Thus the Sunlight brand gained "a respectability and ubiquitousness far beyond the bathroom and pantry."[12] These yearbooks constituted a brilliant giveaway scheme, as each page was accompanied by a unique slogan promoting Lever soap: "Don't worry, use Sunlight soap!"; "See smiling faces all around, wherever Sunlight soap is found"; and, my personal favorite, "The best soap for washing pigeons." It is easy to imagine a child studiously looking through the sections labeled "Rulers of the World" or "List of Cathedrals" and unwittingly absorbing Lever's advertisement rhetoric from the volume's headers and footers.

Some of Lever's literary publications recorded in WorldCat invoke Sunlight Soap's mission through puns and associations. Take, for example, the choice to publish *Sunny South*, by F. C. Armstrong, as well as works by the coincidentally named Charles James Lever (a popular fiction writer who died in 1872 and had no apparent connection to the soap company).[13] Did Austen's *Sense and Sensibility* offer up unseen wordplay in connection with slogans for soap? At first, the catalog approach dead-ended, largely because so few other Lever editions of popular novels apparently made it into academic libraries: one copy of the Lever edition of Defoe's *Robinson Crusoe* is held by Oxford University, one copy of Scott's *The Antiquary* survives at Edinburgh University, and Emory owns a copy of Thomas Cobb's *Wedderburn's Will: A Detective Story*, cataloged to 1895.

Perhaps searching nineteenth-century newspapers for soap ads would yield more information about other titles with the Lever imprint. I turned to the scholarly subscription databases Nineteenth-Century British Library Newspapers and Nineteenth-Century British Periodicals published by Gale. Even though I did not find "Austen" in any soap advertisements, I did find

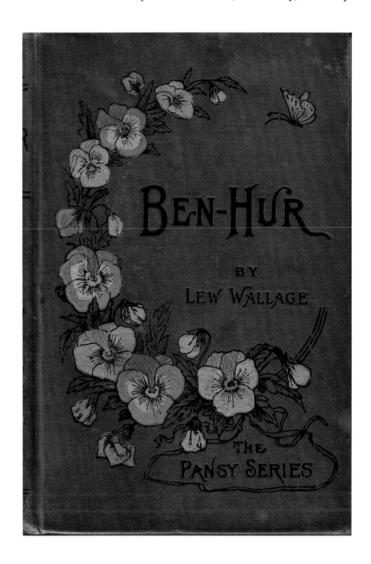

2.6. Lew Wallace, *Ben-Hur*, in grey cloth (London, New York, and Melbourne: Ward, Lock, & Co., Limited, n.d.). Author's collection.

mentions of "books" as prizes in many 1890s Lever ads, and there I was able to track the Sunlight Soap Monthly Competition, which ran from 1890 to 1897. Lever was the first company to design giveaways on such a grand scale. Advertisements announced that the competition was "for young folks only," and they were urged to send in soap wrappers for chances at various categories of prizes. A minimum number of coupons, twenty-four in 1890 and fifty by 1897, guaranteed the sender a prize for his or her efforts—in the first year it was an art print, and it subsequently became a book. The competition started in 1890 with £600 in prizes awarded monthly. For 1894, Lever announced it would award "232,800 prizes in Prizes of Bicycles, Watches, and Books, value £41,904." With prizes reflective of working-class values, it is significant that the bulk of this marketing collateral took the form of books.

The competition's rules divided England, Ireland, Scotland, and Wales into eight (later reduced to seven) geographical "districts" according to population. Newspaper ads and fliers in 1897 explained how every month, "the 1 competitor in each District who sends in the largest number of Sunlight coupons from the District in which he or she resides, will receive £21 cash," the next ten would receive "carriage paid, at winner's option, a Lady's or Gentleman's 'Premier' Bicycle, price £21." Forty further competitors in each district received gold watches, while "the remaining Sunlight Competitors" would each receive "Cloth-bound Books, by Popular Authors, in the proportion of 1 Book for every 50 Sunlight coupons sent in." The ads also detailed rules (boys and girls age 17 or younger; wrappers from sold products only and not dealer's stock), eligibility (not Lever employees or families), prizes, and even the totals awarded in the different districts. In 1897 large ads from February through at least September listed detailed accounts of the "£66,156 in prizes of cash, bicycles, watches, and books given free during 1897" (figure 2.7). This was the soap circus in which Jane Austen was made a participant.

The ads were detailed enough to roughly calculate that Lever gave away a quarter of a million books yearly during the latter half of its long-running campaign. Naturally, the Lever advertisements inflate dramatic totals with headline prices that use retail amounts for the bikes, watches, and books rather than Lever's true cost. Any calculations have to take the poetic license behind advertised figures into account. For the midcompetition year of 1894, the Lever announcements proudly rank their giveaway books into four retail categories, from five shillings at the top end to one shilling at

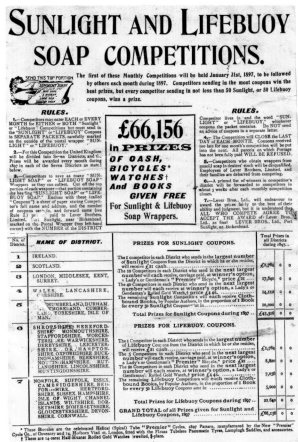

the bottom. Since cheap yellowbacks (or books in picture boards) retailed between one and two shillings and the premium Bentley edition of *Sense and Sensibility* was advertised for six, Lever operated at the low end of the print-culture marketplace, as reflected in the poor production values of its reprint of *Sense and Sensibility*. In fact, Lever appeared to be significantly inflating the market value of their giveaway books.

Nonetheless, from these advertised tallies of books at different price points and the total number given away in each category each month in each of the eight districts, it was possible to calculate that in 1894 (not the peak year for prizes) Lever promised to award 230,400 books.[14] If this middle year in an

2.7. Loose advertisement flier (front and back) for the 1897 Sunlight and Lifebuoy Soap competitions. Author's collection.

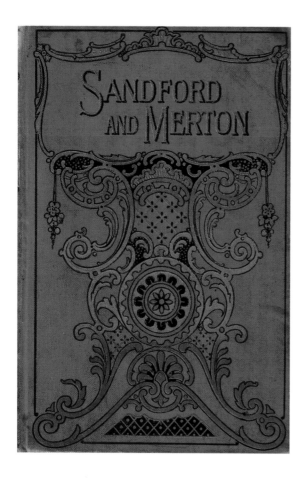

2.8. [Thomas Day], *Sandford and Merton: A Tale for Boys,* in red cloth (Port Sunlight: Lever Brothers Limited, n.d.). Author's collection.

escalating giveaway campaign is taken as an estimated mean, then by the end of the Sunlight Soap Monthly Competitions, which ran for over seven years, Lever might have given away more than 1.5 million books, a staggering number of volumes pumped into working-class communities—of which books there is now surprisingly little trace. Soap advertising, it appears, did more than just fill "the pockets of publishers," it filled the shelves of working-class homes. It is not certain, of course, that all these Lever book giveaways bore a Port Sunlight imprint. The published announcements do not specify the book titles, and some lots may have been bargains struck with other publishers and dealers for Victorian overstock. But every book that Lever could hand out with its own name on the spine or title page would serve as a prominent piece of advertisement in someone's home. Surely it did not take Lever long to start giving away its own branded editions—especially since Port Sunlight was equipped with its own printing house and bindery.

The duration of the competition explained the lack of a date on the *Sense and Sensibility* title page. In a giveaway scheme with no predetermined endpoint, an undated book would continue to look new for years. Searching somewhat blindly for the Lever imprint among book sites, I found a handful of similarly undated Lever Brothers editions for sale online, including a used copy of *Sandford and Merton* inscribed 1898 and another of *Ben-Hur.* Both were advertised as bound with an inventory of the 1897 giveaways, although no images were provided. Since 1897 was the endpoint of the competition, presumably these lists would proudly name the book titles given out. On the outside, the binding styles of these later Sunlight Library copies did not resemble that of my Lever *Sense and Sensibility;* the prominent flowers had been replaced by a stamped binding of abstract design in the same split-fountain color scheme (figure 2.8). Sight unseen, I bought the copies with the bound lists online and waited for their arrival. I reasoned that although the books on this yet-unseen list might span a wide range of popular taste, in isolation each had to sympathize with the Lever mission.

SQUEAKY CLEAN

How might Austen have appeared to young contestants receiving *Sense and Sensibility* as a Sunlight Library book? What were the contemporary associations with the soap that a first-time reader might transfer to Austen? I found that Lever soap advertisements circa 1900 tended toward the self-consciously nostalgic—a style in which Jane Austen's Regency stories could become fit vehicles for the company mission and image. Many Sunlight Soap ads feature young people in outdated collars and costumes, posing with giant mock-ups of the Lever soaps, ostensibly to promote their effectiveness on modern fabrics. The result is often comical, since the nods to history are associative rather than credible: "To Save Time is to Lengthen Life," reads the slogan beneath a long-running ad for Sunlight that shows a girl in the type of massive Elizabethan collar that demands a queenly amount of starch (figure 2.9). Similarly, a magazine ad for Swan Soap, a bath soap marketed especially to "ladies" for the washing of skin and fine fabrics, features a retro couple in Renaissance costume crossing a creek by stepping on a giant piece of floating Swan Soap. The caption reads, "A Stepping Stone to Happiness."

Two popular full-page magazine ads for Swan Soap feature couples in something approaching the Georgian costumes of Austen's era (figure 2.10). In one, the couple seems dressed in early-eighteenth-century attire (the gentleman wears a powdered wig, a ruffled front, and shoe buckles) and sits by a creek, delighted by a giant piece of Swan Soap that floats past. The words "IT FLOATS" are carved on the tree behind them, as befits the tradition of enthusiastic lovers. In another ad a couple ride in a Regency gig—the gentleman in a tricornered hat, knee breeches, and regimentals sitting beside a laughing companion who wears an elaborate bonnet—while a giant piece of Swan Soap is latched to the vehicle by the girl's bonnet strings. These

2.9. Sunlight Soap advertisement from *The Graphic*, December 6, 1902, 781. Author's collection.

2.10. Lever soap advertisements. *Left:* from *Black and White,* March 8, 1902, 359. *Right:* from *The Graphic,* January 12, 1901, 63. Author's collection.

historically specific getups seem intended to draw a sigh of contentment from a female consumer who is duly reminded that modern washable fabrics require comparatively less effort to keep clean, the Victorian equivalent of Virginia Slim's famous "You've come a long way, baby" campaign. Perhaps the company's book giveaways also trained their audience in a historically dependent advertising idiom. Jane Austen does seem remarkably of a piece with the Regency-clad personages in Lever advertisements.

The Lever edition of *Sense and Sensibility* in the 1890s was not the first to yoke Jane Austen to the manufacture of soap. Many of the yellowbacks and sixpenny Austens discussed in chapter 1 featured advertisements for a range of household products, including soaps (figure 2.11). Even the cramped penny *Pride and Prejudice* distilled by Stead had made room for a Pears' Soap advertisement on the final leaf. The cheaper the book, the more likely that it needed advertisements to subsidize production. The "Curious & beautiful optical illusion Presented by the Proprietors of Pears' Soap" on the back of one Routledge sixpenny *Sense and Sensibility* even makes its way *inside* a cheap Cassell's Red Edition of the same novel as a folding leaf.[15] Copies of this popular advertisement also survive as loose Victorian prints on eBay and elsewhere, for this was another long-running advertising

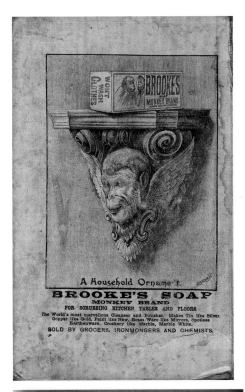

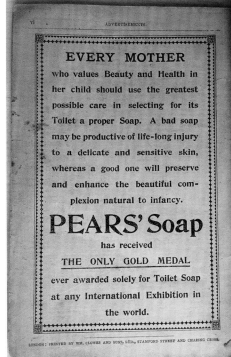

2.11. *Clockwise from top left:* Brooke's soap advertisement on back cover of *Northanger Abbey-Persuasion* (London, New York, and Melbourne: Ward, Lock, & Bowden, Limited, n.d.); Vinolia soap advertisement on back of sixpence *Sense and Sensibility* (London: George Routledge & Sons, Lim, n.d.; circa 1887); Pears' Soap advertisement on back of sixpence *Sense and Sensibility* (London and New York: George Routledge and Sons, n.d.; circa 1884); Pears' Soap advertisement in penny digest of *Pride and Prejudice,* abridged by W. T. Stead (London: Review of Reviews Office, n.d. [1896]). Collections of Sandra Clark and author.

gimmick modified from year to year.[16] Since the optical illusion necessitates rapidly rotating the page and occasionally encourages readers to tear it out for a keepsake, this Pears advertisement might have had readers twirling and tearing their copies of Austen's novel—a curious example of "reader response" and of the type of nonreading activities that, historian Leah Price points out, Victorians took to with their books.[17] Just such innovative marketing techniques earned Thomas Barratt, chairman of Pears, a reputation as one of the fathers of modern advertising.[18] That he practiced his curious art in copies of Austen may be lesser known.

Today, Jane Austen has become an industry in her own right, changing her relationship to advertisement yet again, with uses of her name on nonbook products from toothpaste to gin—as if a posthumous celebrity endorsement. Placing Austen's name and portrait on soap, however, proved a bit of a stickler. The 1994 UK Trade Marks Act (TMA) insists that the use of an artist's name be meaningfully connected to a product's origin. For example, in the year 2000, when a toiletry business sought to register "JANE AUSTEN" as a trademark for a line of toiletries and soaps, the application was refused under s.3(1)(b) of the TMA on the grounds that "it was devoid of any distinctive character." Legal historian Simon Stokes explains how "the application was opposed by the trustees of the Jane Austen Memorial Trust who owned Jane Austen's cottage and museum in Hampshire and who had developed a trade in related souvenirs. It was held that unless educated through use to see the name differently, the public would not regard 'Jane Austen' as a badge of origin" for soap products.[19] This restriction appears to have been lifted or ignored in recent years, for soaps with Austen's name are now a thriving business—selling in tourist shops in the city of Bath and by vendors offering handmade soaps on Etsy, scented with fragrances based on Austen's literary characters. In view of the history behind the Lever edition of *Sense and Sensibility*, such crass commercialization of Jane Austen's legacy proves far less modern and alien than I would have predicted; connections between Austen's books and commercial advertising are older and tighter than I had imagined.

THE COMPANY SHE KEEPS

Only when the Lever Brothers editions of *Sandford and Merton* and *Ben-Hur* arrived was I able to reconstruct the literary context in which *Sense and*

Sensibility was offered as a book prize. Among the advertisement pages at the back I found a handlist of "The 'Sunlight' Library of Books by Standard Authors, given during 1897 for Sunlight and LifeBuoy Soap Wrappers":

Ivanhoe.	Throne of David.
Uncle Tom's Cabin.	Pelham.
Robinson Crusoe.	Vanity Fair.
Swiss Family Robinson.	Handy Andy.
David Copperfield.	Andersen's Fairy Tales.
Old Curiosity Shop.	Opening a Chestnut Burr.
Night and Morning.	Pendennis.
Ernest Maltravers.	Little Women and Good Wives.
Eugene Aram.	Beulah.
Rienzi.	Mother's Recompense.
Last of the Barons.	Barriers Burned Away.
Home Influence.	Pirate and Three Cutters.
The Lamplighter.	Little Savage.
The Wide, Wide World.	Daisy.
Pickwick Papers.	Infelice.
Nicholas Nickleby.	Melbourne House.
Oliver Twist.	St. Elmo.
Old St. Paul's.	Last Days of Pompeii.
Kenilworth.	Paul Clifford.
Bride of Lammermoor.	Scalp Hunters.
Old Mortality.	Disowned.
Waverley.	Devereux.
Rob Roy.	Godolphin.
Vicar of Wakefield.	Alice.
Prince of the House of David.	Barnaby Rudge.
Ben-Hur.	Days of Bruce.
Midshipman Easy.	Bleak House.
Valentine Vox.	The Monastery.
Last of the Mohicans.	Quentin Durward.
Jane Eyre.	Gulliver's Travels.
Twenty Years After.	Black Dwarf and Montrose.
Aunt Jane's Hero.	Guy Fawkes.
Masterman Ready.	Harold.

Tower of London.
Vashti.
At the Mercy of Tiberius.
Pillar of Fire.
Stepping Heavenward.
Pride and Prejudice.
Sense and Sensibility.
Queechy.
Three Musketeers.
Guy Mannering.
Harry Lorrequer.
Jack Hinton.
Naomi.
Vale of Cedars.
Four Girls at Chautauqua.
Chautauqua Girls at Home.
Heart of Midlothian.

Rifle Rangers.
Three People.
Shirley.
Helen Mordaunt.
Flag of Truce.
Woman's Friendship.
Little Fishers and Their Nets.
Sandford and Merton.
Japhet in Search of a Father.
The Roll of the Drum.
The Tiger Hunters.
The Wood Rangers.
The Guerilla Chief.
Did She Love Him?
Windsor Castle.
Antiquary.
The Abbot.

Contestants were warned that not all hundred titles were guaranteed to be in stock and that "lists of books on hand" would be forwarded to those who sent a self-addressed stamped envelope to the "Competition Department, Messrs. Lever Brothers, Limited, Port Sunlight, near Birkenhead." From this list, which did not name authors, I confirmed that *Pride and Prejudice* was indeed another Lever title, although I had not yet traced a copy. After publishing an article about my findings (which shared the information gleaned thus far) two different book collectors contacted me and shared images of their *Pride and Prejudice* Lever books—allowing me to inspect them by proxy (figure 2.12).[20]

Armed with the titles on the list, I also found Lever exemplars in beige, blue, green, and red cloth of both designs. Eventually, another collector found a Lever *Sense and Sensibility* bound in the nonfloral cover style. And I even stumbled upon another Lever *Sense and Sensibility*, this time in blue, stamped with the familiar daisy cloth design (figure 2.13). A few Lever copies of the earlier daisy style were bound with a slightly different "List of Books—Uniform with this Series." This earlier list, which included 108 books, suggests that about 20 percent of the titles were swapped out by the end of the giveaway scheme for similar offerings (the two Austens appear on both lists).[21] Thus the flower design, stamped on titles of various sorts, did not—as I had first suspected—mark a primarily female audience. However, only the Lever copies that contained the advertisement pages for the 1897 giveaway scheme were stamped with the abstract Victorian decoration (not the flowers), as if Lever had marked the final phase of its giveaways, which still included both Austen titles, with the introduction of a new binding style. A comparison of *Ben-Hur* in both binding styles (I then bought the other version too) confirmed that while the exterior binding style differed, the interior text was printed from the same plates. The endpapers in the inspected Lever copies thus far had rarely matched, yet all the 1897 copies contained the same green patterned endpapers, as if produced in one go. Production values differed from book to book: *Sandford and Merton*, for example, was heavily illustrated, but other titles contained no such graphics. There were great internal differences in font, typographical layout, paper, and illustration; only the exterior packaging and the title pages, with their shared Lever imprints, had shaped these books into a unified series—in two distinct binding designs (figure 2.14).

I was surprised at the implied selection criteria for the lists of "Standard Authors," which, while they include many usual suspects and a great deal of Sir Walter Scott, also include a host of titles now almost obscure. In fact, a substantial portion of the company that Austen keeps on these lists did not join her in the next century's canon—eventually not even among juvenile literature. There is nothing yet among the names in this Lever series that suggests Jane Austen was a genius of special status; she had not yet fully separated from the popular herd. And yet the list itself seemed an invaluable index with which to measure Austen's presumed rise. Bibliographically negligible editions such as Lever's prize books, a reflection of popularity in the late 1890s, are time capsules of their cultural moments, even when the copy text may be suspect, the production values

2.12. *Pride and Prejudice* in red cloth (Port Sunlight: Lever Brothers Limited, n.d.). Collection of Lady Martine J. Roberts.

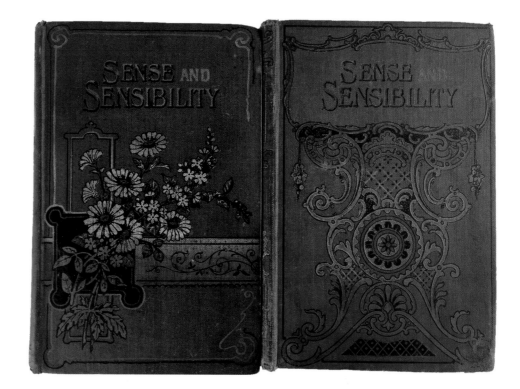

2.13. *Sense and Sensibility* in blue and red cloths of different designs (Port Sunlight: Lever Brothers Limited, n.d.). Collections of author and Sandra Clark.

low, and the editing nonexistent. Books worth keeping for posterity—for the preservation of history—include those no one thinks to keep.

MESSY ENDINGS & MORE UNKNOWN EDITIONS

I thought the story of my Lever copies of *Sense and Sensibility* had ended there, but the typical chaos of nineteenth-century publishing practices soon complicated and extended the narrative. By chance, an eBay search sometime later came across a remarkably similar copy of *Sense and Sensibility* with the unrecorded imprint "London: Miles & Miles, / Foresters' Hall Place, Clerkenwell Road, E.C." (figure 2.15). The binding design is nearly identical to that of the flowered Lever copy, with only the addition of the words "The Marguerite Series" on a strip of gilt on the front cover. Instead of boasting the Lever brand, the bottom of the spine on this copy reads "Miles & Miles," while the words "The Marguerite Series" appear inside the same circle left empty on the Lever spines (figure 2.16).[22] Setting aside

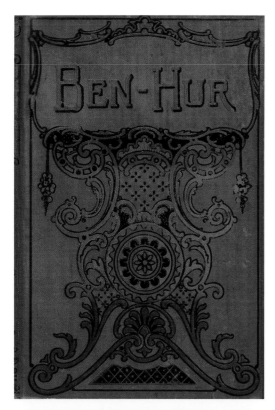

2.14. Lew Wallace, *Ben-Hur,* in red and light brown cloths, and William H. G. Kingston, ed., *The Swiss Family Robinson,* in green cloth (Port Sunlight: Lever Brothers Limited, n.d.). Author's collection.

2.15. *Sense and Sensibility* in the Marguerite Series in tan cloth (London: Miles & Miles, n.d.). Author's collection.

2.16. Spines of Lever Bros. (*left*) and Miles & Miles (*right*) editions of *Sense and Sensibility* printed from the same stereotype plates and in casings with same stamped design. Author's collection.

2.17. *Sense and Sensibility* in red cloth in the Marguerite Series (London: Miles & Miles, n.d.). Author's collection.

the publisher's brand, the stamped bindings on the flowered Lever editions are identical, down to the lettering, design, and split-fountain technique. Soon thereafter, another Miles & Miles copy with the same binding design turned up in red cloth but with a different address in the imprint (figure 2.17).[23] Internally, both my Lever copies of *Sense and Sensibility* and the two Miles & Miles copies were printed from the same poor plates, yet there were differences: the red Miles & Miles copy included an uncaptioned and random-seeming frontispiece illustration (of a couple in Victorian dress) and was a bit heftier, only because printed on thicker paper.

These copies testified that a little-known press called Miles & Miles had, for a time, used the same stereotype plates as those from which Lever Brothers had produced their Port Sunlight Austens. But when? Which series had come first, Lever or Miles & Miles? No Austen edition by Miles & Miles, or any "Marguerite Series," is mentioned in Gilson, and I could not locate the series among those advertised in the *British Catalogue* of books for the years either just before or just after the Lever giveaway years. With much plate wear and low production values evident in both the Lever and the Miles & Miles copies, the physical books did not help fix a definitive order. Did the name "Marguerite," a type of daisy, explain the genesis of the stamped flowered design of the housing (making Miles & Miles the originator), or was the name merely a clever adjustment to the floral design of an inherited stamp (making Miles & Miles the follower)? The search for a "Marguerite Series" published by Miles & Miles in WorldCat (OCLC) yielded only one undated copy of *Melbourne House* by Susan Warner (1819–1885), a title that had also been included among the Lever giveaways.[24] But with so many popular titles, that could be coincidence. Persistence and a bit of luck enabled me to locate copies (purchasing one) of two other titles from the under-the-radar Marguerite Series, both by Dickens—*Bleak House* and *Pickwick Papers*, which are titles also included in Lever's 1897 list (figure 2.18). Perhaps Lever brokered a deal with Miles & Miles for its nascent Marguerite Series, including the stamped housing, adapting everything to a new purpose? This seemed more logical than that another publisher would copy, and even tart up with gilt, a fairly long-running and high-profile giveaway scheme in an identical binding style.

Curiously, the British Library owns the only Miles & Miles edition of Austen listed in WorldCat (OCLC), namely *Mansfield Park*—but not as part of the Marguerite Series. That is why my earlier searches had failed to bring it up. Inside this Miles & Miles *Mansfield Park* is a presentation bookplate that marks it as a school prize for the year 1899–1900, which led the British Library to date the edition to 1900.[25] This suggests that Miles & Miles reprinted Austen after the Lever giveaways ended. Although early on I had assumed that the Lever Brothers name in the imprint signaled that Lever had initiated the selection of its own giveaway titles, the fact that their giveaway books differed so much on the inside should have been a clue to more complex origins. Perhaps Lever Brothers had bought or borrowed the plates not just for its Austens but for all or most of its giveaway books from various publishers. Had Lever, in fact, made *any* selection decisions in the inclusion

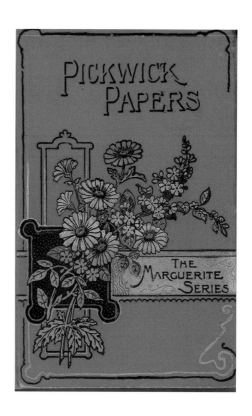

2.18. Charles Dickens, *Pickwick Papers*, in the Marguerite Series in red cloth (London: Miles & Miles, n.d.). Author's collection.

of specific titles for its soap-promoting scheme? Perhaps I had sought interpretive meaning behind Austen's inclusion in the Lever Soap giveaways in vain. Instead, *Sense and Sensibility* may have functioned as a Duchamp readymade in reverse—an object plucked out of its original artistic context to do the sudden bidding of an unanticipated commercial purpose.

A further few months passed before I came across yet another undated copy of *Sense and Sensibility*, printed from the same plates and in the same binding style as used by both Lever and Miles & Miles, but now with a "Standard Authors Publishing Company" imprint.[26] Later, a friend added a hard-lived copy of *Pride and Prejudice* by the same firm to the mystery (figure 2.19). A similar and also undated copy of *Sense and Sensibility* then surfaced, again printed from the same plates, but only vaguely similar now in binding style, this time bearing a "Londoner Press" imprint. Frustratingly, it still lacked a date (figure 2.20).[27] The production values in the Londoner Press reprint are the lowest of the lot; pastedowns and endpapers are crowded with advertisements (including more cleaning products). These plates, it seemed, had served a far longer and more dubious work life than their employment in Lever's seven-year giveaway scheme. None of these derivative Austen reprints are recorded by Gilson. Many months later, an utterly different Miles & Miles copy of *Pride and Prejudice* surfaced. It showed tantalizingly higher production values and was printed in a larger and more solid format than the Marguerite Series—on far thicker paper, with wider margins to made the book wider and taller, a different floral cover design, beveled boards, and all edges gilt (figure 2.21).[28] By then, I was less likely to be misled by the pimped packaging and soon recognized that the internal text was printed from worn plates that resembled my Lever copies of *Sense and Sensibility*. A comparison with one of the privately owned Lever *Pride and Prejudice* copies proved that this larger Miles & Miles copy, regardless of external appearances, was printed from the same hardworking plates used by Lever. Much later, yet another Miles & Miles gift version of *Pride and Prejudice* turned up in a flashy Sundial Series binding, possibly from 1897, extending both the list of reprints not in Gilson and the Miles & Miles mystery still further (figure 2.22).[29] Upon examination, it too proved to be printed from the same stereotype plates used by Lever.

Intrigued by all this turnover, repackaging, and recycling, I searched in the opposite temporal direction. Since all the Lever copies and the Miles

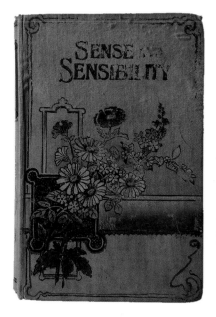  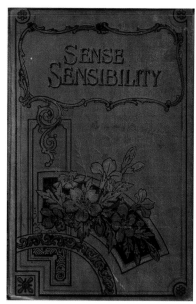

& Miles editions looked to have been printed from tired plates, might either of them have gotten the plates secondhand from an earlier publisher? That's when I realized that the Miles & Miles and Lever imprints matched Routledge's 1883 editions. Lever must have acquired their two sets of Austen plates from Routledge, perhaps via Miles & Miles, after the plates had withstood years of heavy use. Provocatively, the extant copy of the Miles & Miles edition of *Mansfield Park*, the one in the British Library, contains 443 pages—suggestive of another match with the well-worn 1883 Routledge plates, from which even the Thayer sisters' copy had been printed circa 1890.[30] Trade practices would likely have had Routledge selling its Austen plates as a batch, and yet *Mansfield Park* had not been a title offered by Lever. What if Miles & Miles were the true purchaser of the 1883 Routledge plates, holding back some Austen titles when passing them to Lever and reacquiring the plates once the soap giveaway scheme ended, only to print blingy and bloated versions of these same books in bindings that differed from their initial Marguerite Series version—in effect deftly disguising where these texts had been.

I located two additional Miles & Miles books in the same glitzy binding

2.19. *Sense and Sensibility* in tan cloth and *Pride and Prejudice* in red (London: Standard Authors Publishing Company, n.d.). Collections of the author and Jennifer Winski.

2.20. *Sense and Sensibility* in brown cloth (London: The Londoner Press, n.d.). Author's collection.

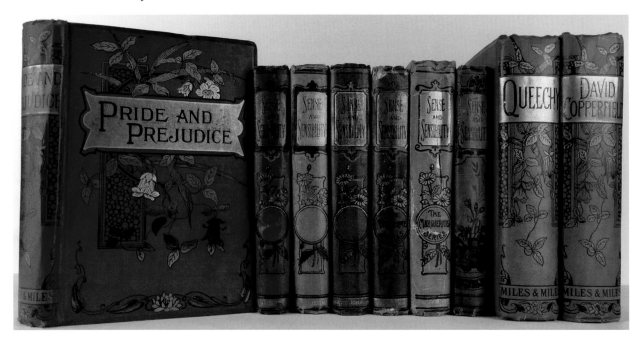

2.21. *Far left:* Pride and Prejudice produced as large gift edition, in red cloth with beveled boards and gilt page edges (London: Miles & Miles, n.d.). The other books (all discussed in this chapter) provide here a sense of the relative size of the inflated Miles & Miles productions. Author's collection.

style: *David Copperfield* and *Queechy*—titles that also appear on the Lever lists (see figure 2.21). Since one of the owners of a Lever *Pride and Prejudice* had, meanwhile, been inspired by the backstory of her book to collect a few more Lever giveaway volumes, to serve as shelf-mates for her Lever Austen, I was able to compare this Dickens title by Miles & Miles to its Lever namesake. It, too, was a match as to stereotype plates. Miles & Miles acquired (or reacquired) more Lever plates than just those for Austen. At this time, I cannot be sure how many, and will leave to others a wider research into the history of these shared plates.

Regardless of the true extent of swaps and sales, the publishing practice of recycling plates comes across as decidedly indecorous, especially when it amounts to trash-to-trash rather than trash-to-treasure. From a modern point of view, seeing old features resurface in "new" books distorts established value judgments and, in Austen's case, makes for an undignified reception narrative at the close of the nineteenth century. If there was just one set of these plates, as I suspect, then Austen's 1883 plates were loaned or sold off by Routledge circa 1889–90, perhaps to begin a new Marguerite series by Miles & Miles, only to spend seven years promoting soap for Lever Brothers.

Alternatively, Routledge may have initially allowed Lever to use the plates by arrangement. After the death of Routledge's two sons in 1899, the firm went briefly into liquidation mode and sold a lot of plates then—or some plates stored with various printers during this uncertain time may have mysteriously fallen into unscrupulous hands. Whatever their journey, the Austen plates do eventually fall into the hands of Miles & Miles to churn out haggard pages that are tarted up with gilt and bulked with wider margins for the juvenile book-prize market. Finally, in their old age, the Austen plates continue to labor for a few more grubby masters down-market, with or without her Lever companions.

The sliding movements of stereotype plates, yet again, blur the lines between Austen editions, but in this instance her texts are not merely shifted from one publisher's series to another within the same firm but are handed off by her original creator to do the bidding of many lesser-knowns. Rather than "rising," Austen in stereotype form seems subject to sinking—serving Routledge, Miles & Miles, Lever Brothers, Miles & Miles yet again, Standard Authors, and Londoner's Press (I cannot be certain of the exact order). Just as this book was going to press, I came across yet another unrecorded example: a ratty *Sense and Sensibility* made from these same plates in the first decade of the twentieth century, undated but with the imprint of "John Heywood Ltd.," a firm based in Manchester. Surprisingly, little or no information survives about some of these small late-Victorian and Edwardian publishing houses specializing in book prizes and stand-alone titles for a working-class audience—this in spite of wide scholarly agreement about the important emancipating force of cheap literature for the working poor. John Spiers, author of *Books for the Million*, points to a gaping hole in the historical record for the following London-based firms, of which at least three printed these unrecorded Austens: R. E. King, Richard Butterworth, John F. Shaw, Croome & Company, Miles & Miles, the London Publishing Company Ltd. (whose imprints included Boswell House Library), the Londoner Press, the Standard Author's Publishing Company, the Standard Library Company, and the Authors' Co-

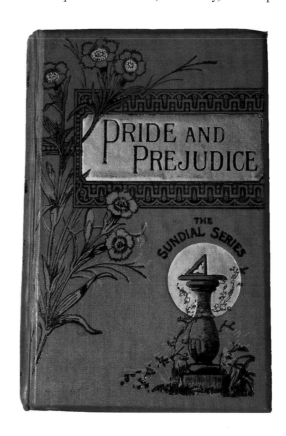

2.22. *Pride and Prejudice* from the same plates and with the same features as the copy in figure 2.21, but now part of the Sundial Series (London: Miles & Miles, n.d.). Collection of Elizabeth Steele.

Operative Publishing Company Ltd.[31] "Alas," laments Spiers, "no commercial archives seem to survive for these firms and so much of their history remains shrouded in mystery."[32] As Spiers's wider investigation into this category of books makes clear, the bibliographical record for Jane Austen is not alone in neglecting lowbrow shapeshifters.

In sum, one haggard Lever soap copy led to the discovery of not just one, but more than a half dozen, unrecorded editions (or should we stick to the less ambitious term *reprints?*) of *Sense and Sensibility*—not yet counting any sightings or suspicions of versions of Austen's other novels by these same publishers. The current record shows only Routledge's use of their *Sense and Sensibility* plates, starting in 1883, but not the subsequent reprintings by five further publishers, counting Lever. These findings reflect the systemic narrowness of the bibliographical record for all manner of cheap reprints that have never found their way into libraries—and not just for Jane Austen.

Vignette IV
Charlotte & a Real Castle

Everyone knows at least one fixer-upper horror story about a home stripped of original architectural features in the name of Danish modern. Here is the book-conservation version of that outrage, sanitized for kid-friendly reading.

Figure V.IV.1 pictures three Austen survivors from the Parlour Library series, originally offered cheaply in boards and cloth by Simms & M'Intyre. The first is a copy of an 1851 shilling edition of *Mansfield Park* identical to that owned by meat-seller Ellen Horwood (see introduction and figure I.12). The second is a copy of an 1850 Simms & M'Intyre *Emma* that anticipated the Routledge Railway Library edition read by young Emma Morris in Largs (see vignette II). The third is a reprint of *Northanger Abbey* and *Persuasion*, also dated 1850. These three Austen volumes do not survive in anything like their original publisher's bindings; they were sold just over a decade ago as a matching set, "handsomely rebound in contemporary style," as dealers tout it. Rather than suffering from neglect, these lost books have been killed with kindness and the slate of their history almost wiped clean.

Because rebinding is costly, makeover crimes are rarely committed on lesser-known authors. The book dealer who assembled this trio of Parlour Library volumes judged that the market would favor good looks over visceral authenticity. Perhaps when found, they were all in a bad way. The instinct to spruce up a book and increase its value is understandable, especially as Simms & M'Intyre's inexpensive reprints were not made to last and survivors often look shabby and threadbare. Ellen Horwood's pristine *Mansfield Park* is the rarest of exceptions among these cheap midcentury reprints. But the conundrum of the collector, dealer, or library is when and how much to intervene: preserve, conserve, or renovate? *Preservation* arrests damage and keeps a book from worsening, as when you remove decay

V.IV.1. Radically rehoused, these are early shilling reprints of *Emma, Mansfield Park,* and *Northanger Abbey-Persuasion* (London and Belfast: Simms & M'Intyre, 1850-51). Collection of Sandra Clark.

or critters and then box up the book. *Conservation* repairs while saving the maximum amount of original materials, so that any additions are reversible and all "old" materials are retained alongside the repaired book rather than discarded. *Renovation* tends to make an old object look like new. My thinking is that if you want a new book, you should buy one from Amazon or, better still, from your local independent bookstore.

In this case, the renovators replaced the original, modest, publisher's bindings of board or cloth with something that fails to resemble anything that Simms & M'Intyre offered as an option: compare the gold decoration on these spines to the tooling on Captain Baird's modest leather-bound copy (see vignette III). Worse still, these books have been made to look like part of a three-volume matched set by combining individual strays, guillotining the page edges to clean them up, stripping the volumes of what remained of their old housing, and giving the trio a look-alike makeover of shiny, colored, marbled boards and tooled leather. Bold red leather labels and fancy gold tooling decorate the new calf spines. Many collectors do love matching sets, even when the grouping is inauthentic. Although these three Austen titles belong to the same 1850s Parlour Library series, they were never companion volumes: *Emma* was sold at No. 6, *Northanger Abbey–Persuasion* much later at No. 47, and *Mansfield Park* delayed until No. 60. Over time, the *Mansfield Park* and the *Emma* lost their prelims and series titles. Seeing that all three books were early-ish reprintings of Austen, a savvy dealer probably considered them worth the investment of new housing. But as a result of sledgehammer logic, these bindings are forever out of joint: three aged paupers now sport jarringly new and princely binding.

Ironically, one of these little volumes, the one dedicated to *Northanger Abbey–Persuasion* actually did belong to a charmed and princely household long before it was renovated into this anachronistic triplex (figure V.IV.2). The inscription, preserved on the series title (missing from its current mates), gives an exact name and address, complete with house number:

Charlotte M. Mills
Octr 14th 1850.
5. Bryanstone Sqre

This book, whatever its original binding style, belonged to Charlotte Maria Mills (c. 1833–1902), who lived with her father, Edward Mills, at 5 Bryanston Square, London.[1] Edward Wheler Mills (1801–1865) was by profession a banker and by birth a blueblood. His wife had died when Charlotte was only 6, and he never remarried, choosing instead to carry on as a single parent. The census of 1851 provides a detailed snapshot of life for father and daughter at 5 Bryanston Square just after the date of Charlotte's inscription.[2] Eighteen-year-old Charlotte and her widowed father resided together not quietly but with a 30-year-old governess named Margaret Beard and eight servants—a butler, two footmen, a housekeeper, a lady's maid, two housemaids, and a kitchen maid. Number 5 Bryanston was a full-service operation that knew no half measures. The house still looks today like the perfect setting for a stern Victorian bonnet drama, complete with gated basement entrance to what was once the kitchen.

In 1858 Charlotte, age 25, marries Edward Henry Cooper (1827–1902).[3] At that time Edward, although born into an elite Irish family and educated at Eton, is but a promising young lieutenant-colonel in the British Army. By 1861, Charlotte and Edward have moved their growing family to a fashionable house at 36 Hertford Street, between Hyde Park and St. James's Palace.[4] Two years later, Edward inherits Markree Castle in County Sligo from an uncle without sons. Edward, now 36 years old, promptly retires from the army to manage his country estate and, together, he and Charlotte embrace

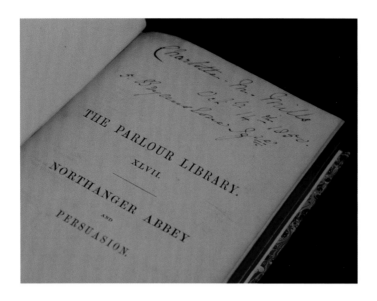

V.IV.2. Ownership inscription by Charlotte M. Mills on the series title of her 1850 copy of *Northanger Abbey-Persuasion.* Collection of Sandra Clark.

life in the enormous Irish castle that was his family's ancient country seat—and yes, they do also keep a London house.

Markree Castle would have satisfied even Catherine Morland's eagerness for the Gothic. With a history dating back to the fourteenth century, a castellated facade, a moat, vaulted ceilings, and many elaborate Gothic touches, old and new, Markree was just the dwelling craved by Austen's teenage heroine. That spring morning in 1863, when Charlotte learns of Edward's sudden inheritance, does she remember this exchange in her copy of *Northanger Abbey*?

"What, is it really a castle, an old castle?"

"The oldest in the kingdom."

"But is it like what one reads of?"

"Exactly: the very same."

"But now, really, are there towers and long galleries?"

"By dozens."

"Then I should like to see it."[5]

Edward becomes a landlord in County Sligo and a Conservative politician, while Charlotte raises their six children in Gothic splendor. The uncle has left behind an observatory at Markree Castle, described by the Royal Astronomical Society in 1851 as "undoubtedly the most richly furnished private observatory known."[6] Edward and Charlotte keep it operational until their deaths in 1902.

Charlotte and Edward grow older together. She dies at 69, with Edward, at 75, following his wife to the grave only four weeks later. Charlotte left £7,200 of her own money to her second-born son—her eldest, Francis Edward, had died during active service in South Africa in the Boer War just the year before. When Charlotte first acquired *Persuasion* and enjoyed Austen's ironic account of Mrs. Musgrove's grief over "poor Dick," the difficult son who died during wartime so far from home, she was only 17. She could not then have comprehended a mother's loss, only the loss of a mother. Did the death of her eldest, her own dear Frank, change her reading or memories of that novel? Was her copy of Austen still with her at the end?

Could the original worn binding, stains, or any notes on the now-lost endpapers and extras possibly have told us more? Did Charlotte also own the other two unsigned books, or are they strangers to each other? After retrieving her story, I am eager to see the book that Charlotte once owned. The central pages in her Parlour Library copy of *Northanger Abbey* remain those she read and turned, but this is not exactly her book anymore.

PRIDE

AND

PREJUDICE:

A NOVEL.

IN THREE VOLUMES.

BY THE

AUTHOR OF " SENSE AND SENSIBILITY."

VOL. I.

SECOND EDITION.

London:

PRINTED FOR T. EGERTON,

MILITARY LIBRARY, WHITEHALL,

1813.

CHAPTER 3

LOOKING DIVINE
Wrapping Austen in the Religious

The original top board of one peculiar 1813 copy of *Pride and Prejudice* reads, "The Life of Jesus Christ," announcing the story of Elizabeth Bennet as if it were a biography of the Savior (figure 3.1). Once owned by American philanthropist and society matron Frances Morgan (1845–1924) and now safely tucked among the collections of the Harry Ransom Center, this bibliographical curiosity constitutes the earliest-known printed binding to attach itself to any Jane Austen novel.[1] Of course, this binding is merely a historical accident resulting from the common practice of reusing so-called printer's waste, faulty-pages-turned-scrap, to reinforce an inexpensive copy in boards. During the process of marbling the no-nonsense boards, the binder recycled pages from Rev. Ezekiel Blomfield's *The Life of Jesus Christ* (1813) to make a sensible, inexpensive Austen cover.[2] Over time, the colored marbling on the outer paper gave way to the underlying darker ink from the repurposed front matter of Blomfield's book. The bleed-through resulted, accidentally, in printed boards long before printed bindings were the norm—a haphazard cover that gives Austen's three-volume novel an unwitting New Testament look.

This religious *Pride and Prejudice* cover is by no means a deliberate marketing strategy. It also belongs among the early copies preserved by institutional libraries that I do not track. Nevertheless, this accident from 1813 exemplifies Austen's subsequent appearances on the shelves of booksellers and readers dressed in the hand-me-downs of religious books. As will become clear, the pop-culture Jane discussed in earlier chapters has quietly kept company with a religious doppelgänger who is equally mercurial and equally unsung. Various devotional features trim a subspecies of Austen reprintings, though not because a growing veneration for the author takes a religious turn. These religiously clad books relate incon-

3.1. *Pride and Prejudice*, 2nd ed., vol. 1 of 3 (London: Printed for T. Egerton, 1813). The original marbled boards of this copy were reinforced with printer's waste. Harry Ransom Center, University of Texas at Austin.

sistently and uneasily to Christianity—from the devout to the irreverent, from pi to cheek.

The poems written by Austen on religious themes and books made from her private prayers are beyond my scope. Instead, this chapter examines the way her novels have circulated in religious contexts in ordinary reprintings. This is surprising because, as one modern critic observes, Austen "ranks among the least proselytizing of Christian novelists."[3] Indeed, her plots show little interest in broadcasting the author's faith. With comical clergyman suitors such as Mr. Collins and Mr. Elton, Austen even dares to lampoon Anglican clergy with a confidence rooted in familiarity, for her father, her brother James, and assorted other relatives were clergymen of the Church of England. Churchman John Henry, Cardinal, Newman (1801–1890), put it more forcefully: "What vile creatures her parsons are!"[4] And yet publishers and reprinters have long marketed and packaged her fictions using strong Christian gestures. Here I explore the uncharted and uneasy intersection of religious bookmaking and Austen's novels during the first century of their reprinting.

The dominant cultural framework for literary appreciation has always been a religious model of devotion—expressed through the familiar language of "relics" and "pilgrimages." In 1891 American critic William Dean Howells (1837–1920) coined the phrase "the divine Jane," echoing longstanding references to Shakespeare as "the God of our idolatry" in the cultural lexicon.[5] With this phrase, Jane Austen took her place among the brightest stars of the literary firmament. The celebrity of "divine Jane" at the turn of the twentieth century prompted devotees to make pilgrimages to locations associated with her life and work. A true pilgrim is willing to put in the miles, and some years earlier Alfred Lord Tennyson had allegedly walked nine of them from Bridport to Lyme Regis, "led on to Lyme by the description of the place in Miss Austen's *Persuasion*." Upon arrival, "refusing all refreshment, he said at once: 'Now take me to the Cobb, and show me the steps from which Louisa Musgrove fell!'"[6] In 1897 his son published this anecdote, just as a growing appreciation for Jane Austen began generating guidebooks for the initial wave of literary tourists. The first major book of this nature is *Jane Austen: Her Homes and Her Friends* (1902) by Constance and Ellen Hill, a sister team of Janeites who narrate a literary "pilgrimage" that follows in "Miss Austen's gentle steps."[7] A contemporary review observes that the book "takes the attitude of an adorer" and offers a "eulogistic" view of Austen.[8] Although this new generation of adoring literary pilgrims would, naturally, be hungry for handsome editions packaged in reverential ways, I do not concern myself here with the sanctimonious luxury editions for Austen's devotees. The religiously packaged reprints discussed in this chapter rarely preach to the choir and rarely occupy the worshipful seating of a reserved pew.

Long before Austen's secular beatification toward literary sainthood, her works already appeared bound and fashioned as religious tomes and sold as quasi-devotionals. More often than not, however, the packaging of Austen's stories in religious robes yields a radical rather than a conservative product, aiming to capture readers outside the mainstream. Traditional religious packaging could be a beard on radical reading. For example, in the 1840s, one London publisher offered miniaturized reprintings of Jane Austen in "illuminated bindings"—making her novels look like small medieval primers for a revolutionary series of proto-feminist books by radical contemporary thinkers. By the 1870s, many versions of Austen began to appear in Sunday schools as earnest book prizes, even as the award labels testified to an uncompromising message about the termination of childhood. By 1890, a religious temperance society commissioned a special reprint of *Mansfield Park* for men employed as laborers in coal mines and potteries who were unable to afford a clean suit of clothes for Sunday church attendance. This edition's mission was reformist rather than conformist. In 1907, at the other end of the reception spectrum, Austen's fiction was printed on Bible paper and bound to resemble hymnals for secular aesthetes interested in avant-garde book arts. Circa 1909, the brand new Selfridges department store offered a diminutive Austen in gilded brown suede similarly reminiscent of small prayer books. By 1930, gratis *Pride and Prejudice* copies greeted guests at a prominent New York hotel—as if a cheeky Gideon Jane. Reprints with a religious dimension dazzle with diversity of commercial purpose and visual range.

Although whole studies are devoted to the religious concerns of Jane Austen's plots, and many more to the emergence of a "Cult of Jane," none has glossed the recurring religious dimension of her books as books, as material objects in a Christian context. Whereas studies of Austen and the clergy focus on her Anglican upbringing and speculate about her private

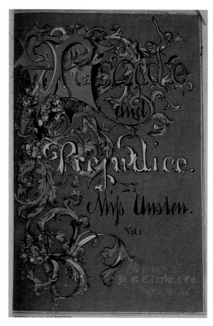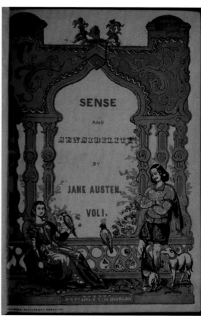

3.2. Special title pages for *Pride and Prejudice* and *Sense and Sensibility,* 2 vols. each (London: H. G. Clarke and Co., 1844). Collection of Sandra Clark.

faith, the religious contexts of Austen's reception have faded from view in our increasingly secular world—especially as the experiments that offered her up in the guises of church hymnals, temperance books, and Bibles are now scarce or unrecorded.[9] Today's readers may associate a religious look with an earnest conservative outlook, but the circulation of Austen in liturgical dress was rarely po-faced. It would also be wrong to assume that early religious guises of Austen's books laid the groundwork for her later secular deification in the literary canon. Some chroniclers of the Cult of Jane have looked back for precursors of early worship—for the first believers in a "divine Jane." Beware, however, the famous logical fallacy *post hoc ergo propter hoc.* Just because these editions were published ahead of today's Cult of Jane, that does not mean they caused her secular saintliness.

MEDIEVALIST JANE

The trappings of religious tradition can serve as a blind for radical ideology. Take, for example, the miniaturized editions of Jane Austen's *Sense and Sensibility* and *Pride and Prejudice* in elaborate "illuminated bindings" of

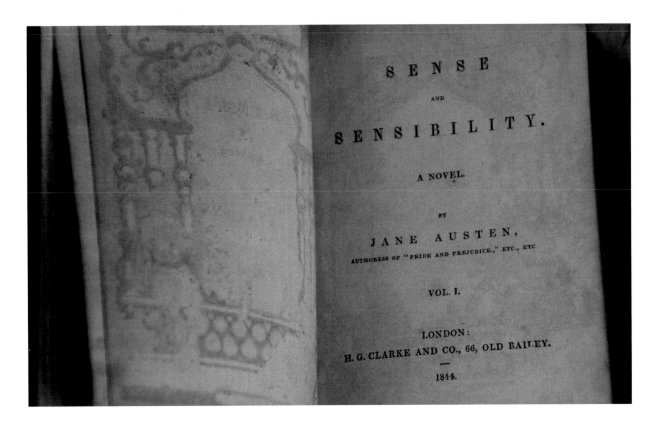

SENSE

AND

SENSIBILITY.

A NOVEL.

BY

JANE AUSTEN,

AUTHORESS OF "PRIDE AND PREJUDICE.," ETC., ETC

VOL. I.

LONDON:

H. G. CLARKE AND CO., 66, OLD BAILEY.

—

1844.

3.3. Additional title page in the opening volume of *Sense and Sensibility*, 2 vols. (London: H. G. Clarke and Co., 1844). Collection of Sandra Clark.

tooled leather complete with fancy colored title pages that made her novels look like small medieval devotionals during a wave of reactionary medievalism in 1844 (figures 3.2, 3.3, and 3.4).[10] These unusual reprintings were the brainchild of Henry Green Clarke (1816–1894), printer and publisher at 66 Old Bailey, where he was the proprietor of what is arguably one of London's earliest feminist bookstores—albeit one in a rigid Victorian mold.

In 1844, when Clarke's Cabinet Series of New and Popular Works appeared, these devotional Austens were priced well below Richard Bentley's better-known Standard Novels, which he was then still offering at six shillings before the introduction of ultracheap books in waxed paper boards forced him to significantly lower his retail price. Even so, at the base price of 3s.6d. for a two-volume novel, Clarke's editions of *Sense and Sensibility* and *Pride and Prejudice* remained an indulgence, especially for a small-format book—palm-sized, or what bibliographers term 32mo. format. The value

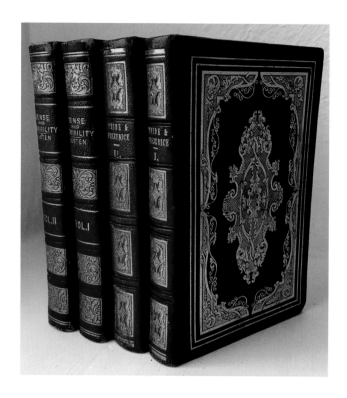

3.4. Copies of *Pride and Prejudice* and *Sense and Sensibility* in tooled publisher's bindings of red leather, as sold by H. G. Clarke in 1844. Collection of Sandra Clark.

proposition of Clarke's Cabinet Series, with its mix of poetry, fiction, and instructional literature, seemed partly to reside in their resemblance to handsome religious books of yore. In the hurly-burly of the nascent Industrial Revolution and among the latest clothbound books, these little retro leather volumes offered an inviting respite.

Clarke's 1840s series of small-format poetry and prose may have looked old-fashioned in appearance, but the content was remarkably modern—even revolutionary. Although the forty-some titles in the series chaotically cross literary genres, national boundaries, and eras, a consistent algorithm is at work, namely the instruction and motivation of female readers. *The English Maiden: Her Moral and Domestic Duties* (No. 12) contains an introductory note that easily doubles as the unifying slogan of Clarke's Cabinet Series: "Upon the right training of the female character depends the future welfare of mankind."[11] Other instructional works, including James Foster's *Duties of the Married State* (1843) and Rev. Henry Edward's *Female Influence in the Nineteenth Century* (1841), make it clear that this timely series promoted female education and influence—at least to the extent allowed by Victorian sensibilities. The authors, including a plethora of women writers, are linked by intellectual networks and kindred ideologies. For example, the opening title was *Psyche; or, the Legend of Love*, a poetic allegory in Spenserian stanzas first published in 1805 by Mary Tighe (1772–1810), an Anglo-Irish poet admired for her long-suffering femininity. Felicia Hemans (1793–1835), the author of *Domestic Affections and Other Poems* (at No. 4), famously penned a tribute to Tighe as a morbid poetess; it was entitled "The Grave of a Poetess." In her turn, Hemans is said to have influenced American poet Henry Wadsworth Longfellow (1807–1882), who keeps close company with her at number 3. From today's modern perspective, these authors may not qualify as radical feminists, but this series, packaged as sedate books of hours or devotionals, amounted to an explosive syllabus of nonconformists and free-thinkers aimed at women readers.

Early in 1844, a bold Gothic flyer in red and green lettering announced the first thirty-one titles in the Clarke's Cabinet Series of New and Popular Works, available in "Imperial 32mo., in an Illuminated Binding."[12] Miss Austen's *Sense and Sensibility* was number 21. By October 1844, newspaper ads listed forty-four titles, with *Pride and Prejudice* at number 34, poised between the first English translation of *The Amber Witch: The Most Interesting Trial for Witchcraft Ever Known* and *Poems by Frances Ann Butler.*[13] The most likely reason for Austen's inclusion in this eclectic mix was opportunistic: *Sense and Sensibility* and *Pride and Prejudice* ran out of copyright in 1839 and 1841, respectively. As David Gilson observes, Clarke's volumes were the first separate editions to appear after these expiration dates.[14] Produced between Bentley's versions of Austen as Standard Novels, starting in 1833, and the spate of railway editions that, for one or two shillings, would soon transform her work into cheap penny dreadfuls by the 1850s, Clarke's intermediate Cabinet Series cut a new facet in Austen's public image: the religious look. It also aligned her with women's rights long before "suffragists took Jane Austen to the streets of London" in 1908.[15]

Clarke's Cabinet Series was highly esoteric, short-lived, and—to judge from what happened next—a financial train wreck for its creator. Advertisements stop abruptly after 1845. On January 21, 1846, a legal notice dissolved Clarke's business partnership, announcing that he had left the publishing concern at 66 Old Bailey in the hands of others.[16] And in 1848, only four years after the series launched, the firm's remaining stock was sold at auction, apparently to clear debts.[17] The origin story of the edition begins in 1843, when Clarke took over an existing printing and publishing business at 66 Old Bailey.[18] At that time, Clarke was a minor author of popular guides to the Dulwich Picture Gallery and National Gallery, a genre to which he contributed until the 1860s. He may also have authored that manifesto promoting women's education, *The English Maiden*, himself; it was first published anonymously in 1841.[19] He married twice, once in 1843 and again in 1862, after the death of his first wife.[20] As a new publisher, Clarke took competitive risks, or so I interpret his 1843 piracy conviction involving a handbook about Hampton Court. A few years into the business, possibly because of his outlay for the Cabinet Series, he was declared insolvent after being sued for debts. Little more is known about Henry Green Clarke beyond the circumstances mentioned in his insolvency announcement of January 1847.[21] By 1849, however, he was back on his feet with a new publishing concern, again as H. G. Clarke, at a different address in the Strand. There he ran a healthy business in guides, maps, and engravings for another two decades, focusing on visually innovative products such as model kits for Shakespeare's birthplace and Anne Hathaway's cottage.[22]

Clarke's reprints of Jane Austen, like others in the Cabinet Series, was a publisher's mashup of secular fiction in biblical packaging. When it came to the text block printed by Clarke, his small letter-press books, apart from their compact size, were ordinary and devoid of page decoration: no fancy initial letters, no printer's ornaments at the heads or tails of chapters, and no Gothic lettering or historically evocative type. But the unusual publisher's bindings transformed Clarke's small plain Janes into medieval jewels, complete with ornately colored title pages bound at the front. The phrase "illuminated binding" repeated in most advertisements refers to the option of a leather publisher's binding with ornate gilt tooling—a term and style borrowed from the contemporary realm of Bible-making.[23] Such an elaborate binding was not usually a standard option for "popular works."

Clarke's illuminated bindings, visually striking, set them apart from other reprints and caught the eyes of enough collectors to make for a substantial number of survivors in rare-book libraries and private hands.[24] The densely gilded designs were variations on old-fashioned, hand-tooled, binding styles used for serious books (see figure 3.4). Although only one of Clarke's designs boasts an explicitly Christian cross at the center, all resemble the elaborate tooling associated with prayer books and Bibles. Brown leather seems to have been the most popular choice, although the books could also be had in slightly flashier green or red morocco. Perhaps because "illuminated bindings" appear so out of keeping with popular fiction, the phrase seems to have bewildered Austen's bibliographers. Gilson, for example, refers instead to this edition's "illuminated wrappers," admitting, "No copy has been seen in original wrappers or in original cloth."[25] In line with established norms and practices, Gilson reverts to familiar options and assumes that his copy's binding of "dark morocco gilt" represents an unusual extra, or custom binding. His assumption confirms the standout oddity of

Clarke's packaging. In a midcentury world of proliferating "cheap" fiction in publisher's cloth bindings of fairly uniform sizes, Clarke's series of popular works, miniaturized and sold in publisher's bindings of elaborately tooled leather, stood out in defiance of norms.

Any Austen reader might do a double-take at the illustrated title pages of Clarke's Cabinet Series. Bound into each volume between the plain half title and title pages is a page of gilded ornate design that appears hand-colored—as if a time-traveling medieval monk took up Austen's novels and decorated them with sumptuous illuminations. But these designs are definitely the printed products of a machine age. On the bottom edge, trimmed off in some copies by the binder, the imprint of the specialist in colored printing remains visible in tiny type: "Gregory, Collins and Reynolds."[26] For *Pride and Prejudice,* the special page mimics medieval illuminated lettering, while in *Sense and Sensibility* it portrays a man and a woman in what Gilson terms a "Moorish/Gothic scene"—one that might better serve *Romeo and Juliet* as a fanciful set design for the balcony scene. The image reflects the adaptation of medieval motifs about to feed into the aesthetics of the Pre-Raphaelite Brotherhood of the late 1840s. In these copies, medievalism meets Jane Austen.

In Clarke's series, the two reprints of "Miss Austen" keep company with at least six contemporary novels by "Miss Bremer." Fredrika Bremer (1801–1865) was a Swedish writer who rose to prominence as an early feminist reformer. Translated into English, her novels were wildly popular in Britain and America during the 1840s and 1850s. Owing to her realist style, she was dubbed the Jane Austen of Sweden. In April and June of 1844, lists of five or six Bremer titles made up separate advertisements for the Clarke's Cabinet Series, implying that the series pinned special commercial or intellectual hopes on Bremer's popularity.[27] In her late 30s, Bremer had successfully petitioned the King of Sweden for emancipation from her brother's guardianship. Her activism subsequently prompted a social movement that granted Swedish women legal majority at age 25 and led to the establishment of a women's academy.[28] Clarke had a penchant for Swedish fiction, it seems, for in 1845 he also included *The Magic Goblet,* by Emelie Carlen. An anonymous reviewer panned that novel for not living up to standards of propriety set by Bremer: "Evil predominates, and admiring virtue bows before it. Among other scenes described are some love passages with a married man who makes no concealment of his guilt, which are an outrage on all womanly delicacy."[29] Bremer, an advocate for women's rights palatable to the Victorians, and Carlen, not so palatable, were at a great remove from the traditional liturgical atmosphere signaled by Clarke's medieval packaging. As a trio, Austen, Bremer, and Carlen already make up a challenging and formidable ABC of transformative early fiction by women.

If Austen's inclusion in Clarke's edgy Cabinet Series was a considered choice, it may provide new evidence that, as early as 1844, her work was recognized as a model of proto-feminist thought and urgent social satire, rather than as a forerunner of Saint Jane. Only three years later, George Henry Lewes (1817–1878), progressive thinker and proponent of religious skepticism, wrote his review praising Jane Austen and Henry Fielding as the two greatest novelists in the English language, famously irking Charlotte Brontë. Austen's just-out-of-copyright status may, of course, have made her mere filler for Clarke, but his selection algorithm seems honed. He bundles progressive works by and for women into a deceptive historical garb, dressing new ideas in the guise of old tomes. By binding his chosen texts in a manner invoking reverence and conservative authority, Clarke neatly borrows that authority for his series. Perhaps the project was too cerebral as well as too costly for "popular" appeal. Given the oddity of the devotional format, the entrepreneurial Clarke must have planned for special distribution—perhaps via a society, a club, or a school—that fell through. I even dare to speculate that the close proximity of the formidable Sunday School Union at 56 Old Bailey kindled hopes of a large order for use in the education of female schoolteachers or for adoption as prize books.[30] If he calculated that the pious packaging would attract notice from the nearby Sunday School Union, did management balk at the content? Doubtless the launch of Simms and M'Intyre's cheap Parlour Library books in 1846 contributed to Clarke's financial woes.

Advertisements for Clarke books not in this same series suggest, surprisingly, that the bulk of Clarke's entire inventory targeted a clientele of women. In addition to the Cabinet Series and his guides to local London sites—Hampton Court Palace, Thames Tunnel, and Westminster Abbey—he advertised a large proportion of books specifically to or for women. A separate series called Clarke's Ladies' Handbooks included small volumes devoted to domestic crafts and aesthetics: *Fancy Needlework; Knitting, Net-*

ting & Crochet; Plain Needlework; Baby Linen; Embroidery; Millinery; The Toilet ("A Manual of Elegance and Fashion"); and *Berlin Wool Work*. In one advertisement Clarke groups together *The Ladies Handbook of the Language of Flowers, Woman's Worth, Music Explained to the World, The English Wife*, and *The Married State*. He also pushed Miss Louisa Stuart Costello's illustrated guidebook *The Falls, Lakes & Mountains of North Wales*. His business at 66 Old Bailey seems to have specialized along gender lines, a precursor of the women's bookstore. Yet it proved an unmitigated failure. Scholarship's failure to take his remarkable series into account compounds Clarke's financial disaster.

PRIZING JANE

Pretty copies of Austen awarded in a religious context can conceal grim realities. Many a copy of late-nineteenth-century reprints of Austen contains a school award label or gift inscription, testifying to their popularity as book prizes, especially in Sunday schools, or as Christmas presents. Only recently has technology made it easy to triangulate the names found in such books to census records that might provide details about these young readers of Austen. Although I have not studied ownership marks in prize books systematically, I was surprised by the strong working-class context in which Austen's novels were often received as Sunday school prizes. Since nineteenth-century schooling, both secular and religious, officially stopped at age 14 for all but the elite, award labels usually document the end of childhood for working-class recipients. In a gift-book context, a school prize of Austen signaled not an encouragement to further study as much as a passport to adult toil. For most recipients, these pretty but inexpensive reprints were not an innocent starter Jane but an ironic welcome to Worker's Paradise.

In 1870 the Elementary Education Act introduced universal education for ages 5 to 12 in England and Wales, promising British publishers an uptick in readers among the young. By 1900, America had compulsory schooling laws in at least thirty-four states, usually through age 14. These legislative events frame the window through which gift books for children took flight. Earlier, I mentioned a gift-book version of Routledge's *Sense and Sensibility* from the 1870s, which showed a picture of a mother and a daughter at prayer, with a meal on the table behind them. The publisher integrated the pretty

3.5. Award label from St. James Sunday School in a copy of *Mansfield Park* presented to Clara Smith in 1883 (Philadelphia: Porter & Coates, n.d.). Author's collection.

paper illustration into the stamped binding as a central on-lay (see figure I.6 in the introduction). The iconography is not subtle; the mother's bright blue skirt invokes the Virgin Mary's robes of lapis lazuli in Renaissance painting. Eyes closed and head bowed, the mother appears to be taking the hands of the child between her own, teaching the young girl, wide-eyed and kneeling, how to pray before the meal. This scene, which does not appear in Austen's accompanying novel, points to a devout Christian pedagogy reinforced by juvenile gift books.

For nearly five decades, from about 1870 through the 1910s, prize books constituted a significant segment of the publishing market. As reward series mushroomed, Jane Austen became a popular Sunday school prize. On "Dec 31st 1881," pupil "Louisa Hernshaw" received a Ruby Series copy of *Sense and Sensibility,* the one with the cannabis look, from "Minton Sunday School." Austen was given away on both sides of the Atlantic, for during Christmas celebrations in Philadelphia in 1883, "Clara Smith" at "St. James' Sunday School" received a copy of *Mansfield Park,* issued by the local firm of Porter & Coates in a handsome binding of black and gold (figure 3.5). In 1885, back in England, "Mary S. Gettings" was awarded a gilded new Ward & Lock reprint of *Mansfield Park* as "A Prize for Elocution" at St. Timothy's (figure 3.6). At this time, parochial schools still outnumbered state institutions, and all primary schooling retained a strong religious dimension.

In the form of pretty prize books, Austen entered austere domestic spaces as a harbinger of adult life. Take, for example, a modest copy of *Northanger Abbey* in a later iteration of Routledge's long-running Ruby Series (figure 3.7). By 1910 this series had been reset several times and updated with a cover design showing a bonneted girl surrounded by foliage. The book is inscribed:

Gladys Shipley
Xmas. 1912

On the bottom of the page is added "From mother." If this is Gladys Shipley of Darlington, Durham, the census of 1911 suggests she was 14 years old when she received this Christmas gift of an inexpensive but pretty volume of Austen in a publisher's binding of blue cloth. Although 14 seems a suitable age to start reading a book with a 15-year-old heroine and begin to develop a taste for fiction, Gladys was then embarking upon her final year of girlhood.

The 1911 census records show that Gladys Shipley lived at 28 Surtees Street, Darlington, in a narrow, two-story, working-class, brick tenement consisting of five rooms, counting the kitchen, that were shared among ten Shipleys—husband and wife, both age 39, and their eight children, ranging from 18 to 3. That small home still exists, and even a quick glance on Google suggests a cramped life for the Shipleys in 1911. But their home must have been clean and well-run, for the census reports that there had only been eight births total in their house, suggesting that all the babies thrived. At 13, Gladys is the fourth child and the eldest of those still in school. Her 15-year-old sister Tessa no longer attends school and is already listed as "single," as is their 18-year-old brother Bertram, who works as a clerk, and 17-year-old Enoch, who is in training as an "apprentice fitter," perhaps under the supervision of their father, also Enoch Shipley, an "engine fitter" at the locomotive department of the Eastern Railway Company. Little 3-year-old Mary, still too young for school, remains at home with her mother. While Evelyn, 10, Martha, 9, and Geoffrey, 6, would have walked to school with Gladys in the mornings, Tessa's life as an adult has already begun, at 15. The census information on the Shipleys is typical of the working-class households to which the names in gift-book Austens often point. Society turned boys into men and girls into women at 15, ready or not, ushering many of them into the workforce. Fourteen marked the last year of a girl's childhood because it was her last year of book learning—her last year with ink pots rather than cooking pots or manual labor. In 1912, this Christmas gift, a book that today seems the perfect start to worthy teenage reading, was probably Gladys's final girlhood book.

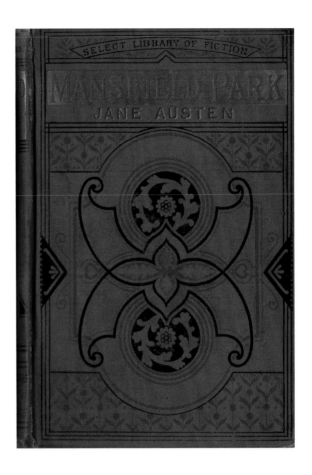

3.6. Ward & Lock reprint of *Mansfield Park* awarded as "A Prize for Elocution" to Mary S. Gettings by a British Sunday school in 1885. Author's collection.

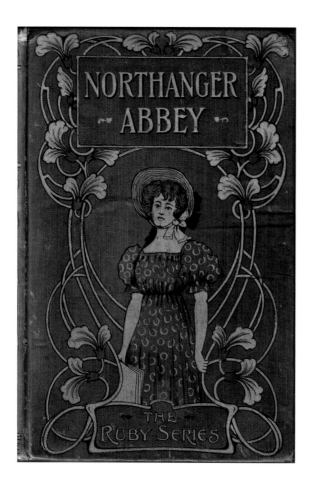

3.7. Gladys Shipley's copy of a Ruby Series reprint of *Northanger Abbey* (London: George Routledge and Sons, Limited, n.d.), gifted to her in December 1912. Collection of Sandra Clark.

The bright cover art of these books, offered as school prizes, rarely matches the recipient's harsh domestic reality. Take the Blackie's Crown Library Series, for example, which included dozens of juvenile titles, some of them *Dog Crusoe, Hans Brinker,* and *Little Women,* bound in cloth casings of eye-popping colors and stamped with an art nouveau design.[31] Two Crown Library copies of *Northanger Abbey,* awarded as attendance prizes, survive with their original school certificates pasted inside. In 1911, one was awarded to "Annie Munro" as an "attendance prize" from a school board in Forfar, Scotland, and the other is made out to "Winnie Valentine" during "Advent 1916" by the vicar of Kimberworth Parish Church Sunday school, presumably in South Yorkshire (figure 3.8). For the tragic story of 12-year-old Annie Munro, who died (along with a younger sister) in a diphtheria outbreak in a crowded working-class neighborhood within months of receiving her school prize, see vignette VII, entitled "Annie's Prized Gift." Winnie, if short for Winnifred, was 11 years old when she received her colorful *Northanger Abbey.* "Winnifred Valentine" appears on the 1911 census, along with four brothers and sisters; their father is listed as "clog maker and boot repairer." For girls from working-class families, a handsome clothbound book of their very own would have been a proud trophy indeed.

Inside, the bright gift edition of *Northanger Abbey* strikes a cheery tone. The brief introduction claims that the book is a fun read, "chosen for our Library, because of her works it appears the one most likely to interest young readers by its amusing records of everyday life in our grandfathers' days." The purpose of Austen's original, explains the writer, was "to make fun of a heroine whose head has been turned by reading the romantic fiction then in fashion—Mrs. Radcliffe's *Mysteries of Udolpho,* and such like, which dealt with haunted ruins, secret passages, cloaked desperadoes, midnight crimes, and other incidents of a class now pretty well abandoned to 'Penny Dreadful' literature." For all its lowbrow analogies and bright packaging, the copy also warns that "there are many readers that do not relish Jane Austen, whose quiet humour has a flavour often lost upon dull palates."[32] Reverse child psychology, circa 1910.

In spite of their "amusing" content, book prizes conveyed a serious message. Although the significance of these trophies depended upon local economic circumstances and the age of the recipient, these books reflect as a group how, for most working-class families at the turn of the twentieth century, elementary school was the limit of formal schooling, and apprenticeship in a trade came soon after. Children graduated to adulthood at 14—and often by means of just such a book. Hugh Thomson, Austen's most famous illustrator, grew up in rural Ireland and left school at 14.[33] Census records rarely call a working-class child of 15 a "scholar," adding their new profession to their names instead. A few girls avoided manual labor but, once identified as "single," left school to help at home or enter the domestic marketplace. The modern assumption that universal schooling should extend to 18 had not been fully articulated, let alone the idea that attending university should no longer be reserved for the elite.

In good economic times, some 14-year-olds received a reprieve. One copy of an earlier 1895 reprint of *Northanger Abbey* in another Blackie and Sons gift series was not, like so many, the terminal Jane of youth. Its school prize label, from "Dundonald Road / Ladies School," awards the book to "Miss Sarah Granger" for "Grammar" during the session of 1898–99. At 20 Dundonald Road, in the town of Kilmarnock, Ayrshire, in Scotland, existed a middling school for girls run by Miss Mary Garriock.[34] Sarah received the book at age 13, and the 1901 cen-

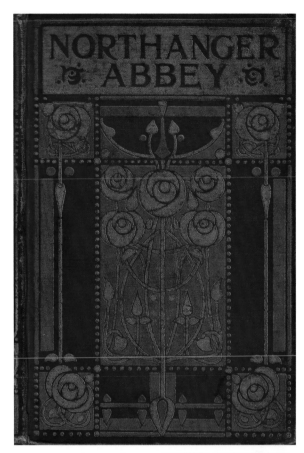

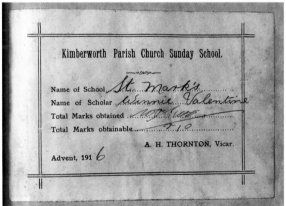

3.8. Winnie Valentine's copy of *Northanger Abbey* in Blackie's Crown Library Series, awarded in 1916 by her Yorkshire Sunday school. Author's collection.

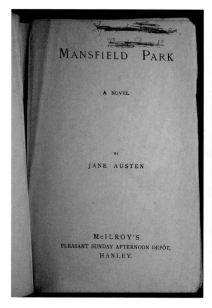 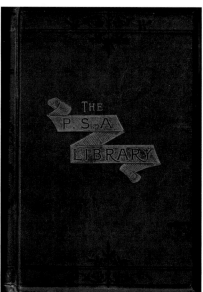

3.9. Title page of 1890s reprint of *Mansfield Park* (Hanley: McIlroy's Pleasant Sunday Afternoon Depôt, n.d.). Author's collection.

3.10. Cloth casing with insignia of the Pleasant Sunday Afternoon temperance society stamped in gold. Author's collection.

sus records her, at 15, as remaining in school. Her occupation and that of her younger sibling is still "scholar." She was lucky. Her father, James Granger, was a wool broker with his own business, then training his 19-year-old son, also named James, in the trade. Business for the Grangers, who lived in a thriving agriculture area, was good enough to allow childhood to be a little prolonged.

TEMPERANCE JANE

Jane Austen in a religious guise or context was not reserved for women and schoolchildren but was actively proffered to working-class men, particularly men of the estimated 40 percent of the population who, while not destitute, hovered just above the poverty line—often unable to afford the extra suit of clean clothes expected for church attendance. Such were the rough readers for whom this late-nineteenth-century reprint of *Mansfield Park* was commissioned (figure 3.9). It bears a quizzical publisher's imprint on its title page: "McIlroy's Pleasant Sunday Afternoon Depôt, Hanley." The imprint and the book's original cover, with its central scrolled design in gilt that reads "The P.S.A. Library," date it to the 1890s, when a religious temperance society tied to the Congregationalist church organized wholesome alternatives to publican culture for laboring men (figure 3.10). The Pleasant Sunday Afternoon society became the reformer's answer to working-class men lingering in the pubs after church on Sundays or, yet worse, avoiding church altogether.[35]

The PSA movement owes its origins to an ambitious linen draper named John Blackham (1834–1923), a young deacon of the Ebenezer Congregational Church in West Bromwich, who became an activist in the Adult School Movement prevalent in the Black Country, so named for the pollution generated by its coal mines, iron foundries, potteries, and steel mills during the Industrial Revolution. Inspired by the lively preaching style of visiting American evangelicals in 1875, Blackham experimented locally with new forms of Sunday school activities aimed exclusively at men from the laboring classes. At the start, he buttonholed men on the street who were not attending church to form what became the Pleasant Sunday Afternoon society, or P.S.A. for short. Adopting the motto "brief, bright, and brotherly," the PSA provided "convivial musical worship and male fellowship within a religious framework." Regular attendees paid "a small weekly amount" to become eligible for inclusion in a benevolent fund and for prize gifts of books. The popularity of these meetings spread over the next ten years throughout the Black Country, across the Midlands and beyond. PSA societies, some instigated by other nonconformist denominations, offered a wide range of social activities and classes. Since individual chapters of the society were "self-governing and autonomous," activities varied. Most local societies offered lectures and concerts. Some "taught basic sanitation and hygiene"; the Nottingham society in 1891 demonstrated "pigeon-flying."[36]

The municipality of Hanley, named in the imprint of this copy of *Mansfield Park*, was home to the deepest pit in the North Staffordshire coalfield as well an abundance of producers of ceramics, now known collectively as the Potteries. Laborers in these industries lived on the edge of penury. The Dickensian job titles of pottery workers conjure up hardship and monotony: batter man, barrow loader, biscuit kiln man, clay blunger, flat knocker, mould runner, pugman, slabber, treader, thrower, and wedger—just a few of the officially designated jobs in a pottery.[37] The Hanley PSA society boasted thirteen hundred of just such men as members by 1890.[38] This total seems the right order of magnitude for the aggregate membership, though the number of attendees at any particular meeting was surely far smaller.

Meetings need not have taken place in a church building, but in this case the Congregational Tabernacle Church on Hanley's High Street, built in 1883, had ample classrooms and meeting rooms, as well as a library.

Founder Blackham insisted that PSA "especially aimed to reach those . . . who were above destitution, but who could not afford Sunday clothes and were therefore reluctant to attend church or chapel services," a group he estimated at 40 percent of the population.[39] Regardless of whether dress or dullness was the reason for truancy, his target audience of young workingmen was beyond the age of Sunday school, in the range of 15 to 25. These members contributed "a penny payment every Sunday" toward a fund for "useful and attractive prizes" awarded for regular attendance. To be included in a PSA Library series, Jane Austen's fiction had to be deemed "useful and attractive" to clay blungers, coal miners, and slabbers. For these young men whose jobs often did not require literacy, and for whom a penny was a significant weekly sacrifice, such books (and this copy has all its edges gilded) were a badge of honor and, like the membership cards stressed by Blackham as an important aspect of PSA, totemic of personal discipline and aspirations.

The Pleasant Sunday Afternoon society grew into a worldwide network of Christian social groups, closely tied to the Congregational Church but nominally open to men of other persuasions.[40] In some locations, the society even offered its own monthly magazine. References to the PSA enter parliamentary debates in 1905 and 1908, when politicians gesture to a block of voters in favor of regulating intoxicating liquor, confirming that by then the society had earned a reputation as committed abstainers and teetotalers. In 1909, when William Ward became president of a unified National Council of PSA Brotherhoods, the society counted six hundred PSA Brotherhoods strewn throughout England, including those groups who met under "Men's Own" or other names.[41] Detractors among the mainstream Church of England, resenting the implication that standard church services were boring or unpleasant, dismissed the PSA as cheap entertainment.

The Hanley edition of *Mansfield Park* is therefore a nonalcoholic and aspirational Jane with a religious twist and a dash of radical thinking. It formed part of a library of reading materials held or awarded by the PSA Brotherhood in Hanley, Staffordshire. The imprint's prominent mention of McIlroy's, a large department store located along Hanley's Stafford Street since

1883, suggests sponsorship by the merchant, whose slogan was "The People Providers." Perhaps the local PSA chapter approached the prominent Hanley department store for help with the purchase of books. McIlroy's chain of successful department stores began with the first store in nearby Swindon in 1875, founded by Irishman William McIlroy (1851–1915), linen draper and fellow Congregationalist. Given the family's vested interest in the region, their philanthropy included donating to Congregationalist-related causes.[42]

Unfortunately, no annotations in the surviving copy record how members of this PSA Brotherhood reacted to *Mansfield Park*, with its limited references to the working classes in the Plymouth section and a healthy share of rakes and debauchees along with the main story about the landed gentry. The copy is well worn, however, with a spinal laxity that suggests it was read through many times. Four different ownership signatures, with some so scratched out that only the signatures of "Florrie Williams" and "Frank Turner" remain legible, indicate that women also owned the book, presumably either after the PSA Library for the working men of Hanley dissolved, or because they became secondhand owners of a prize book originally awarded to a PSA member.

Might the Hanley PSA have picked out this Austen title for a perceived affinity between its story and reformists, including, as Blackham's inspiration shows, a touch of evangelicalism? Of all of Austen's works, *Mansfield Park* "contains Austen's most extensive discussion of the clergy, and indicates her sympathy with Evangelicalism."[43] The Sotherton close-ups of a rich but neglected chapel from a former age, Mary Crawford's objections to becoming the wife of a mere country cleric, and the gluttony of the food-oriented clergyman Mr. Grant, who dies of an apoplexy brought on "by three great institutionary dinners in one week"—are all examples of jabs at mainstream Anglicanism that PSA members might well have appreciated.[44] Above all, evangelicals had historically been a strong voice in the abolitionist movement, a topic raised prominently in *Mansfield Park*. For what it's worth, Austen's personal views on evangelicals appear to have evolved. In 1809, when she wrote to her sister Cassandra about a new novel by Hannah More (1745–1833), she declared outright, "I do not like the Evangelicals."[45] Faith was a personal matter and not, she implied, fit food for proselytizing via novel writing. By the time she completed *Mansfield Park*, however, she writes to a niece in 1814, "I am by no means convinced that we ought not all to be Evangelicals, & am at least persuaded that they who are so from Reason & Feeling, must be happiest & safest."[46]

Regardless of the way the story spoke to PSA members, this well-worn copy of *Mansfield Park* is a rare example of Austen's participation in yet another feature of the publishing trade visible only in cheap reprints: white labeling. That business term derives from vinyl record labels in the twentieth century, so it would not have been in circulation in the 1890s. But the term fits the circumstances, since it refers to the practice of a manufacturer leaving a label blank, to be filled in by the consumer's own trade dress or name. When applied to the printing of books, it amounts to a title page flaunting the name of the buyer rather than that of the actual printer or publisher, making a book look as if it had been privately printed by the customer—in this instance, for "McIlroy's Pleasant Sunday Afternoon Depôt, Hanley." Only on the bottom of the book's final page, known as the colophon, does the volume reveal the true publisher-printer in small type: "Printed by Walter Scott, Felling, Newcastle-on Tyne."[47]

The Scott firm practiced white labeling in its reprint business. Walter Scott Publishing Company, Ltd., of Felling, at Newcastle-upon-Tyne, started in 1882. Its proprietor, Walter Scott (1826–1910), no relation to the famous author of the Waverley novels, was a self-made entrepreneur and building contractor who seems to have fallen into publishing by accident. During an impending bankruptcy of the Tyne Publishing Company, Walter Scott stepped in and took over the existing business. The venture expanded to several hundred additional titles in just the first few years. Scott grew the provincial business into a national brand founded upon cheap reprintings "intended for the self-improvement of working-class readers."[48] Jonathan Rose describes the firm as "an important immediate precursor" of J. M. Dent, another working-class autodidact, whose Everyman's Library followed Scott's instincts about audience.[49] The great majority of Scott's publications "were perfectly normal books," observes bibliographer John R. Turner, but "a few copies survive which are unusual."[50] It seems that from his start as a publisher, Scott produced some popular titles in his stock with no mention of his own printing house on the title pages. Instead, the imprints on the special title pages of these bespoke copies listed only the customer.

Except for the title page and lack of advertisements, the 440-page central text of the PSA copy is identical to Scott's standard 1889 reprint of *Mansfield Park* that was sold in the normal way and appears in Turner's comprehensive bibliography of the output of the Walter Scott Publishing Company.[51] The customized title page in the PSA "edition" of *Mansfield Park* is what bibliographers term a cancel. Scott would still have printed standard title pages as usual, but in custom copies like those sold to the PSA Brotherhood of Hanley, the firm's usual title leaf "was cancelled and was replaced by the customer's title leaf."[52] This tailor-made title page could be glued in at the stub of the razored-out leaf of preprinted stock or inserted by the binder. In the only known PSA copy, the custom title is indeed tipped in, or pasted, to the inner edge of the first free endpaper, where it now hangs on for dear life by the last few inches of remaining glue.

The Scott special reprints could be bound to suit the customer's tastes or purpose. In this instance, the Hanley bindings consist of blue cloth with beveled edges and a central gold stamp on the top board with the words "P.S.A. Library" inside a scrolled design. The name "Mᶜ ILROY," rather than PSA, takes the publisher's place at the bottom of the spine, a modest advertisement for the department store on the shelves of Hanley readers—a case of philanthropy-turned-advertising. Aside from these gilded extras (including page edges), it looks like a generic publisher's binding, with minimal Eastlake decoration in black. I found only three further volumes similarly commissioned by the PSA society in Hanley from the Walter Scott Publishing Company, each with custom title pages and in bindings stamped with the "P.S.A. Library" scroll: Scott's reprints of Charles Dickens's *Pickwick Papers* and Sir Walter Scott's *Heart of Midlothian* and *Old Mortality,* bound in red or blue cloth of the same design.[53] Jane Austen was not therefore singled out, but appears to have been part of a larger PSA order of a modest number of popular fiction titles, all neatly subsidized by McIlroy's department store. Of course, a picaresque adventure by Dickens and two historical novels by Scott filled with religious intrigue and violent conflict are far less surprising choices than Austen for the working-class men of PSA. Turner's inventories of Scott's regular books and reprintings suggests that the PSA had dozens of popular titles from which to make their selection, many of them dealing with social concerns of interest to a dominantly rural and working-class clientele. Yet survivors from the PSA Library stock seem rare; none are listed in WorldCat (OCLC). Unless an inventory of all the books once at the PSA

"Depôt" in Hanley fortuitously appears, it cannot be known what literary company *Mansfield Park* kept on the shelves of PSA members. Regular off-the-rack copies of Austen and other authors also occasionally surface with PSA labels of various towns, in the form of prize announcements.[54] The PSA commissioned specially printed and bound books for the membership of Hanley (and perhaps other towns like it), but it also gave away many standard reward series as prizes to members. Austen, bless her, was right there at the site of this religious working-class community—as temperance reading for men who might not otherwise afford books.

The practice of tailoring title pages continued at the Walter Scott printing house, says Turner, only through 1904. Bespoke reprintings differ from vanity publishing and from the Lever product giveaways discussed earlier. During the 1890s, the Lever Soap company needed tens of thousands of tailor-made reprints for the titles in their giveaway contest, all packaged in matching bindings with the Lever name on the spine. But societies with a modest educational mission such as the PSA might order small batches of books with their name in the imprint and stamped with their own logo and brand on standard casings. Did other churches or companies do so frequently? "Presumably," argues Turner, "there would have been a minimum order below which Scott would not supply tailor-made title pages, but this must have been fairly low." It is hard to know how low. Turner balks at "thousands."[55] So, what about hundreds?

The coal miners and pottery workers of the Blacklands, rewarded with possibly hundreds of copies of *Mansfield Park* commissioned by the Hanley PSA chapter, were not the only mining community to develop a taste for Jane Austen. Jonathan Rose, in his examination of the records of miners' libraries in Welsh coal towns, cites a ledger maintained by the Markham Welfare Association from September 1923 to December 1925 that shows Jane Austen, along with the Brontës, Dickens, and George Eliot, among the most popular authors borrowed by pit workers.[56] Sadly, no record remains of actual editions read by those miners.

BIBLICAL JANE

Religious features of books step in and out of vogue—sometimes merely accessorizing a secular author. A three-in-one copy of *Sense and Sensibility, Emma,* and *Persuasion,* first published in 1907 by T. Nelson and Sons of

London, sports a "yapp" binding (figure 3.11). The elaborate scrollwork and gilt decoration on the limp red suede leave room only for the title of *Sense and Sensibility*. As the *Dictionary of the Book* explains, the limp or turned edges in a yapp binding, made from soft leather, tend to touch or overlap; the style derives its name from late-nineteenth-century bookseller William Yapp. "The Yapp style is especially associated with books of devotion."[57] Yapping was expressly created for prayer books and Bibles, originally to protect the pages when carried in a pocket. On Austen, this type of binding seems to venerate. In addition, the Nelson edition of Austen is closely printed on thin, light-

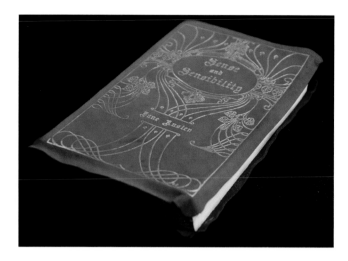

weight paper known in the trade as Bible paper. The rubricated title page, printed in black and red, is yet another traditional print feature borrowed from the appearance of Bibles, one that dates all the way back to Gutenberg. He, in turn, was imitating the red lettering practices of medieval scribes. Starting in 1899, old printing habits were newly adapted in modern Bibles to isolate in red the words spoken by Christ in the New Testament, initiating a rubrication practice still popular today. Combine all these physical elements with the ornate style of the gilding on the front suede cover, and this 1907 copy of Austen seems redolent of religious atmosphere.[58]

On the back of the reprint's title page, this volume explains that it was sold in "Two Volume Sets in Special Bindings," along with a companion volume containing *Pride and Prejudice*, *Mansfield Park*, and *Northanger Abbey*. In January 1907, a full-page advertisement for this edition in *Publishers' Weekly* confirmed what anyone looking at the binding might only dare suspect, namely that the American publisher explicitly and deliberately intends to offer its edition of Austen as the literary equivalent of a venerated Bible.[59] The advertisement shows only two categories of books: Bibles and The New Century Library. The top half of the advertisement lists the variety of binding styles for Nelson's best-selling American Standard Bible and Red Letter Teacher's Bible. The bottom half is devoted to touting the New Century Library series: Austen in two volumes, George Eliot in twelve,

3.11. Three-in-one copy of *Sense and Sensibility, Emma,* and *Persuasion* in a "yapped" publisher's binding of limp red suede (London: T. Nelson and Sons, 1907). Author's collection.

Shakespeare in six, Thackeray in fourteen, Scott in twenty-five, Dickens in seventeen, and the Brontës in five. The secular authors of the literary series are "handsomely bound" to resemble the publisher's own packaging of the word of God. The advertisement even explains why the Red Letter Bible prints Christ's words in red type, thus contextualizing the rubrication of secular texts such as Austen's within that same tradition. Not subtle. Like the Vatican gift stores selling "Popeners"—bottle openers with images of the current pope—this brazen commercializing of religious trappings enthusiastically pushes profanation aside.

For modern book buyers or lovers of the contemporary book arts, the binding style may fail to conjure up veneration in a religious sense, but it still signals a book bought to own as much as to read. The limp binding is best suited to being laid flat on a table as a decorative object, indicating a particular kind of collectibility for Austen in 1907, post-Howells. The fact that American poet e. e. cummings owned Jane Austen in a Nelson edition may indicate the firm's deliberate avant-garde appeal.[60] At $1 per volume in "leather limp," Nelson's Austen is a middle-class edition, and the special packaging points to participation in the culture of collecting, marking Austen's book for admiration beyond everyday reading. The Nelson binding is a publisher's affectation, a strategic marketing tactic that borrows the religious trappings of veneration for secular use.

From the perspective of book historians, Nelson's yapp bindings are crass commercializations of the Arts and Crafts movement. Circa 1907, examples of yapp bindings among the works of the Roycroft colony in New York—with its loose medievalism and participation in the late Arts and Crafts movement—can help contextualize this self-conscious binding style. For a few years at the start of the twentieth century, floppy suede bindings could be found on shorter Roycroft works, especially poetry. Another term for these faddish bindings is "limp ooze," a phrase apparently determined to depart from a venerating mode (Nelson's advertisement stayed clear of any ooze). Hardcore fans of William Morris look down upon the secular popularization of this style, such as in the Nelson bindings of Austen, because they see his many imitators as watered down, even lowbrow. Librarians also hate books bound in limp suede, because the bindings tend to crumble with red rot and are hard to house. All in all, Austen's biblical apparel failed to become a long-lasting, sought-after look.[61]

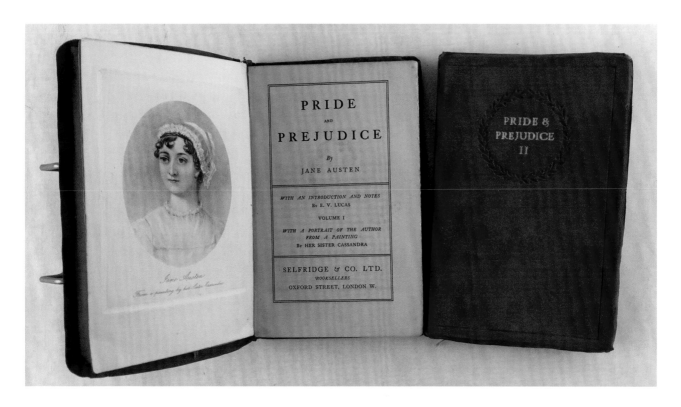

Nonetheless, and not long after opening its first store in 1909, the fashionable Selfridges ordered suede-bound copies of *Pride and Prejudice* as an exclusive for their book department (figure 3.12). Printed by Morrison and Gibb of Edinburgh, this special-order Selfridges edition, in two small volumes, also imitates the style of compact devotionals or hymnals, complete with yapped bindings of limp brown suede with "PRIDE & PREJUDICE" in gilt on each top cover inside a blind-stamped laurel wreath. The books were a reissue of the Methuen & Company edition of 1900, edited by Edward Verrall Lucas, and identical to that text but for the imprint on the custom title pages, which read: "Selfridge & Co. Ltd. / Booksellers / Oxford Street, London W."[62] The top edges of these white-labeled volumes are lightly gilded and each volume contains a built-in orange ribbon for use as a bookmark. Here too the religious look for Austen is a secular merchandising gesture, some might say gimmick.

3.12. Selfridges department store's edition of *Pride and Prejudice* in two suede volumes (London: Selfridge & Co., Ltd., n.d. [circa 1909]). Collection of Sandra Clark.

3.13. Hotel Taft's gift edition of *Pride and Prejudice,* circa 1930, in bright orange cloth with art deco design in black. Author's collection.

GIDEON JANE

Even a marked secular look may intersect with a religious context. Just before 1930, proprietors of the largest hotel in Times Square custom ordered editions of *Pride and Prejudice* strikingly bound in bright orange cloth with the building's facade stamped in black on the front cover—to offer to guests as giveaways. Built in 1926, the Hotel Taft was twenty-two stories tall, a high-rise of its time, with seventeen hundred rooms.[63] Inside their complimentary copy, patrons of the landmark hotel found the full text of Austen's novel as well as an advertisement for the salt water pool at the nearby Hotel St. George, informing them that, for a dollar, they could enjoy a "healthful" swim, "sun and suits" included. Think of this hotel edition as a cross between a souvenir ashtray and a Gideon Bible. Telltale stains suggest that this particular Austen copy doubled as a coaster, so not a lot of veneration is evident here (figure 3.13). Eventually, it was regifted and inscribed on the inside cover "*From Dave to Zelma,*" complete with a December 1931 date. Regifted books were common and welcome presents during the Great Depression. In the Hotel Taft series, Jane Austen kept company with Edgar Allan Poe, Sir Arthur Conan Doyle, Robert Louis Stevenson, Jonathan Swift, and Rudyard Kipling.[64] The series, entitled Tarry at the Taft, consisted of fewer than two dozen titles, with all authors bound in the Art Deco design of orange and black—as if dressed in stylish hotel livery. The same edgy orange saturated the hotel decor.

Was this hotel giveaway a wry take on a religious gesture? On the one hand, just when the Taft Hotel produced these giveaway reading materials for guests, the Gideon Association's Bible Project was still a relatively fresh and much-discussed evangelical phenomenon. Most first-generation members of the Gideon Association, which came into being around 1900, were traveling Christian businessmen and salesmen who spent a lot of time in hotel rooms. *The Bible Project* was an evangelical device tailored to the hotel environment. The Gideons wanted to place a Bible in every hotel room in the United States, starting with the first Gideon Bible in a hotel in Superior, Montana, in 1908. Since then, the Gideons claim to have placed more than 2 billion Bibles in hotels throughout the United States and in more than two hundred countries, with editions in more than ninety different languages. By 1930, the Gideons were well on their way to making their mark on the hotel industry, although the Depression slowed down donations even as it added a sense of urgency to their cause. The fact that the Taft reprint of Jane Austen, or Kipling or Swift for that matter, was a secular substitution for the proliferating hotel Bible might have been especially visible to the first wave of Taft hotel guests.

On the other hand, this book giveaway is simply a variation on the merchandising of many authors that, by the 1920s, was in full swing. Various department stores already offered custom copies of Austen: McIlroy's department store had subsidized the PSA's prize books to gain modest commercial visibility on the books' spines and title pages, while Selfridges sold their own white-labeled edition of *Pride and Prejudice*. Circa 1900, the flagship store Boots pharmacy in Nottingham, which then maintained a book department, sold flashy copies of *Emma*, cheaply printed from old plates by Edward King, with the imprint "Nottingham: / Boots Limited, / Bookselling and Stationery Department, / Pelham Street." And let's not forget how in the 1890s the soap company Lever Brothers gave away more than one hundred popular titles. While the British Lever was the first company to award books as prizes in a massive advertising campaign for soap products utterly unconnected to books, the concept of yoking literature to any and all commercial products immediately took off in America. In Chicago, the New Home Sewing Machine Company started giving away booklets of *Shakespeare Boiled Down* with a purchase.[65] In 1907 the Horlick's Malted Milk Company gave away wall calendars of "Shakespeare's Heroines."[66] By the 1930s, American kids were collecting cigarette cards to place in *An Al-*

bum of Celebrities of British History, with portraits of Austen, Shakespeare, Chaucer, and Byron.[67] A landmark hotel such as the Taft must have been awash in self-promotional goodies. The architectural image on the Gideon Jane also appeared on hotel luggage tags, souvenir postcards, matchbooks, and bookmarks. If the proprietors intended their book giveaways to convey a deeper religious message, it surely drowned in a sea of bright orange swag.

FADING

Over time, the meaning of a book's packaging fades as a religious signal. Among all those nineteenth-century reward series named for flowers, I probably missed untold liturgical hints, for the Victorians' language of flowers assigned emotional messages or symbolic significance to different flower species, such as the lily signaling purity and virtue. And in Matthew 6:28, the "lilies of the field" are reminders of God's promise to provide. Might the gift of a book from the popular Lily Series by Ward & Lock have different resonances as a reward book in a Sunday school setting than as a gift from a friend at a birthday party? How did the schoolteacher Helena Hawley, of Bury, near Manchester, present *Northanger Abbey,* in its pretty Lily Series binding of blue cloth, to "Master Henry Boal" in 1891? Did she stress the religious or secular symbolism of the lilies on the cover? The floral design was not, as it might be now, intended for a female audience.

The so-called Peacock Edition of *Pride and Prejudice,* the most famous and collected of the gift books, once signaled a bold Christian message that has now faded. Published by George Allen in 1894 and brimming with ornate illustrations by Hugh Thomson on the inside and out, this edition's front cover and spine boast a peacock (see figure 2.4). Christians adopted the peacock, already a symbol of immortality in some ancient cultures, as emblematic of Christ's resurrection. As a result, peacocks surface as familiar architectural motifs on churches and decorative religious objects. Whether illustrator Hugh Thomson (1860–1920), who grew up in Ireland attending a school with pupils "of mixed religious denominations," intended the peacock on his Austen cover to reinforce a Christian message remains unknown.[68] Since peacocks are also associated with pride, perhaps I risk overreading. Modern bibliophiles and Janeiacs sporting this famous cover on everything from tote bags to T-shirts seem innocent of any possible religious symbolism. But when George Allen and Company marketed the lavishly gilded edition among their many Christmas books in 1894, the firm inserted the Peacock Edition into a seasonal gift book market already replete with religious associations. For what it's worth, novelist Evelyn Waugh, another admirer of Austen with a penchant for Catholic aesthetics, owned a Peacock edition of *Pride and Prejudice*.[69]

Further orphan reprints of Jane Austen either with a lost pious purpose or marketed with the borrowed trappings of religion must exist. If such books suffered long journeys spread over great distances, they might now be so alienated from their original homes and contexts as to be similarly misunderstood.

V.V.1. Heman Burr's complete set of the Tauchnitz editions of Jane Austen, acquired by him in Paris in August 1879.
Collection of Sandra Clark.

Vignette V
Young Heman's Summer in Paris

An unassuming grouping of Tauchnitz reprints proves a delicious example of Austen being reprinted cheaply on the Continent—where she was binge-read in 1879 by a young American on break from his studies at Harvard Law School.

Bernhard Tauchnitz's inexpensive English-language reprints of British and American authors were distributed only in continental Europe, to avoid copyright conflicts. Most of his books sold for the equivalent of 1s.6d. as unreinforced texts in floppy paper wrappers, the same price point at which the upgraded Railways and Parlours sold in glazed boards or publisher's cloth in England. As discussed in chapter 1, the Tauchnitz price reflected the good-quality paper used by the firm, allowing these books to be privately bound and integrated into permanent home libraries. Only the wrapper was intended as ephemeral. Pictured in figure V.V.1 are five volumes of individually sold Tauchnitz Austens. Although the leather at the spines may have been recently repaired, the worn brown boards are surely not new. This mannish brown binding was likely the first of its kind for these works, probably chosen by the consumer.

Internal clues in these five Tauchnitz copies confirm that they were acquired at the same time and read by the same person, who wrote on the top right-hand corner of the flyleaf at the front of each volume: "*H. M. Burr.*" Each volume also contains further annotations in pencil, in the same hand. The inscriptions reiterate the owner's name more fully, along with his location at the time of acquisition and a specific day in August of 1879:

Heman M. Burr
Paris, France
[the date ranges from 11 to 30] *Aug., 1879*

Surely the penciled notes came first, before the owner decided to commit his name to these volumes in permanent ink—after integrating them into his home library. In 1879 Heman Burr was a man on holiday in Paris, reading material in his own language but remaining, at first, uncertain whether he wanted to take these cheap books back home in his luggage. Home was surely America, as best befits the endearing disambiguation of "*Paris, France.*"

If the dates in the volumes correspond to the time when Heman started the books, he read them over the course of a month in the following order:

> *Northanger Abbey–Persuasion* (dated in pencil "*Aug. 11, 1879*")
> *Emma* and *Mansfield Park*
>   (both volumes dated in pencil "*Aug. 15, 1879*")
> *Sense and Sensibility* (dated in pencil "*Aug. 21, 1879*")
> *Pride and Prejudice* (dated in pencil "*Aug. 30, 1879*")

Burr read fast and for many hours daily, if it took him only six days to deplete his supplies of *Emma* and *Mansfield Park*. Did he become ill during the crossing, creating a desperate need for reading material in his native language during a long and boring recovery in a foreign land? Whatever the catalyst for this binge, he did not abandon these volumes.

Who was this apparent Austen fan? Heman Merrick Burr was born July 28, 1856, in Newton, Massachusetts, the third child of a well-to-do merchant family, and lived until 1933. The census record of 1865 suggests that he was one of six children, three boys and three girls, although a later census shows only five. Heman, the eldest son (he had two older sisters), studied at Harvard Law School from 1877 to 1879 and again from November 1879 to February 1880. According to the career updates he periodically sent in to his Harvard Law Class of 1877, he emphasized the substantial break in his studies: "In summer of 1879 went abroad."[1] These Tauchnitz volumes tell us what his cryptic summary for his classmates did not, that he recharged his batteries by reading all of Jane Austen while in Paris.

His August of Austen, even if associated with illness and convalescence, was no deterrent to future travel, for he returned to Europe in the summer of 1880 and soon "lived in England and France for nearly a year." After coming home in November of 1881 to wed Mary Frances Ames, he whisked his bride almost instantly back with him to Europe, where together they "spent two years in Germany, Switzerland, and Paris."[2] Their first child, Roger, was born in Rheinbach, Germany, during that extended honeymoon-cum-Grand-Tour. Reading Austen in Paris evidently started a European romance that Heman was eager to share with Mary.

In Boston, Mary and Heman lived a successful life together, filled with passport applications, ship manifests, and more trips to Europe. I could tell you about Heman's law career, how he served a stint as mayor of Newton and sponsored the Boston Symphony orchestra with Mary, and how their two sons excelled at school and athletics at Harvard. But nothing in his life now fascinates me more than that August of 1879, when he was just 23—a Boston bachelor on his first solo trip to Europe spending a whole month of his precious time in the culture capital of Paris inhaling six novels by Jane Austen, that exquisite paragon of Britishness. He then carted the volumes home to America, where he had them bound in these sturdy brown boards for his personal library. Sadly, none of Heman's US passport applications involve a photo, not required then, but his 1895 application records that he was 5 feet and 8 inches tall, with a high forehead, grey eyes, and a straight nose.[3] He had brown hair, a fair complexion, and a round chin, and at age 39 he wore a moustache. This description must satisfy our curiosity. As for the rest, we can picture him reading and rereading these precious books.

CHAPTER 4

SELLING WITH PAINTINGS
A Curious History of the Cheap Prestige Reprint

The most ubiquitous visual marker of modern literary prestige—the signal that a book is a weighty literary classic—has its roots in yet another set of cheap unrecorded Austen reprintings. Those neglected reprints also provide a window onto an unanticipated aspect of Jane Austen's nineteenth-century American reception: long periods of virtually zero public interest. I believe that critics may have misjudged the market for her books during the latter half of the nineteenth century because they based projections exclusively upon widely hailed American firsts. Only neglected reprints reveal fault lines unique to the nineteenth-century American book trade. The meager way that Austen was initially marketed and produced on this side of the Atlantic in no way resembled the crowded competition of nineteenth-century editions in Britain.

Look around the classic literature section of your local bookstore, and you encounter a plethora of book covers decorated with paintings of people and scenes that, even with little or no interpretive connection to their content, still send an unmistakable signal, sometimes aspirational, about a book's claim to literary canonicity. This popular synesthetic marketing tactic is illogical. When and how did reproductions of oil paintings become associated with highbrow literature and serious editions, especially in an educational environment that increasingly isolates art history and painting from the reading of literature? Major publishers of paperbacks for today's college schoolroom—including Oxford, Cambridge, and Penguin—predominantly place images of master paintings on the covers of their literary classics. The fact that many of these earnest volumes are inexpensive paperbacks rather than traditional hardbacks barely seems to matter. Price is no longer an index of a book's canonical seriousness or importance. Quite the opposite, for the successful redesign of Penguin's Black Classics paperbacks, a line of classic literature that in 2002 was decked out in matching black jackets ornamented with old paintings, successfully forged in the mind of the contemporary consumer, especially students, a strong link between master paintings and worthy canonical reading.[1]

Paintings as cover art for serious reading may be a relatively new marketing tool in the history of publishing, but it has embedded itself quickly into the very genome of bibliophiles and readers. Whereas the difference between hardback and paperback format once designated prestige, the divorce of content from physical book format with e-publishing and e-commerce increasingly emphasizes the cover graphic as the dominant signal of literary value. A few years ago, after I showed several hundred Jane Austen book covers during an evening slide lecture, one man enthusiastically responded that it was all very well to see so much creativity being exerted on behalf of a beloved author, but he, gesturing to a black-jacketed Penguin, preferred his classics to look like classics. He had missed the point of the lecture, in which I had tried to show that, during two centuries of reading Austen, her appearance as a printed book ranged across a wide spectrum, from highbrow to lowbrow. In my opinion, no fixed look for Austen is more legitimate than the rest—not until such time as someone can show me that Coco Chanel secretly designed book suits. Nonetheless, publishers of canonical authors try to dress the part as defined by contemporary consumer expectation. For the next generation, those expectations may change. Our first encounter with a serious book imprints upon us (excuse the pun). By the time we recall the old adage to not judge books by their covers, it is too late. Our expectations have hardened.

Paintings on Jane Austen editions are now everywhere. Pushing aside the author's own portrait controversies, which were released from their moorings by her recent appearance on the ten-pound note, portraits of unknowns and little-knowns currently dominate the covers of Austen reprints. Oil portraits of all manner of Georgian women, and a few men, provide design fodder for contemporary marketeers of her novels, including scholarly classroom editions as well as lush coffee-table reads, such as Harvard's handsome Annotated Editions. Recently, the greatest variation within this approach has been to zoom in upon a painted detail in a high-res image, blowing it up to emphasize the craquelure of age. Tagging books with grand works of art helps signal textual legitimacy and quality. To cover a fiction with an old oil, or just a tiny visual quotation from a painting, is to mark it instantly as serious literary art—even if it's an inexpensive paperback.

Consumer response makes covers of contemporary fiction swing as far away from master paintings as possible. An ambitious new work of fiction cannot present itself as edgy and original if fronted by a traditional oil painting. Designers were forced to make an exception for Donna Tartt's *The Goldfinch* (2013), a Pulitzer Prize–winning story that revolves around a theft of the famous 1654 painting by Carl Fabritius. Even so, Brown and Littlefield revealed only a fragment of the famous painting through a trompe l'oeil on a plain cover—creating the illusion that the canvas hid behind a roughly torn book wrapper. They then placed a standard reproduction of the painting on the first leaf before the half title, belatedly offering up the full central image of Tartt's bildungsroman. To reproduce the Fabritius painting straightforwardly on the cover would have made a brand new story look like a stodgy old classic.

Viewed through the lens of Jane Austen's publications, the history of this type of prestige cover starts in 1904, with a little-known reprint series published by Henry T. Coates of Philadelphia. An established publisher of fiction, Coates glued small reproductions of master paintings onto the cloth bindings of his cheapest publisher's series devoted to popular works, old and new—including Jane Austen—for 50 cents per clothbound book. Coates's inexpensive series, so undistinguished as to go unrecorded by Gilson, was not merely the first to try what became a popular modern marketing technique but also produced the last descendant of a long-lived American family of Austen editions. This is because Coates was the final publisher to print Austen's books from one particular pre–Civil War set of American-made stereotype plates that served for many decades as the sole source of Jane Austen reprints on the American market. The ownership history of Coates's plates lays bare not only the longevity of stereotypes but also the habits and courtesies specific to the American book trade. Moreover, print runs from these plates contradict Austen's assumed steady climb in American popularity after the first local editions of Austen were published by the leading firm of Carey & Lea, also of Philadelphia, in 1816, 1832, and 1838. In the absence of data about print runs in nineteenth-century America other than these firsts by Carey & Lea, Austen's fame by century's end looked like a straightforward incline drawn between two points. New data, found by tracing the lineage of Coates's seemingly illegitimate lowbrow reprints, adjust Austen's presumed "rise" from a smooth upward curve of gradual ascendance to a spikey, uneven graph of punctuated equilibrium in the American marketplace. Cheap reprints point out how, for a number of decades in nineteenth-century America, Austen lived life below the curve.

AUSTEN IN PHILADELPHIA, 1876-1904

From September 24 to November 26, 1904, Henry T. Coates and Company of Philadelphia advertised in *Publishers' Weekly* their new autumn series, the New Acorn Library, as containing 123 "world famous books, carefully printed on excellent paper and substantially bound in cloth, with elaborate and effective cover designs." The series retailed for only 50 cents in publisher's cloth of dark colors, each stamped with a two-color design of autumnal acorns and oak leaves in black and orange on the top board and spine. A colored paper reproduction of an old master painting was glued onto the middle of the front cover, framed by the stamped design. Although the publisher's rhetoric overpromised with regard to the quality of the printing, the eye-catching cover design was a definite selling point, and Coates paid extra for a small "cut" in his advertisement to show off the look of his stylish but cheap reprints.

Coates hoped to make a final splash. After decades in the publishing business, he intended to retire, and a last surge with a novelty series would prove to a potential buyer that his long-running publishing house had not stalled in innovation, positioning him to fetch a better price for his thriving concern. The New Acorn Library series was indeed a hit, and on December 3, 1904, *Publishers' Weekly* announced that publishing giant John C. Winston had purchased the company from Coates, who would remain on the board as adviser.[2] The Acorn list grew to more than two hundred titles. Paper onlays, as a technique, had been around for decades, but only for sophisticated books, Christmas specials, or superior gift books at twice Coates's price or higher.[3] Perhaps Coates hit on the idea of gluing old paintings on the covers of his series when he was taking inventory in preparation for his retirement. He was known for amply illustrated books and inexpensive popular fictions. It made sense to combine his two strengths as he made his exit.

Whatever his inspiration or impetus, the Acorn books looked smashing on the outside—and sold at a remarkably low price. While 50 cents then

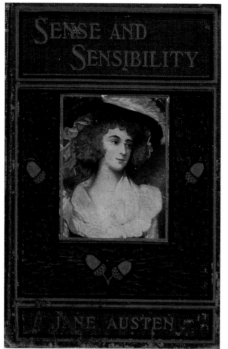

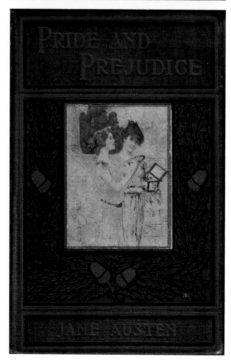
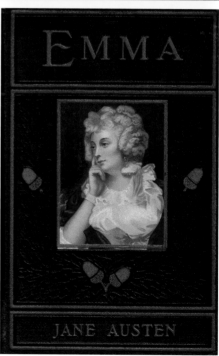

4.1. Jane Austen's six novels appeared in four volumes in the New Acorn Library series published by Henry T. Coates of Philadelphia in 1904. Author's collection.

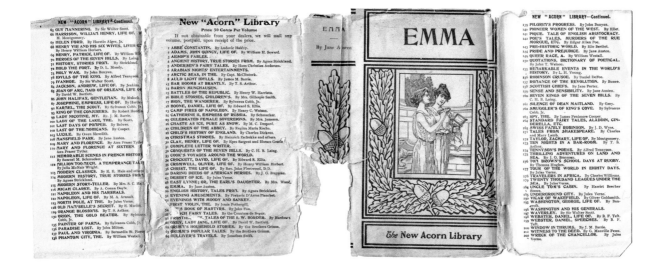

4.2. Surviving Acorn series dust wrapper, circa 1904. Author's collection.

may be close to $14 of buying power now, hardbound books in flashy covers of this nature usually retailed at twice that price. Pictured here in figure 4.1 are copies of the four Austen volumes printed as part of the Acorn series under the aegis of Henry T. Coates. *Sense and Sensibility* shares a volume with *Persuasion,* and *Pride and Prejudice* with *Northanger Abbey,* allowing all six novels to be present in four volumes. All copies lack dates, but their shared Henry T. Coates & Co. imprint confirms that production took place before Winston took over in December 1904. Simple paper wrappers protected the cloth covers, with their fragile paper onlays. The wrappers, listing other titles in the Acorn series, were meant to be thrown away once the books reached their destination. Figure 4.2 shows the only surviving book wrapper of the series that I have seen.[4] Even when stripped of their protective wrappers, most Acorn volumes have aged well, still frequently appearing among used books in secondhand stores and online retail sites. Wrappers are typically a lost feature of early cloth books, because before the advent of long-wearing dust jackets with color graphics, author photos, or supplementary text of their own, they were a standard packaging element rather than a part of the purchase.[5] In 1904, a book wrapper was intended to be removed to reveal the handsome cover beneath—more like today's shrink-wrap or gift wrap than a modern, well-designed, book jacket.

At first, the portraits on these four Coates volumes appear well chosen to grace Jane Austen, especially the Georgian ladies. Coates does not identify his images, but the pictured copy of *Sense and Sensibility* is suitably fronted with a portrait by George Romney (1734–1802), while *Mansfield Park* boasts a painting by Francis Cotes (1726–1770), and *Emma* a portrait by Sir Joshua Reynolds (1723–1792). [6] Although these paintings depict real people unconnected to her fictional protagonists, their portraits belong roughly to the right historical period, neatly invoking Austen's milieu. In fact, a hard-core Janeiac might recognize Jane Austen's sister-in-law among them, making the choice of paintings look increasingly intentional—almost as if the cover rewards insider knowledge of Austen's life. [7] But, to steal from Nabokov, that would be wrong—an interpretive fallacy to deceive the overeager reader.

Acorn covers cannot resist the interpretive pressure of modern readers. As proof, see two further copies of *Emma*, one printed by Henry T. Coates and the other sold under the brand-new ownership of John C. Winston (figure 4.3). Landscapes, seascapes, cityscapes, and portraits are haphazardly glued onto the casings of every book in this inexpensive series. An owner of an isolated volume of *Emma* may well imagine that the street view with public house connotes Highbury, or that the boats recall Jane Fairfax's dramatic rescue on the water at Weymouth, but knowing that Jules Verne's *Underground City* contains the same absurdly inappropriate seascape destroys the magic. There were simply not as many images of paintings glued to these books as there were titles in the Acorn series, and both the duplication and the occasional mismatch of story and painting can be jarring to a modern reader. In 1904, however, bindings on publishers' series served a different function, flaunting the brand of the publisher rather than that of the author. Readers were not accustomed to seeking deep meaning in cover art, especially on a series binding.

At 50 cents a volume, irrespective of a consumer's interpretation of the artwork on the binding, Henry T. Coates was not offering a prestige product. In 1904, the reason Henry T. Coates could drop his price dramatically, while simultaneously investing in these flashy bindings, was that the New Acorn Library was not in fact "new," but aggressively recycled. As seen earlier, nineteenth-century publishers' series on both sides of the Atlantic were often reprints of reprints of reprints of reprints. Using the same hardwearing stereotype plates to reproduce an identical central text at intervals,

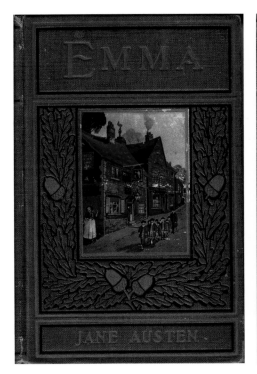
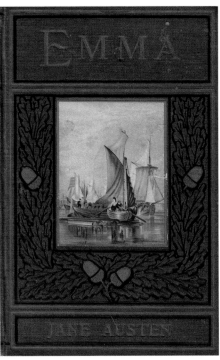

4.3. Two identical copies of *Emma* sporting different cover images in the New Acorn Library series by Henry T. Coates of Philadelphia. Author's collection.

publishers seasonally outfitted familiar books in fresh binding styles. Like the firms of Routledge or Miles & Miles of London, Coates of Philadelphia printed from plates that had churned out Jane Austen titles, variously dressed in the covers of multiple series, for several decades. His firm had sold the exact same texts as part of its Laurel Series in 1897 (figure 4.4). Bound in understated uniform green cloth, with a top board modestly stamped in gilt and two colors, the Laurel books had sold for 75 cents each—identical in central text to the Acorn versions. In 1897 advertisements stressed, and surely exaggerated, the production values of "about 140" Laurel volumes, printed on laid paper with a special Laurel Library watermark: "so well constructed mechanically, that even the fastidious booklover will not object to possessing them."[8]

The Laurel Series was not the only forerunner of the New Acorn Library series. Before 1895, Henry Coates had worked for many years alongside partner Robert Porter, publishing books as Porter & Coates. The biggest

 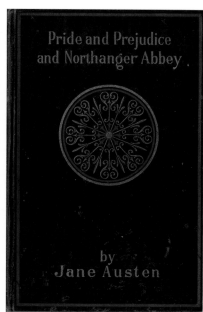

4.4. Austen reprints for the Laurel Series in 1897, also published by Henry T. Coates, were printed from the same stereotype plates as the Acorn series. Author's collection.

seller for Porter & Coates was its standard offerings of "popular 12mos," sold individually and as part of the Alta Series. First advertised in 1881, but with new titles added seasonally thereafter, the Alta Series sold initially for 75 cents, briefly for $1, and then for 50 cents by 1895.[9] Austen had been present in the long-running Alta Series, which experienced at least one radical makeover, as books already printed from these same plates—which looked a little less tired on the inside then (figures 4.5 and 4.6). In November 1888, Porter & Coates struck a deal with the *Ladies Home Journal,* which announced it would send any one of the "150 volumes" in the Alta Series, postage paid, as a reward for recruiting four new subscribers to the journal. If a "journal sister" was unable to recruit new subscribers, she might instead order any Alta Series book for 45 cents, postage paid, the journal having "made arrangements to buy these books in very large quantities."[10] By 1888, therefore, these Austens, along with the rest of the Alta Series, were discounted books in a commercial giveaway scheme.

Porter & Coates worked their plates hard, for in August of 1880 they had also advertised the same Austen titles in "New and Beautiful Bindings.

Printed on fine paper. Large, clear type. Beautifully illustrated. Cloth extra. Black and Gold."[11] The reference to illustrations is a tad misleading, because the images touted were limited to the frontispieces recycled in the later versions. In 1880 these Austens, always the same four volumes printed from those familiar stereotype plates, retailed for $1.25, bound in strong covers that reflected the influence of architect and furniture designer Charles Locke Eastlake (figure 4.7).[12] Roughly 90 percent of the titles advertised in the Black and Gold series in 1880 survived among the New Acorn Library books taken over by Winston in 1904.

I cannot be certain of all the early binding styles and runs by Porter & Coates. The copy of *Sense and Sensibility–Persuasion* in green cloth in figure 4.8 contains the bookplate of the Williamsburg Library Association (Williamsburg, Massachusetts), with an accession number that dates to April 1877.[13] Next to it, the Porter & Coates copy of *Mansfield Park* contains a Sunday school prize label dated 1883. In addition to ramping up their packaging, the firm offered their popular works in bindings of plain unstamped publisher's cloth in red or blue with paper labels that give the author's last name (in red gothic letters) and the title of the book (in black). In spite of the paper labels and the likely date of 1880s, the clean look of these undated copies is, judging from listings on commercial sites, easily mistaken for twentieth-century printings (figure 4.9). In sum, Porter & Coates, later Henry T. Coates and Company, had been recycling and repackaging its books for nearly three decades, adding to and rarely subtracting titles from its list of popular works in 12mo and various publisher's series. All of the Porter & Coates editions of Jane Austen, printed from the same plates—except for the title pages and an occasional advertising section or frontispiece—were therefore internally identical.

THE AMERICAN AUSTEN, 1855–1876

These stereotype plates went back well beyond the history of a single firm, for the Austen plates that Coates owned in 1904 dated from before the Civil War. For much of their long working life, they had remained unchallenged as the sole source of all American reprintings

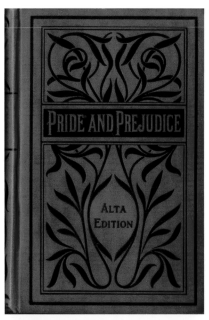

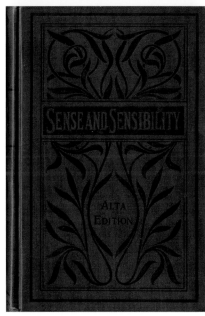

4.5. The titles of the Porter & Coates Alta series were also printed from these same stereotype plates during the 1890s. Author's collection.

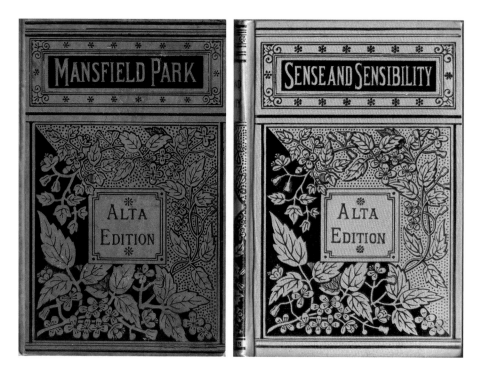

4.6. Earlier iteration of the popular Alta series from Porter & Coates, also printed from these same stereotype plates as far back as the 1880s. Author's collection.

of Jane Austen, owing to a trade courtesy unique to the American publishing industry. Unearthing the complete ownership history of these stereotype plates reveals new data about Austen's reception in America—data that complicate and redirect assumptions about her presumed momentum on American soil.

Porter & Coates neither set nor cast their first Jane Austen texts themselves. In March 1876, the Philadelphia firm had acquired the four sets of stereotype plates for their Austens, via George Leavitt and Company's busy New York auction rooms, from publisher James R. Osgood & Company. In turn, Osgood had printed his own Austen editions from these plates since 1870 (figure 4.10). One Osgood copy of *Sense and Sensibility–Persuasion* from 1875 survives in its original green cloth binding with a bookseller's inked stamp on the inside front cover that conjures up life in a bygone American era: "Trading Post / Hubbard, Ore."[14] In 1871 a new railway line connected the small mining settlement of Hubbard in Oregon to the larger

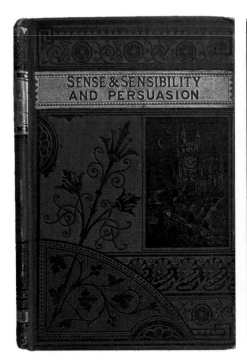

4.7. *Sense and Sensibility-Persuasion* and *Mansfield Park* in Eastlake binding styles of "black & gold" circa 1880, also published by Porter & Coates of Philadelphia from the same plates. Author's collection.

world, prompting the building of new stores and businesses stocked with goods from the East Coast. If Osgood's reprint arrived there by 1881, the year Hubbard's first and only hotel was erected, Austen entered a hamlet with a population under two hundred.[15] Jane Austen, after traveling by train from Massachusetts to Oregon, may have sold alongside mining and farming equipment in a dusty general store of the American West. In this Osgood copy, drawing rooms and saloons collide.

In 1876, Osgood declared his intention to devote his business to American literature, offering up for auction his plates of more than four hundred volumes by British authors.[16] One reason to unload this vast stock may have been increased competition from foreign imports, for by then the London publishing house of Routledge was distributing some of its own staples, including its Austens, directly to the American market from offices in New York. Porter & Coates reportedly paid $105 per volume for the metal plates that, it turns out, for two previous decades had already generated American

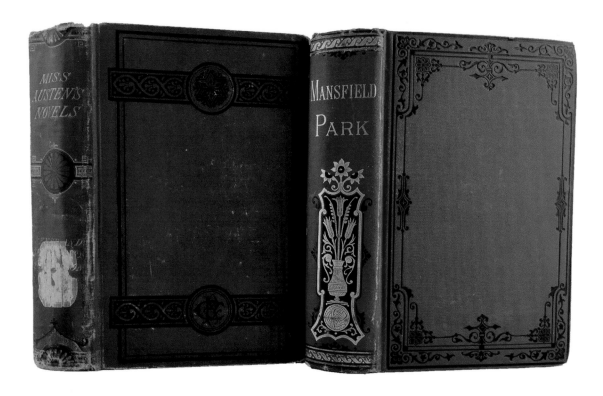

4.8. *Sense and Sensibility-Persuasion* and *Mansfield Park* (Philadelphia: Porter & Coates, n.d., 1877 and circa 1883, respectively). Again printed from the same plates, in two of the firm's earliest publisher's bindings. Author's collection.

reprintings of Austen's novels.[17] As the Civil War raged, even literature publisher Ticknor & Fields, a firm synonymous with high standards and elegant books, had owned these selfsame plates, printing its Austen editions from them starting in 1863. This earlier handoff was not a sale, because in 1868 Ticknor & Fields became Fields, Osgood & Company, to which James R. Osgood succeeded as the sole proprietor in 1870. At the time of the transfer to Osgood, "Fields, Osgood & Co." remaindered their stock of bound books in publisher's cloth, selling them in lots at the September 1870 trade sales. Austen even held her value as remaindered stock, selling at 95 cents per bound volume wholesale to members of the trade.[18] So far, such information about repeated trading and solid auction pricing seems to reinforce rather than challenge current assumptions about Austen being solidly valued in nineteenth-century America, but the print runs tell a different story.

As Ticknor & Fields, the firm owned the Austen plates during a time when America's book market was desperately trying to cope with wartime inflation and a sharp drop in production.[19] In 1863, when Ticknor & Fields first published Austen, far fewer books were being produced than during the robust antebellum years (figure 4.11). For the year 1863, the firm's fair Cost Book records the runs, printed by Welch, Bigelow & Company, for each of the four Austen volumes: approximately 500 copies of each volume, for a starting total of 2,000 from the complete set of plates. With production costs averaging 44 cents per volume across the four titles and a common retail price of $1.25 in the firm's trademark binding of ribbed brown cloth, Ticknor & Fields made Austen a quiet, no-frills wartime investment.[20] These isolated numbers are meaningless without

4.9. The same familiar Austens from Porter & Coates, but in plain bindings of unstamped publisher's cloth with paper labels. Author's collection.

further context, however. Compare, for instance, Nathaniel Hawthorne's much-quoted exasperation of 1855, in a letter to his publisher William D. Ticknor, about the "mob of scribbling women" who "sell by 100,000." While *The Scarlet Letter* sold, to Hawthorne's chagrin, only 11,800 copies during the 1850s, Harriet Beecher Stowe's *Uncle Tom's Cabin* sold 310,000 during the same decade and Maria Susannah Cummins's novel *Lamplighter* sold 75,000 in 1854 alone. True, these earlier sales of contemporary fiction reflect a prewar prosperity that, for most authors, dropped sharply during wartime, but the Civil War alone does not explain Austen's comparatively slow reprint sales. Although in England during the 1850s, 1860s, and 1870s, multiple publishers printed Jane Austen at multiple price points in batches that might have fueled Hawthorne's misogynist outrage at public taste, in America she presented no such threat—either before or after the war.

From October 1862 through March 1876, when the Austen plates were

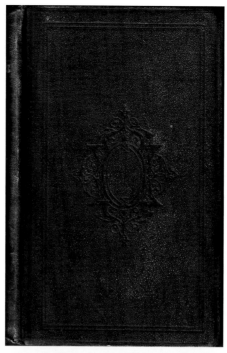

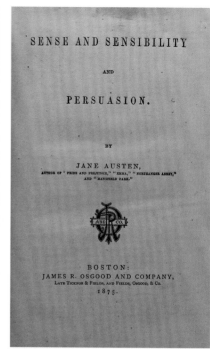

4.10. *Sense and Sensibility-Persuasion* volume (Boston: James R. Osgood and Company, 1875). This earlier Austen reprinting, too, was made from the same plates later used by Porter & Coates of Philadelphia. Author's collection.

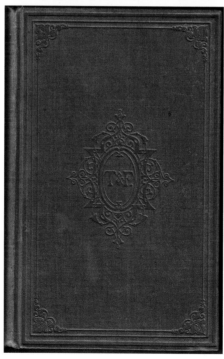

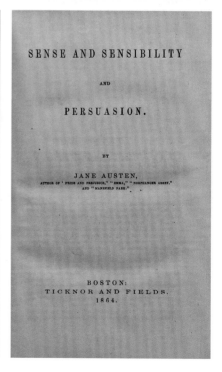

4.11. *Sense and Sensibility-Persuasion* volume (Boston: Ticknor & Fields, 1864). Reprint made from the same plates, this time during the American Civil War. Collection of Sandra Clark.

in successive possession of Ticknor & Fields, then Fields, Osgood & Company, and then Osgood's solo concern, the Sheet Stock Book shows a total of 6,696 volumes of Austen printed by the historic firm in very small batches.[21] The total copies across fourteen years, and for four titles rather than just one, is exceedingly low—especially accounting for professional exclusivity. By this, I mean the unique extralegal courtesies that self-regulated the publishing trade in nineteenth-century America, preventing publishers from pirating each other's books or cutting in on reprinting until plates were sold. The possessor of these particular stereotype plates was therefore the only American firm printing copies of Jane Austen.[22] This professional courtesy, periodically reaffirmed through advertising, helped artificially to retain the value of stereotype plates and related overstock. The Boston firm relied upon the uniqueness of its product to make a small profit on an author for whom there appears to have been only a trickle of demand.

Once the extralegal exclusivity is factored in, the Boston firm's Sheet Stock Book records the exact number of copies of Austen's books printed not just by one firm as it evolves but in all of America between October 1862 and March 1876. For close to a decade and a half, America's publishing industry produced fewer than 6,700 new copies of Jane Austen's novels. This information alters the curve. Up to now, Austen's reputation in America has been measured only by the print runs of Carey & Lea of Philadelphia in 1816, 1832–33, and 1838—which before the adoption of stereotyping were hand-press books.[23] Carey & Lea's first edition, printed in 1816 as a modest run of 500, had not sold well, but the firm's larger reprinting of all six of Austen's novels, each in two volumes, in 1832–33 hails "a turning point in Austen's American reception," according to Juliette Wells, who reckons that "the 7,000 total copies represented a huge influx into a market that had previously contained only occasional imported volumes and the 500 copies of the 1816 Philadelphia *Emma*."[24]

Critical enthusiasm for the size of Carey & Lea's print run differs, for Gilson called the same 7,000 run "small" as a combined total for all six novels and as a supply to satisfy demand for the next five years.[25] Nevertheless, the 1,500 further copies of the all-in-one opus *Novels of Jane Austen*, published in 1838 by the same firm, by then Carey, Lea & Blanchard, has been pointed to as evidence of Austen's additional reputational traction.[26] Between this promising start in the 1830s, then, and her strong showing by the century's end (the only concrete information hitherto available), the shape of Austen's reception curve across nineteenth-century America looked like a steady upward trajectory—a straightforward climb between these two points. But the accounting books of Ticknor & Fields, arguably the most important publishing house in America at that time, provide sobering numbers that fall steeply below the supposed incline for many years. Instead of enjoying an ever-rising reputation, what Austen experienced during the 1860s and 1870s was an extended plateau, a very low one by Gilson's standards. In spite of "passionate American readers" like the Quincy sisters of Boston, for a decade and a half Jane Austen was an author with little or no pulse in America—a virtual flatliner.[27] At the centenary of America's independence, one hundred years after her own birth, Jane Austen's literary reputation stood still inside the busy hub of American publishing.

The Austen plates take us still further back, however, to before the Civil War, for even the fastidious Ticknor & Fields had acquired their Austen plates secondhand. The cost books record that in October 1862 the firm purchased the four sets of Austen stereotypes for $220, or $55 per volume, via the same auctioneer, G. A. Leavitt, who sold them again a decade and a half later.[28] A report of the 1862 auction, billed as "The Great Auction of Stereotype Plates," confirms that, taking into account depressed wartime pricing, these sums—roughly half what Porter & Coates of Philadelphia paid later, in 1876—still amounted to a substantial outlay for any publisher, no matter how optimistic about the future.[29] Per volume, Jane Austen fetched at that wartime auction slightly more than Daniel Defoe, less than Madame de Staël, and about the same as Ann Radcliffe and Hannah More. All these dead authors were free of copyright fees in America—the low-hanging fruit of the reprint business. In other words, Ticknor & Fields expected Austen to sell well. But she didn't.

Before the war, the Austen plates had been part of the asset liquidation of the New York firm Derby & Jackson, which printed from these identical plates as early as July 1857, advertising Austen's six novels in their Standard Female Novelist Series as a four-volume set "with Steel Illustrations" (figure 4.12).[30] The price per volume varied according to binding style: "cloth $1; sheep $1.25; half calf, gilt $2; half calf, antique, $2."[31] Derby & Jackson also sold Austen in the "People's 12mo Edition" of Classic Authors, priced at $1 each in publisher's cloth.[32] Whatever its print runs of Austen, Derby

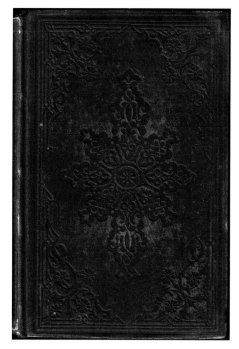

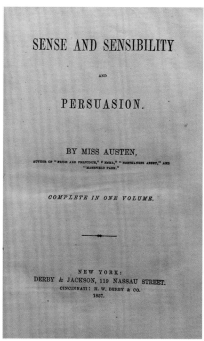

SENSE AND SENSIBILITY

AND

PERSUASION.

BY MISS AUSTEN,

AUTHOR OF "PRIDE AND PREJUDICE," "EMMA," "NORTHANGER ABBEY," AND
"MANSFIELD PARK."

COMPLETE IN ONE VOLUME.

NEW YORK:
DERBY & JACKSON, 119 NASSAU STREET.
CINCINNATI: H. W. DERBY & CO.
1857.

4.12. *Sense and Sensibility-Persuasion* volume (New York: Derby & Jackson, 1857). Again, same book, from same plates, now pre-Civil War. Author's collection.

& Jackson failed to sell out, because Ticknor & Fields's cost books show that the firm also acquired several hundred copies in sheets of each Austen novel via the large publishing house of D. Appleton & Company, probably the winning bidder on the loose Derby & Jackson stock unloaded at the same time. Ticknor & Field then folded these hundreds of preprinted sheets into its first print runs of each novel, binding them uniformly with its own title pages. The total of 6,696 copies recorded in the sheet stock book thus included those made directly from the earlier firm's leftover sheets bought via Appleton. All this again demonstrates the trade courtesy of allowing the holder of stereotype plates to absorb any related stock and thus control market share of specific titles.

In its turn, Derby & Jackson had taken over at least two of its stereotype plates from a short-lived firm called Bunce & Brother, also of New York, that printed from scratch, and had cast in stereotype, new editions of *Pride and Prejudice* and *Sense and Sensibility*, advertised for 75 cents each in September 1855 and January 1856, respectively (figure 4.13).[33] With its

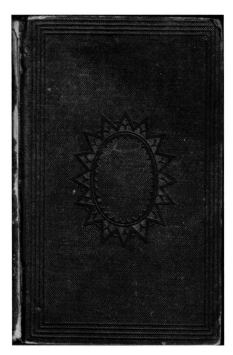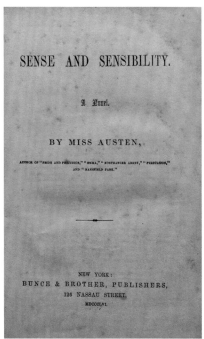

4.13. *Sense and Sensibility* (New York: Bunce & Brother, Publishers, 1856). Already those same plates were hard at work in 1856. Author's collection.

proud announcement of an intention to issue a full new edition of all six of Austen's novels, Bunce & Brother was the first to claim the trade right to exclusivity that then clung, for some decades, to the set of Austen plates on which this firm had begun production (figure 4.14). Before 1855, the only other known Austen reprinting in America took place in 1849 in Boston, a stereotyped solo production of *Pride and Prejudice,* reprinted from plates that had been used in 1848 by another Boston publisher.[34] Between that *Pride and Prejudice* in 1848 and the six-in-one volume by Carey, Lea & Blanchard of 1838, there had been yet an earlier gap in Austen activity lasting a full decade.

Alas, the records of the smaller firms do not survive. By 1856, Bunce & Brother went bankrupt, which explains why they abandoned the scheme for a full edition of Jane Austen.[35] By July 1857, Derby & Jackson advertised the "works" of Austen in four volumes as "now ready," having taken over the Bunce & Brother plates and, apparently, its optimistic mission to offer a complete Austen. Although Bunce & Brother had sold *Pride and Prejudice* as

REPUBLICATION OF MISS AUSTEN'S NOVELS

BUNCE & BROTHER,

In pursuance of their design to publish an uniform edition of Miss Austen's celebrated novels, announce that two of the series are already issued :—

I.

PRIDE AND PREJUDICE.

II.

SENSE AND SENSIBILITY.

Which will now be followed rapidly by the remainder, consisting of

III. NORTHANGER ABBEY.
IV. EMMA.
V. MANSFIELD PARK.
VI. PERSUASION.

Miss Austen is emphatically the novelist of Home. The truth, spirit, ease, and refined humor of her style, have rarely been equalled. She will always retain a leading position in literature, as the representative of the domestic school of novels, of which she was the founder, and notwithstanding the brilliant successes of many recent imitators, she still remains undisputed mistress of this class of composition.

Pride and Prejudice, and Sense and Sensibility, are issued in uniform volumes, 12 mo. Price, 75 cents each.

BUNCE & BROTHER, PUBLISHERS,
126 NASSAU STREET, N. Y.

4.14. Announcement of intent by Bunce & Brother in 1856, bound in with copy shown in figure 4.13. Author's collection.

well as *Sense and Sensibility* individually, Derby & Jackson now bound these novels with the shorter *Northanger Abbey* and *Persuasion*, respectively. This is how Austen's novels remained bundled until 1904. Readers in nineteenth-century Britain predominantly encountered *Northanger Abbey* alongside *Persuasion* in one volume, but in America these two shorter novels hid behind the author's better-known works for a half century.

In sum, the history of these crucial stereotype plates is a string of hand-offs from publisher to publisher—from New York to Boston to Philadelphia. Here is an overview timeline with corresponding retail prices per volume:

1855–56	Bunce & Brother, New York	75 cents
1857–61	Derby & Jackson, New York	$1.00 to $2 (in calf)
1862–3 to 1867	Ticknor & Fields, Boston	$1.25 (also $1.50)
1868–70	Fields, Osgood & Co., Boston	unknown
1871–76	James R. Osgood & Co., Boston	$1.75
1876–1895	Porter & Coates, Philadelphia	$1.00 to 50 cents
1896–1904	Henry T. Coates, Philadelphia	75 to 50 cents

The list shows, yet again, not merely the longevity of stereotypes but also the variations in prices of different, although internally identical, cloth editions. Since only the account books of Ticknor & Fields are known to have survived, and the print runs of these American firms might have differed greatly, I remain cautious about redrawing the curve. Context and marketing also differed: while Bunce & Brother advertised the publication of a stand-alone edition, Derby & Jackson slotted Austen into a convenient spot in its Standard Female Novelists Series. Ticknor & Fields were known for fastidious bookmaking, but Porter & Coates took more of a fiction-by-the-yard attitude with its popular 12-mo series of more than a hundred titles. The needed numbers and details are not yet in. Even so, this list of consecutive rather than simultaneous editions looks nothing like the heady and varied market for Austen in England. Between 1855 and 1880, hardback Austens in London sold anywhere from 6s. to 1s., but during that same time in America the price pendulum swung up rather than down and traveled a much shorter distance between 75 cents and $1.75—for identical texts that remained available only in cloth bindings. For decades in America, a gentlemanly cartel rather than fierce competition in an unregulated marketplace traded in Jane Austen. She became both beneficiary and victim of price fixing.

Even without knowing the numbers of every print run, the ownership history of this one set of American stereotype plates, in active use for close to five decades from 1855 to 1904, stretches rather than defies known trade practices. On both sides of the Atlantic, stereotyping allowed for the proliferation of cheap books during the latter half of the nineteenth century, and plates were aggressively traded in England as well as America. But in America, the selling, exchanging, or auctioning of used stereotype plates did not necessarily move down-market. In America, Austen plate sales differ from the handoffs of the London plates of the 1883 *Sense and Sensibility* that slid, as seen in Chapter 2, downward from Routledge to Lever to Miles & Miles and to Londoner's Press. Guarded by trade courtesies, American plates held their value, and repairs, such as those recorded in the Ticknor & Fields cost book, fixed obvious breakage or damage by replacing lines of text neatly with slugs.[36] But it seems possible, even likely, that the very trade courtesies that guarded American investment in Austen by individual publishers also slowed down the author's popular reception. American trade practices, an exclusivity amounting to price fixing, limited the unbridled competition for Austen at the price spreads witnessed in Britain—where Bentley sold deluxe Austens at six shillings to the middling classes at the same time that Routledge and others peddled her books at train stations for one or two shillings to a very different clientele. The narrower American trade practices surely contributed to Austen's loss of momentum for long stretches of the nineteenth century, in spite of the initial push from Carey & Lea in the 1830s.

Around 1880, the trade courtesy granting exclusivity to any active user of the Austen plates ended, along with many self-regulating extralegal understandings among the old guard of the American publishing trade. Not only is this the moment when New York firms such as Harper & Brothers and George Munro printed dime novels of Austen in dailies and weeklies, thumbing their noses at established courtesies with flimsy and indiscriminate paperbacks, but in addition the forces of globalization brought more cheap books from England into America.[37] As luck would have it, once Porter & Coates acquired Austen in 1876, and her American reputation took off in earnest—as evidenced by the ringing endorsement from American tastemaker William Dean Howells, who called her "the divine Jane" in 1891, and the green-eyed attentions of Mark Twain in 1898—changes in the publishing landscape and increased competition made those old Austen plates less valuable because less unique. By the early 1890s, both imported and homespun editions of Austen competed for readers in the American marketplace at a healthy range of prices.

CAVEAT EMPTOR

Flash forward to 1904. The plates for Coates's "New" Acorn Austens were, professionally speaking, ancient relics. His hand-me-down Austen plates were nearly fifty years old and had spawned at least a half dozen imprints and many more publisher's series. Although few working exemplars could have been as old as these Austen plates, most titles in the Acorn series were printed from aging and secondhand stereotypes. My guess is that many more books in Coates's Acorn series came out of that same 1876 auction of Osgood's plates of British authors. Reusing aging assets allowed Coates to lower his end-career prices. In 1904 he could match his own lowest-ever retail price for a cloth book while still investing in the extra material and labor of gluing eye-catching onlays onto fancy new cloth casings. Place the same Austen titles with different imprints in a chronological sequence, and the type wear and deterioration of the plates across their long lifespan of forty-nine years becomes obvious. Gilson occasionally claims to see plate wear in reprints that are only a year or two apart; I confess that I cannot. But even a nonexpert can see at a glance that, while the covers of the Acorn Austens in 1904 look smart for a 50-cent purchase, the printing quality on the inside is shockingly poor, with the impression unevenly inked on type no longer as sharp as that in, say, the Ticknor & Fields copies. Pretty on the outside, Coates's books proved hard on the reader's eyes. There is no trace of the worn plates after 1904, when they were probably sold as scrap metal by Winston and melted down.

All this selling and recycling of stereotypes creates more textual duplication, which inevitably undermines questions of status and blurs bibliographical accounts (figures 4.15 and 4.16). Gilson sums up the Philadelphia productions as "numerous undated imprints issued apparently in the 1870s," tossing a mention of the Alta Editions into entries for the 1863 imprints of Ticknor & Fields of Boston. But, as just shown, after these plates sold in 1876, they were kept warm by the firm of Porter & Coates, later Henry

T. Coates, through multiple imprints and publisher's series until 1904.[38] I do not blame Gilson for his summary. Technically, the different names in the imprints require separate entries, but with so much duplication, further listings for the Porter & Coates, and Henry T. Coates, reprints from these same plates may have seemed redundant. Judging by the number of survivors, however, the Alta, Laurel, and Acorn productions were among the best-selling cloth series in America—where Porter & Coates stood out among the most prolific publishers of juvenile books and cheap fiction. In Gilson's chronological bibliography, the many British editions obscure and interrupt the unique importance of this one set of American plates that for many decades and in different guises served up exactly the same Austen text on one side of the Atlantic. The East Coast libraries that Gilson relied upon for the American copies he examined did not, however, bother to systematically collect 75-cent or 50-cent series reprints of textually identical Austens. Why should they? Coates and his partners were, after all, putting lipstick on the proverbial pig. Nonetheless, these unworthy tacky reprints now lead the way to a clearer understanding of Austen's reception in America. The nineteenth-century public in America did not reject Jane Austen. Rather, the American consumer did not buy Austen in the static textual format in which publishers consistently served her up for decades—at an artificially inflated price. Only around 1880 did indecorous and messy market forces set her free in America.

When inexpensive reprint series readily recycled the innards of books, the outside had to be seasonally refreshed. Ticknor & Fields cultivated an association with one particular cloth binding style, the "brown 'ribbed T-cloth' binding" that Osgood faithfully continued to reproduce, down to the blind-stamped arabesque ornament from which he removed the previous firm's initials. But later publishers such as Coates changed their cloth casings seasonally, to catch the eye.[39] Already, this minihistory of one set of plates has shown, in reverse, the visual evolution of the cloth publisher's binding in nineteenth-century America. Coates's modifications occurred during the so-called Golden Age of American book design, and yet his inexpensive publisher's cloth bindings were lowbrow knockoffs of high-end fashions—trendy without being stylish.[40] In 1904, the novelty of Coates's bindings was that, at little extra cost, different books could carry different pictures without breaking the uniformity of a series cover. The publisher's brand so far

SENSE AND SENSIBILITY.

CHAPTER I.

THE family of Dashwood had been long settled in Sussex. Their estate was large, and their residence was at Norland Park, in the centre of their property, where, for many generations, they had lived in so respectable a manner as to engage the general good opinion of their surrounding acquaintance. The late owner of this estate was a single man, who lived to a very advanced age, and who, for many years of his life, had a constant companion and housekeeper in his sister. But her death, which happened ten years before his own, produced a great alteration in his home; for to supply her loss, he invited and received into his house the family of his nephew Mr. Henry Dashwood, the legal inheritor of the Norland estate, and the person to whom he intended to bequeath it. In the society of his nephew and niece, and their children, the old gentleman's days were comfortably spent. His attachment to them all increased. The constant attention of Mr. and Mrs. Henry Dashwood to his wishes, which proceeded not merely from interest, but from goodness of heart, gave him every degree of solid comfort which his age could receive; and the cheerfulness of the children added a relish to his existence.

By a former marriage, Mr. Henry Dashwood had one son: by his present lady three daughters. The son, a steady respectable young man, was amply provided for by the fortune of his mother, which had been large, and half of which devolved on him on his coming of age. By his own marriage, likewise, which happened soon afterwards, he added to

outweighed the importance of the author that most series bindings do not bear names of authors on the covers, only book titles. The logic was that, if you enjoyed the Alta Edition of *Pioneer Women of the West*, you might return for a matching copy of *Pride and Prejudice*. If sold in a matching binding, *Ten Nights in a Bar-Room* would look like the perfect follow-up to *Mansfield Park*. Then as now, consumers liked sets and matching books. Coates's innovation for a lowly 50-cent book created enough variety to tease with interpretive possibilities without the burden of an original illustration to suit each title. Reusing assets he already owned, Coates offered a shortcut compromise between expensive illustration on cloth covers and the brand recognition that came most easily with the rigidity of a single look.

Coates's use of paintings to sell fiction in 1904 did not immediately catch on, however, nor could his recycled reprints raise his pictorial covers to the hallmark of canonicity for serious reading. Oddly, the books that shaped the modern prestige cover were the far cheaper paperbacks of the 1950s—but only after returning to the Coates style of covering books in old paintings. We will now follow the lowbrow book cover as it becomes embroiled in three further experiments to capture prestige for the cheapest of reprintings: Penguin's short-lived affectations with the woodcut; Pocket Books's borrowings of Hollywood's glam; and Bantam's trendsetting return to master paintings.

PAPERBACK AMBITION, 1938

As chapter 1 explains, the early history of Austen in paperback format, from yellowback to penny delightful, does not align with prestige. But in 1938, the paperback format, by then well established, made its first major cosmetic move toward attempted seriousness with a rarefied style of pictorial cover art—the woodcut. This makeover proved to be an unmitigated failure in a world where serious reading of canonical works remained stubbornly synonymous with hardbacks, and where the pictorial cover had not yet transitioned from juvenile books to hearty classic fare.

On May 18, 1938, British publisher Allen Lane experimented with the first ten volumes of a new paperback series, the Penguin Illustrated Classics (figure 4.17). Nine classic titles joined the hundreds of existing Penguin paperbacks, color-coded by genre, that mushroomed after Lane founded Penguin Books in 1935. Leading the Penguin Illustrated Classics lineup at

4.15. *Top row:* Bibliographically identical pages from three different editions of *Sense and Sensibility. Left to right:* Bunce & Brother, 1856; Derby & Jackson, 1857; Ticknor & Fields, 1864. Author's collection.

4.16. *Bottom row:* More bibliographically identical pages, from three additional editions of *Sense and Sensibility. Left to right:* James R. Osgood and Company, 1875; Porter & Coates, c. 1880; Henry T. Coates, 1904. Author's collection.

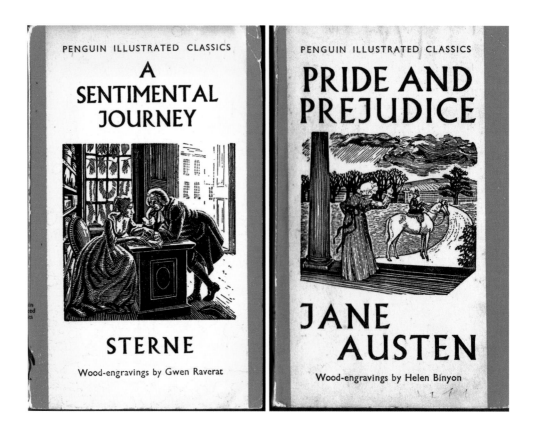

4.17. Sterne's *Sentimental Journey* and Austen's *Pride and Prejudice* in the Penguin Illustrated Classics series of 1938. Author's collection.

number C1 was *Pride and Prejudice.* The other books were Sterne's *A Sentimental Journey,* Poe's *Some Tales of Mystery and Imagination,* Thoreau's *Walden,* Browning's *Selected Poems,* Defoe's *Robinson Crusoe* in two volumes, Melville's *Typee,* Jefferies's *The Story of My Heart,* and Swift's *Gulliver's Travels.* Released simultaneously, the books sold at the low cost of "sixpence each," the equivalent of $1 today. Every book featured a woodcut on the cover and at least a dozen further cuts inside. The woodcut illustrations were commissioned from established contemporary wood-engravers.

The 1930s had witnessed a woodcut revival among expensively illustrated hardback books, and the idea of merging this sophisticated aesthetic with economical bookmaking came from within the Lane family. John Lane, Allen's uncle, was cofounder of the Bodley Head publishing company, which specialized in top-of-the-line illustrated hardbacks selling as collectible books in small print runs. Perhaps, thought Allen, the moment had

THE ARTIST

Helen Binyon

is the daughter of Laurence Binyon, the poet, who was for many years Keeper of Prints and Drawings at the British Museum. Most of her childhood was spent in his house at the Museum. She has a passion for puppets, and has toured with her travelling marionette company all over England. She took her diploma in book illustration at the Royal College of Art, London, and has also worked in Paris and the U.S.A.

Reading-case label

Penguin Books keep better in bookshelf if they are protected by the special Penguin reading-case (6d. from any bookseller). Cut out this label and paste it on to the back of the case.

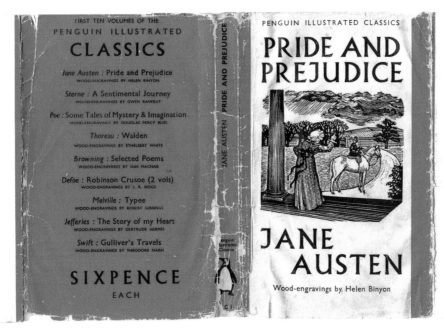

FIRST TEN VOLUMES OF THE
**PENGUIN ILLUSTRATED
CLASSICS**

Jane Austen : Pride and Prejudice
WOOD-ENGRAVINGS BY HELEN BINYON

Sterne : A Sentimental Journey
WOOD-ENGRAVINGS BY GWEN RAVERAT

Poe : Some Tales of Mystery & Imagination
WOOD-ENGRAVINGS BY DOUGLAS PERCY BLISS

Thoreau : Walden
WOOD-ENGRAVINGS BY ETHELBERT WHITE

Browning : Selected Poems
WOOD-ENGRAVINGS BY IAIN MACNAB

Defoe : Robinson Crusoe (2 vols)
WOOD-ENGRAVINGS BY J. R. BIGGS

Melville : Typee
WOOD-ENGRAVINGS BY ROBERT GIBBINGS

Jefferies : The Story of my Heart
WOOD-ENGRAVINGS BY GERTRUDE HERMES

Swift : Gulliver's Travels
WOOD-ENGRAVINGS BY THEODORE NAISH

SIXPENCE
EACH

PENGUIN ILLUSTRATED CLASSICS

**PRIDE AND
PREJUDICE**

**JANE
AUSTEN**

Wood-engravings by Helen Binyon

Jane Austen

was one of the pioneers among women writers. *Pride and Prejudice* is her best-known book, and one of the great novels of the English language. Delicately and humorously flavoured with the formal romanticism of her times, her work has a strength of character and a beauty of expression which ensure its immortality. It is a subtle tale of love and the marriage mart, sparkling with satirical wit and situations of intrigue.

PENGUIN BOOKS LIMITED
(ALLEN LANE)
HARMONDSWORTH, MIDDLESEX
ENGLAND

come to illustrate familiar works with trendy wood engravings in the new, accessible, and inexpensive paperback format he was helping to popularize. It was time to dial up the aesthetic sophistication of Penguin Books—and, by extension, raise the intellectual reputation of the paperback format.

Remarkably, in spite of being paperbacks, the Illustrated Classics—like the rest of the Penguin line before wartime paper restrictions were imposed in January 1942—came with dust jackets (figure 4.18). That is, Lane was still dressing up his cheap books in the familiar clothes worn by serious hardbacks. The sheer redundancy of a paper jacket, 75 percent of which duplicates the fixed paper cover, looks now like another sign of the project's schizophrenia and visual excess, but the practical benefit included side flaps that provided Lane with extra space to explain his choices. He placed an author image and minibiography on the front flap and an artist photo plus work description on the back flap. In this manner, he insisted upon the legitimacy of the illustrator nearly as strongly as he promoted the "classic" status of the writer. The blurb for artist Helen Binyon, illustrator of *Pride and Prejudice,* however, may have erred on the side of quirky when stress-

4.18. Rare surviving Penguin Illustrated Classics dust wrapper for *Pride and Prejudice.* Jackets on these paperbacks protected the fragile covers and provided additional information on flaps. Author's collection.

185

ing her "passion for puppets" and how she had "toured with her travelling marionette company all over England."

The Penguin Illustrated Classics floundered. As the war approached, the elitism of the woodcuts frustrated consumers looking to cheap paperbacks for the distractions of light reading or for information about current affairs—since Penguin's "Specials" about politics and practical issues sold well. The stodgy woodcuts did not mix well with the projected egalitarianism of the paperback format. The woodcuts may also have uncomfortably resembled the aesthetics of the new propaganda stylings from Germany. Either way, the woodcut sent a confusing consumer signal, and the project failed to secure a place for paperback "classics" packaged in rarefied artistic fashion. These colorful floppy books aspired to status but made for an awkward betweenity, since the woodcut failed to reconcile the cheap utility of a paperback with elegant canonicity. Penguin's Classics line did not relaunch until 1946, and then it led with a new translation of Homer's *Odyssey* in a sedate cover with a "rather clumsy" layout that reduced any residual illustration impulse to a thin decorated border and a small roundel.[41] After the unmitigated failure of Penguin's radical woodcut experiment, most European paperbacks quietly returned to the safe austerity inherited from Tauchnitz or, in England, to color-coded books devoid of graphics except for a publisher's logo.

BORROWING HOLLYWOOD'S PRESTIGE

American paperbacks, as we saw in chapter 1, swung the other way. The look that Pocket Books chose for their entire line in June 1939 seemed as far from stately or minimalist as possible. The garish pink cover for the initial printing of *Pride and Prejudice* exemplifies the splashy colors and eye-catching graphics that came to define Pocket Books (see figure 1.28). Nonetheless, and almost immediately, Pocket Books made a grab for the refracted prestige of Hollywood when marketing their classic literature. Although Pocket Books's designs remained unabashedly brassy, their covers reflect complex struggles for cultural status in the arts. To boost the film industry's gravitas and legitimacy, Hollywood was remaking canonical works of literature into screenplay material as its own prestige commodity. Conversely, the books depicted by these movies began referencing the silver-screen versions of themselves as a way to reenergize the cultural currency of old au-

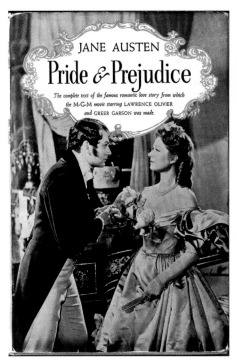

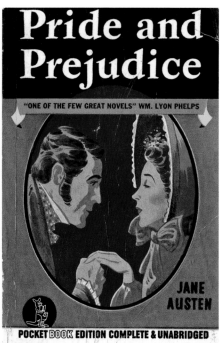

4.19. *Left:* An MGM-sanctioned tie-in edition from Triangle Books with a still from the 1940 film. *Right:* Pocket Books edition of *Pride and Prejudice* invoking the same movie moment. Author's collection.

thors. When it comes to Austen, on July 26, 1940, MGM released its feature film of *Pride and Prejudice,* starring Laurence Olivier and Greer Garson. By then, Austen was already doing well, as number 63 among the hundreds of Pocket Books selling as paperbacks for 25 cents via magazine distributors at newsstands, subway stations, drugstores, and media outlets. On the back of their *Pride and Prejudice,* Pocket Books had already integrated a shout-out to the upcoming MGM film. Once the film played in theaters, the cover of *Pride and Prejudice* changed to connect it more directly to the movie, with a drawing that modified, with bonnet, a still of Olivier and Garson also found on hardback tie-in editions (figure 4.19). In this manner, Pocket Books neatly rode the coattails of the film's success.

Pocket Books tied many of its editions of classic literature to books-turned-movies, cloaking 25-cent reprints in moments copied from popular films. Other publishers followed suit, some with a movie company's blessing and some with a circumlocutory strategy that used drawings evocative of movie moments to avoid a copyright fuss. The following year saw MGM's

Dr. Jekyll and Mr. Hyde (1941), starring Spencer Tracy, Ingrid Bergman, and Lana Turner. When Pocket Books integrated a cutout of Tracy into the cover of their Stevenson reprint, Vladimir Nabokov was driven to distraction. In his literature lectures at Wellesley College and Cornell, starting in 1951, Nabokov instructed students to ignore the misfit:

> First of all, if you have the Pocket Books edition I have, you will veil the monstrous, abominable, criminal, foul, vile, youth-depraving jacket—or better say straitjacket. You will ignore the fact that ham actors under the direction of pork packers have acted in a parody of the book, which parody was then photographed on a film and showed in places called theatres; it seems to me that to call a movie house a theatre is the same as to call an undertaker a mortician.[42]

When these 25-cent editions made their way into the country's elite schoolrooms, they jostled with academic authority. Nabokov may have loathed the film, but a full decade later, he still found himself teaching students whose readings of the fiction were influenced by the image of Tracy on their books. Cheap editions of classical authors found their way into lofty and scholarly venues—as books not to be collected and treasured, but rather held up as dangerous and inauthentic. Intellectuals such as Nabokov did not find the books' editorial content wanting; no mention was made of any misprints or the lack of editorial guidance. The packaging alone was what gave offense, just as it had done for Henry James. Moving pictures, for the ranting Nabokov, would not assist the legitimacy of the mass-market reprint.

Even so, movies moved books. They still do. Tie-in editions that appropriate stills of films remain a staple of the Jane Austen reprint, especially in the wake of the many screen adaptations in the 1990s. Silver-screen influences on covers are easy to spot and are so familiar that I do not need to provide contemporary examples from recent years. Celebrity author and celebrity actor symbiotically augment each other's cultural powers with movie-based cover art. Older or manipulated movie stills, such as those on Pocket Books titles, however, make for an invocation of Hollywood authority that can, after many years, be harder to pinpoint. During the coming of age of the paperback format in the 1940s, 1950s, and 1960s, Hollywood exerted an extraordinary force upon the design world, including many covers for reprinted literary classics. When it came to inexpensive foreign editions of Austen, the aim was often not to reference a specific movie, but to invoke Hollywood glamour in general. When foreign designers drew upon the aesthetics of American films or the generic allure of screen celebrities, the specific source could become increasingly clandestine or irrelevant. In some contexts, it no longer mattered whether the movie scene placed on a Jane Austen book had anything to do with her story.

4.20. Italian paperback of *Emma* for a teen market (Torino: SAIE, 1959) and a Spanish paperback of *La abadía de Northanger* (Barcelona: Bruguera, 1945). Author's collection.

One set of examples of the many furtive film references on mid-twentieth-century Austen translations, in which the movie fronting a book is unrelated to the accompanying text, consists of two reprints covered with repurposed movie stills (figure 4.20). The 1959 Italian paperback of *Emma* boldly appropriated a movie still from a noir Western set in post–Civil War Wyoming. Entitled *Devil's Doorway* (1950), the movie was a box-office failure in America but had modest runs in Europe.[43] The Italian designer colorized the black and white still of actress Paula Raymond, cropping out the film's central character, the Native American played by Robert Taylor. The erasure of Taylor from the still is painfully ironic, since the movie's main tragedy concerns the denial of the Native American's rights of citizenship. The Spanish paperback, on the other hand, seems to appropriate the "wrong" movie for Austen, although the use of Olivier-as-Heathcliffe from the film *Wuthering Heights* (1939) as the face of *Northanger Abbey* is perhaps not that great a gaffe—if intended to invoke shared Gothic elements rather than confuse Austen with a Brontë sister.

4.21. *Orgoglio e pregiudizio,* translated by L. Corsini and illustrated by Cassinari (Milano: Piccoli, n.d.); *Ritorno a te* (Bologna: Capitol, 1962); and *Orgullo y prejuicio,* translated by Costa Clavell (Barcelona: Mundilibros, 1973). Author's collection.

The next trio consists of cheap translations whose covers invoke movies less directly and by means of hand-drawn illustration rather than photo still (figure 4.21). The cover of the Italian edition of *Pride and Prejudice,* part of a juvenile series for teens, looks racy for a teenage Austen, what with Lizzie knowingly holding that whip. But the cover gathers together multiple movie moments from the Italian-American film of *War and Peace* (1956), starring Audrey Hepburn and Henry Fonda. The hat, the stare, and the whip are copied directly from the popular film. Simultaneously released in Italy and America, with a strong Italian presence among cast and crew, this Hollywood hit bolstered Italian pride. The visual reference would have been caught for many years. How are Tolstoy and Austen connected? Well, that doesn't matter. There is also zero attempt to connect the cover image to the internal illustrations by Cassinari, which take a more literal, if Italianate, attitude to the plot. The Italian teen edition of *Persuasion,* from 1962, similarly appropriates a classic movie moment as a cover graphic. I recognized only the Hollywood-style pose, not the source, but a clever colleague pointed to the film *Captain Horatio Hornblower* (1951), with Gregory Peck and Virginia Mayo, as the likeliest referent.[44] Kudos to the anonymous Italian illustrator, since C. S. Forester's setting is perfectly contemporaneous with Austen—although, again, that probably is not the point.

The third member of this trio of examples shows how, when movie references veer outrageously off-topic, bad choices can tip over into great. This Spanish translation by Costa Clavell of *Pride and Prejudice*, printed in Barcelona by Ediciones Mundilibros in 1973, announces the illustrations of Maria Paz Garcia-Borron on the title page, although her artwork is limited to the book's striking jacket. No one would mistake this cover illustration for an intentional representation of Lizzie, or even Lydia. Instead, in 1973, everyone would have recognized the pouty blond bombshell Brigitte Bardot as the likely celebrity inspiration for the cover. The specific visual reference may be to the Bardot film *Le Mépris* (1963), released in Spain as *El Desprecio*, or "contempt," for the movie poster bears a striking resemblance—in style, color, and pose. From a linguistic perspective, an allusion to a popular movie about a couple's mutual contempt on a book called "pride and prejudice" is wonderfully apt. The synergy between film title and book title prompts a smile, but the Janeite mind reels.

Movies continue to sell books, and even to lure students into classrooms about Jane Austen, but many university teachers still share Nabokov's prejudices. Movie tie-ins are not the serious editions ordered for college students, and moments stolen from movies rarely appear on the books collected by libraries. The moving pictures did not lend the cheap reprint authority or prestige.

BANTAM BREAKS THE CODE, 1958

Not until September 1958, when Bantam Books of New York introduced their low-cost Bantam Classics series, did the modern paperback find aesthetics with enough gravitas to balance literary canonicity. Assisted by advances in color printing, the classic paperback reprint rediscovered the power of selling books with master paintings, first attempted by Coates. *Publishers' Weekly* tags the series as "the world's great literature, priced from 35c to 75c." Stressing the word "CLASSICS," the advertisements assume a teacherly tone: "authoritative editions, sound new ones and accepted old ones, chosen from the whole span of living literature." The selected authors are "writers who have made an indelible impact on Western culture."[45] Four books were chosen each month, including Austen's *Emma* in November 1958—admit-

4.22. Bantam Classic reprint of *Emma* (New York: Bantam Books, 1958). Author's collection.

tedly after Henrik Ibsen and Arthur Miller but respectably before John Steinbeck and Honoré de Balzac. Bantam announced that their covers "will be simple and clean in design and will reflect, by the use of appropriate artistic masterpieces, the period, the tone, and the context of each work."[46] A few titles were reissued from previous Bantam editions, standard practice for any publisher's series.

The advertisements sound a tad heavy-handed now, but in the context of the late 1950s, the marriage of canonical literary works and visual masterpieces reassured book buyers. Bantam insisted that the paperback remain a radical democratizing force, one that could appropriate the most elite badges of privilege for 50 cents. Armed with a Bantam book decorated with a master painting, any reader might detect connections between painting and literature, insights hitherto reserved for those with a university degree. Such was the implied promise. The particular choice of cover art for each title was explained inside, including, for Austen's *Emma:* "The art work on the cover of this Bantam Classic is a reproduction of the charming portrait Miss West, by Sir Thomas Lawrence (1769–1830), which shares the crispness and refreshing quality of Miss Austen's Emma. The original painting hangs in the Pennsylvania Museum of Art in Philadelphia" (figure 4.22). For a person who knew that the full title of this painting is *Portrait of Harriott West,* and who also was familiar with the story of Emma Woodhouse, it might seem odd that a portrait of a mere Harriet trumps her eponymous friend. But Bantam's point is their concerted effort to link cover image to printed text. Masterworks of painting and serious literature, according to Bantam, go together—especially in the liberating format of the paperback.

Using paintings to pledge the educational value of a text proved so effective that it did not take long for other publishers to do likewise. Suddenly, many paperback "classics" series, including one from Penguin, began to dress their authors up in old works of art. The result remains visible on today's shelves and in bookstores, so I will wrap up with one example to stand for the whole phenomenon. Fronted by old artworks, reprints do not become dated so quickly as when they wear trendy covers requiring seasonal retouching or updating. Paintings on classic texts effectively slow down the frequent makeovers typical of pre-1950s reprint series. Some paintings were apparently so effective in conveying the style or promise of a particular classic read that they stuck to the same title for years, even decades, through many reprintings. Sir William Beechey's portrait of Marcia Fox, for example, may have fronted the Penguin

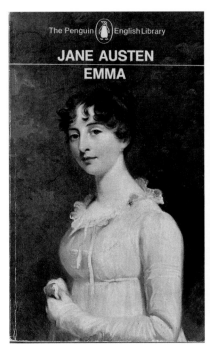 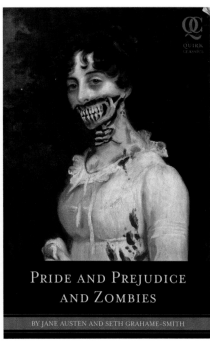

4.23. Sir William Beechey's portrait of Marcia Fox, as it appears on the Penguin English Library edition of *Emma* (1966 to 1985) and on the 2009 Quirk Classic spoof *Pride and Prejudice and Zombies.* Author's collection.

English Library paperback of *Emma* for nearly two decades, from about 1966 to 1985 (figure 4.23). In modern publishing terms, such longevity is astonishing. No wonder that, when it came time for Quirk Books to spoof Austen with zombies, this was the cover image tweaked by Doogie Horner, a designer who moonlights as a standup comedian. An aging Penguin paperback of *Emma* probably sat on Horner's shelves.

As Coates discovered early on, a serious painting on a cover does not need to connect to a book in order to catch the consumer's eye and stimulate a purchase. Advertising is not always cerebral or logical. Kindle's cheekily named Vexin Classics label, used for public-domain e-books, took advertising to a new level of conspicuous kitsch with its racy choices of old paintings for the promotion of classic authors. Since 2008, Kindle has used a nineteenth-century pre-Raphaelite masterpiece by John Collier (1850–1934) as their e-book image on Amazon for *Pride and Prejudice* (figure 4.24). Truly worrying is that Vexin advertises this edition as the "Complete Illustrated Edition." One online reviewer observes, "That is the most jawdroppingly

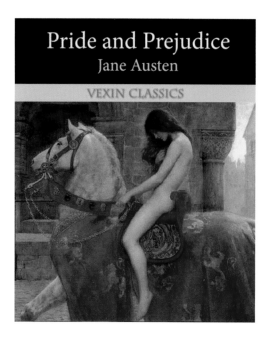

4.24. Screenshot of Vexin Classics advertising image on Amazon.com for e-book of *Pride and Prejudice* (the same image has been used since 2008).

inappropriate cover for Pride and Prejudice that I've ever seen. So far as I can recall, the legend of Lady Godiva is not mentioned in this novel, nor do any of the Bennet sisters (even Lydia) go in for naked horsemanship displays." The reviewer gives it five stars and closes with "I'd almost buy the book for the cover alone," failing to acknowledge the possibility that this image shows us exactly why Jane Bennet catches cold on her way to Netherfield in the rain.[47]

Not all great paintings—and Collier's is a doozy—make for authoritative book covers, even if they help sell more Austen. Authority is slippery, and prestige resides in context. What makes the Vexin spoofs so effective (yes, plural, because their choice of a master painting for *Northanger Abbey* is just as shocking) is that their covers overturn deeply engrained trust in paintings as conveyers of artistic authority—even when that trust is unconsciously given. Coates and Bantam started something big.

PAINTING ON THE EDGE

Historically, prestige paintings first appeared not on the front board or top cover, but on the edges of a book's pages. As far back as the Middle Ages, when books were scarce and large tomes were shelved horizontally with their spines inward, owners or librarians might write on the page edges of a closed book the type of information, such as names of authors or titles, now printed on vertically shelved spines. The practice soon invited decoration, and some of the oldest, most valuable books boast elaborately decorated and painted book edges. For example, in seventeenth-century Italy, the Pillone family commissioned Cesare Vecellio (c. 1530–1600), a cousin of the great artist Titian, to paint scenes on the edges of the books in their Renaissance library. For obvious reasons of cost, even when this style of decoration continued to be practiced, it was reserved for the finest bindings or richest commissions. Later, long after books began to be shelved with spines outward, truly important tomes might also be augmented with a secret painting on the edges, what booksellers call fore-edge painting. These images, in watercolors or ink, are painted on the edges when the pages are slightly fanned. When the book closes normally, the painting disappears.

Over the centuries, expensive bindings and gift books continued to be ordered with edge decorations of all sorts—gilded, goffered, stained, marbled, or painted.[48] During the 1950s, publishers of pulp fiction revived a tongue-in-cheek version of this prestige tradition by dyeing the edges of their cheap paperbacks with bright greens, blues, and reds. More recently, artist Mike Stilkey has given existing traditions of decorating the outsides of books a further twist—by painting portraits directly on the spines of stacked throwaway books. Stilkey especially created his book sculpture *Jane Austen* for use as the cover image on the book you are reading. His work, like mine, calls attention to castoff and unwanted books, in his case by repurposing salvaged books discarded by libraries. Many of his books are "reclaimed from library trash heaps as canvas for his whimsical paintings."[49] A recent profile of Stilkey in the *New Yorker* opened with the conundrum that whereas "books are sacred objects," this artist "paints all over them."[50] At first glance his work may look like a despoiling of books and their authority, but Stilkey, too, points to the manifold ways in which books are already endowed—on their outsides—with authority by painters, designers, and all manner of artists, whether legitimate or not.

In this chapter, tracing the curious heritage of the dominant style of prestige book cover via unrecorded and seemingly unworthy Austen editions has unearthed information that complicates and corrects prevailing assumptions about Austen's reception in nineteenth-century America. Chapter 5 will turn to the cheap paperbacks of the twentieth century, to demonstrate exactly when Jane Austen's books became uniquely gendered, or "pinked." The tenacious gendering of her audience is yet another aspect of Austen's reception best viewed among the groundlings of the book world rather than in a lofty box filled with firsts.

MANSFIELD PARK.

CHAPTER I.

FANNY had by no means forgotten Mr. Crawford, when she awoke the next morning; but she remembered the purport of her note, and was not less sanguine, as to its effect, than she had been the night before. If Mr. Crawford would but go away!—That was what she most earnestly desired;—go and take his sister with him, as he was to do, and as he returned to Mansfield on purpose to do. And why it was not done already, she could not devise, for Miss Crawford certainly wanted no delay.—Fanny had hoped, in had quite overlook__ __'s visit, to hear her apartment, till he, stopp___ ____

he

V.VI.1. Torn and repaired page from a poor copy of the first edition of *Mansfield Park,* vol. 3 of 3 (London: Printed for T. Egerton, 1814). Collection of Sandra Clark.

Vignette VI
Lady Isabella's *Mansfield Park*

This battered first-edition copy of *Mansfield Park* (1814) lacks prelims and titles in its first two volumes. Marred throughout with clumsy repairs and handwritten substitutions of missing text and torn bits, this copy barely made it into a private collection, and then only because it was judged so incomplete and in such poor condition as to be deemed of little value by a bookseller, who let it go "for a song" (figure V.VI.1).[1] The current owner's husband gave this imperfect copy to his wife "as a joke," having cheekily promised her a first edition at a bargain-basement price.

The ownership signature, written in brown ink in a flowing hand at the front of the first volume (figure V.VI.2), reads,

> *Isabella St. John*
> *Hampton Court Palace*

The lofty address is a bit misleading. In Victorian times, Hampton Court was occupied by a set of people whose families had performed great services for Crown and country. Members neither owned the accommodation outright nor paid market rents, but were given "warrants" to live at Hampton Court for a certain length of time, providing they were in residence at least half the year and did not keep dogs. Census records show Lady Isabella St. John (c. 1792–1875) residing in an apartment in Suite XII, Hampton Court Palace, from 1839 until her death at age 83—attended by one housemaid, a lady's maid, a footman, a cook, and her daughter Antonia.[2] Her husband Henry died in 1857, and her unmarried daughter remained her companion. Although Lady Isabella's pedigree was impeccable and contained some deliciously illegitimate royal ancestors, she was not a member of the royal household but lived in grace-and-favor accommodations.

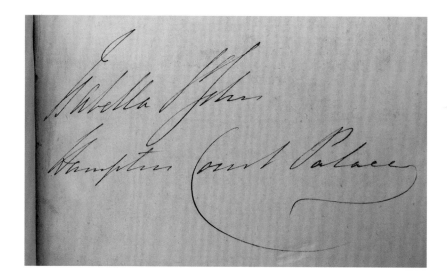

V.VI.2. Ownership inscription: "Isabella St. John/Hampton Court Palace." Collection of Sandra Clark.

While I cannot be absolutely certain that all the handwritten insertions of lost text, penned hither and yon over the many repairs in this copy, are in the same hand as the ownership signature, a full page of penciled comments in a hand similar to Lady Isabella's confident flourish is found at the back of the third volume.[3] Although the pencil has faded, these horizontally written comments on one of the book's final blanks remain perfectly legible. Lady Isabella, it appears, had some notes for Miss Austen: "*There are three defects in this otherwise perfect novel. Fanny sh.d have been described as more than pretty lovely to attract such a man as Crawford—D.r Grant sh.d not have been killed with so little feeling— and Crawford sh.d have married Maria—not for his or her happiness but punishment—Maria of course should marry again—*" Lady Isabella, without any sense of humor about an author deftly killing off a clergyman by gluttony to conveniently bestow his clerical living on her heroine by marriage, chides Austen for failing to adhere to her own personal philosophy about how three-volume novels should end. In her outrage that the bad have not been properly punished, Lady Isabella bears more than a passing resemblance to Oscar Wilde's novel-writing Miss Prism: "The good ended happily and the bad unhappily. That is what fiction means."

Lady Isabella takes her objections a step further when she crosses out—in ink—the offending punishment of Dr. Grant, excising the incident from her copy: "~~and when Dr. Grant had brought on apoplexy and death, by three great institutionary dinners in one week, they still lived together~~" (3:345). On the penultimate page, marking with an X the mention of Dr. Grant's living going to Edmund upon his death, she laments, "*X Poor Doctor Grant! Why kill him?*" (3:353). Opposite, the same familiar hand inks another X at the spot where Lady Bertram's fondness "gradually" shifts from Fanny to Susan, when the younger sister proves the more attentive to her needs. At the foot of the page, Lady Isabella complains: "*X Miss Austen might have spared any increase in Lady Bertram's selfishness*" (3:352). She also makes her mark beside the words "mutual punishment" on page 336, glossing her displeasure below at the improbability of aunt and niece living out their lives together: "*—It is just but not probable Maria's punishment. Of course she married again—she did not marry Crawford—but some one—where age and looks*" (3:336–37). Austen's final chapter, which ties things up with "tolerable comfort" for all her characters, most annoyed this Victorian reader.

Lady Isabella's use of "*Miss Austen*" in these notes confirms that she knew the identity of the author of *Mansfield Park*, even though hers was an old damaged edition published anonymously. She also presumes to know about Austen's life and her reputation for realism. Earlier in the third volume, she has marked an X at "Mr. Crawford's business had been to declare himself the lover of Fanny," explaining her objection over the next few pages: "*In Miss Austen's life it is said that all her characters are imaginary—lifelike as they are—with one exception Crawford's love for Fanny is a perfect impropibility* [*sic*]" (3:7–9) (figure V.VI.3). This section is heavily stained; perhaps she spilled her tea in frustration at Austen's defiance of the probable. The next dark splashes of tea occur when Mary Crawford teases Fanny about the romantic attentions paid to her brother Henry by the women of London, as if Lady Isabella veritably choked on the impropriety of both brother and sister (3:108–9). Only once, during the scene at Sotherton, does Lady Isabella appear to indulge in a rare moment of wry good humor. Near Fanny's focalized disapproval of Edmund's walk with Mary, she places an X and remarks, "*Poor Edmund never had in all probability so pleasant a walk again*" (1:214).

Throughout her copy, Lady Isabella objects to the sparseness of Austen's descriptions—especially as to people. When William enters the story as a young man "of open, pleasant countenance," she writes: "*Miss Austen's slowness in making her personages handsome is most strange—why not say William was tall and goodlooking—*" (2:128–29). This reader obviously expects to be told immediately whether a lad is of the strapping sort. Similarly, in response to the description of Miss Crawford as "very lovely" during a rehearsal of *Lovers' Vows*, she writes, "*lovely is quite a wonder for Miss Austen to use, tho' only applied to* [word cut off]" (1:331). During the ball scene, Lady Isabella has apparently tired of Austen's economy of description and inserts remarks about Fanny's looks, placed here in square brackets: "Young, [*extremely*] pretty, gentle, however, [*plainly drest*] she had no awkwardnesses that were not as good as graces, and there were few persons present that were not disposed to ~~praise~~ [*admire*] her" (2:224). Toward the end of the book, she underlines the word "bewitching," adding, "*Poor Fannys looks are rarely mentioned—so* bewitching *is now brought in*" (3:216). According to Lady Isabella, the heroine is never properly described. This late-stage word becomes for her the rare and insufficient exception, catching Austen out in the tardy desire to fix her own authorial neglect toward the heroine.

Lady Isabella, whose corrections also extend to the occasional printer's error and small matters of phrasing, may have felt entitled to correct Miss Austen because she was a published novelist herself.[4] Over the course of several decades, Lady Isabella penned one novel and some stories in which, as expected, many exceedingly pretty girls and strapping young men parade by, and only the good are rewarded. Surprisingly, Richard Bentley himself advertised the novel in the 1830s, right alongside his new reprintings of Jane Austen. Lady Isabella's stories are peppered with names such as Willoughby, Musgrove, and Morland, and with women who lament that men can lead an active life while they must sit at home, so it seems that she had taken her Jane Austen reading to heart. I would never have noticed

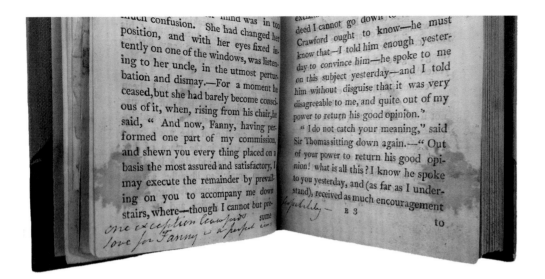

Lady Isabella's intellectual proximity to Austen, as it were, if not for the inscription in her battered copy of *Mansfield Park*.

Lest anyone think that this copy belonged to a neglected literary genius, I shall quote from a contemporary review of *Mrs. Cleveland, and The St. Clairs,* a three-volume novel published in 1836 by Bentley and aggressively advertised as by Lady Isabella St. John, even though some catalogs today record the author as "unknown."[5] After classifying all contemporary novels as literary fungi, the reviewer singles this "deleterious fungus" out as a nonedible member of the poisonous "toad-stool species." His definitive postmortem claims, "Everything is improbable. The characters are . . . colourless, insipid, and vague . . . the incidents are either unnatural, or dull and common-place—and the language is such as would disgrace a daily governess at Whitechapel, in her feeblest efforts at English composition." The reviewer finds it "extremely" puzzling that "novels of this description find a market," but then compares its literary fabric to pocket handkerchiefs sold at the "warehouses at Redriff" as compared to the quality products purchased at "Howell & James," an elite jeweler on Regent Street.[6]

Not everyone who critiques Jane Austen, or finds inspiration in her work, becomes the next great literary sensation. Worse, if you fail as a novelist, history will also ignore your marginalia as a critic.

CHAPTER 5
PINKING JANE AUSTEN
The Turn to "Chick Lit"

Jane Austen has never been just for girls. During the first century of Austen's reprintings, men and women alike owned and critiqued, gave and received, the inexpensive copies of her novels discussed so far. Among lesser-known readers during the nineteenth century, Austen's familiars included J. Owen Woodward, who proudly inscribed a shilling edition of *Sense and Sensibility;* bachelor Heman M. Burr, who binged on all of Austen in Paris; Captain Andrew Baird, who cherished an old reprint of *Mansfield Park;* young Master Henry Boal, who received a Lily edition at school; and the potters and coal miners of Hanley, Staffordshire, who were members of the Pleasant Sunday Afternoon Society. The inexpensive copies owned by these ordinary men must stand in for the substantial group of early Austen consumers who were neither women nor elites, supplementing the association copies of literati preserved by libraries. From those precious library copies, scholars have long understood Austen's works to be a staple in the diets of men as well as women among would-be intellectuals.

Starting sometime in the 1940s, however, Austen's work became increasingly gendered, culminating by the end of the 1960s in swaths of pink ink on pictorial paperback covers that proclaimed her exclusively for women readers. The dressing up of Austen in pink paper frocks occurred precisely when color-coded fashions solidified gender distinctions in the culture—assigning blue to baby boys and pink to baby girls. But just as Shakespeare never got blued, neither has any other female author among the literary classics been as definitively pinked as Jane Austen. What singled her out for this segregation? Clues to this mystery of Austen's reception history can be found only among the cheapest reprints of the twentieth century.

At the turn of the twentieth century, the scholarly force that could lever a modern author such as Austen into the literary canon was male. She would not be studied now in universities if important men had not, at just the right time, read and championed her. Celebrators like William Dean Howells, Sir Walter Scott, and even the surly Henry James helped establish Austen's academic significance. The term *Janeite* referred originally to men—it was not, as today, a mild opprobrium directed at female fans. Although an early Austen editor in 1894 had coined the word "Janite" (spelled slightly differently) to refer generically to the author's ardent fans, Rudyard Kipling is credited with launching its wider use in his short story "The Janeites" in 1924.[1] There, Kipling flung the term at rough World War I soldiers. In fact, during both world wars, Jane Austen's books were sent to men serving at the front lines, as suitably entertaining reading for troops on active duty.

Devoney Looser recently reminded us that turn-of-the-century women also championed Austen for feminist political causes: "On June 13, 1908, suffragists took Jane Austen to the streets of London," carrying her name, along with those of other women writers, blazoned upon banners as they marched.[2] Being appropriated as an icon of first-wave feminism by suffragettes did not, however, turn Austen's novels into "chick lit"—a term now reserved for books dominantly, indeed almost exclusively, marketed to women readers. The segregation of Austen to a female readership came much later. In the late 1940s, one high-profile London reprint series picked up the early feminist banner, but it was the explosion of new paperbacks in the 1960s for coed college students that definitively altered Austen's public appearance forever. Gendered marketing strategies for cheap paperbacks indelibly pinked Austen, creating today's false sense that she has only ever been read by women.

Whether found on flamingoes or on books, pink does not, of course, intrinsically mark anything as female. In Austen's own era, "it was perfectly masculine for a man to wear a pink silk suit with floral embroidery," says fashion scholar Valerie Steele.[3] If anything, pink was considered boyish rather than girlish, being a diminutive of red, a warring color many traditions associate with masculinity. Before 1900, most infants wore white, which could be boiled and bleached. Pink and pale blue were simply two among a range of pastels appropriate for young children—as muted versions of the deeper hues worn by adults. "Pink and blue symbolism is so firmly embedded in American popular culture that it's hard to believe that their gender associations are relatively new," explains Jo Paoletti in *Pink and Blue: Telling Boys from Girls in America*.[4] The evidence that pink was originally neutral is everywhere in art, all the way up to *The Great Gatsby* (1925), where Tom Buchanan derides Gatsby's pink suit to impune not his masculinity but his social class, because pink seersucker fabric was then associated with the uniforms of the working class: "An Oxford man . . . Like hell he is! He wears a pink suit."[5] In 1927, department stores across America still sold blue and pink clothing for babies in equal measure for boys and girls.[6] "By the 1950s, however, pink was strongly associated with femininity."[7] In the 1970s, fashion abandoned pink briefly for the unisex clothing promoted by second-wave feminism, but the gendered association stuck.[8]

This chapter looks at Austen's inexpensive reprints to discover exactly how and when Austen made the turn toward "chick lit." In her first century of reprints, Austen served all manner of audiences and commercial purposes with an astonishing variety of editions in a range of formats, colorful designs, and price points. While early publishers occasionally directed these books at women readers, gendered marketing was only sporadic and did not limit expectations about Austen's readership. Something changed, however, in the second century of her reprintings. Even though Kipling's Janeites were soldiering men, three additional wartime legacies in the twentieth century nudged Austen's audience toward women: in Britain, the profound feminism forged by the experiences of women on the home front in World War II; in Spain, the flowering of the escapist romance novel, or *novela rosa*, during the early Franco regime; and, in America, the impact of the GI Bill on college classrooms. Around the globe, unintended consequences of war narrowed and gendered Austen's perceived audience, even as her appearance on syllabi and shelves continued to multiply. In the 1960s, when universities increased the number of women studying literature, publishers recognized a marketing opportunity, making Austen the convenient leader of series for the new generation of college-educated women. To lure female readers, publishers reached lavishly for pink. With many publishing houses competing for a share of the newly exploding paperback market, the strikingly pinked cover art on Austen's novels effectively altered public perception of both her style and her audience. These cheap pinked paperbacks forged a legacy that benefited and marred Austen's reputation in equal measure.

WOMEN AND CHILDREN FIRST

The twentieth century was by no means the first historical moment when Austen was marketed directly to women. Already, we saw that as early as 1844, Henry Clarke of London published Austen alongside other women and radical thinkers, disguising his clandestine proto-feminist series in the conservative dress of religious devotion, with touches of medievalism. In 1855, the short-lived firm of Bunce & Brother of New York announced plans for a "uniform edition of Miss Austen's celebrated novels" with advertisements stressing how "Miss Austen is emphatically the novelist of Home." By calling Austen the "undisputed mistress" and "founder" of "the domestic school of novels," Bunce & Brother employed a consciously gendered marketing strategy.[9] It hit home with one reviewer, who complained of *Pride and Prejudice* that Austen's mothers and daughters displayed "the disgusting folly and miserable result of miseducated and misdirected female life" more than either pride or prejudice.[10] In 1857, Derby & Jackson took over the Bunce & Brother plates, slotting Austen into their existing Standard Female Novelists Series, an early series presented directly, although not exclusively, to women readers. And in 1888, the *Ladies Home Journal* offered Austen's novels among 150 popular titles for a mere 45 cents per volume, including postage, "to journal sisters only."[11] But none of these earlier marketing strategies ensured that Jane Austen would be exclusively read by women, nor did they tilt her popular reach on either side of the Atlantic sharply away from men.

Instead, by the 1890s, Austen's strong presence among the many series of gift books and school prizes for juvenile audiences may have threatened to align her more with children's literature than with any nascent corpus of women's literature. At the start of the twentieth century, a potentially troubling association with children's books burdens Jane Austen's literary reputation. In 1896 and 1897, for example, the largest publisher of books in the United States included *Pride and Prejudice* in their St. Nicholas Series for Boys and Girls, which sold for 50 cents a volume in seasonal bindings stamped with sprigs of red and green holly.[12] Many affordable reprintings of Austen's works occurred within such publisher's series and gift books for the juvenile market—as if Austen's popularity stemmed from being a conservative, effortless writer suitable as literature for the young. In 1893, Austen comes immediately to W. T. Stead's mind at the start of a survey of

"Gift Literature. A First Batch of Christmas Books" in the London *Review of Reviews*. His distilled pennyworth of *Pride and Prejudice* presented Austen to Britain's working poor only a few years later. Stead times his appraisal of the season's new gift books to enable his readers "to send presents to the colonies and abroad," opening with a compliment to the publishers of the "tasteful" new exemplars of "illustrated and beautiful editions of old classics," especially the "dainty editions of Jane Austen, Maria Edgeworth, and Fanny Burney, which Messrs J.M. Dent and Co. publish."[13] He then leaps directly to the nursery shelves: "To many it has seemed a pertinent question whether the constantly increasing crowd of children's books does not elbow out the older and perhaps better favourites, the classics of the nursery bookshelf?"[14] Why is Austen mentioned, along with Burney and Edgeworth, in the same breath as books intended for children? The answer may lie in a third-party payer dynamic.

Purchasers of the gift books for Victorian-era children were mostly women. Although juvenile reading levels and interests were factored in, neither the packaging nor the content of such gift books appealed directly to the whims of the boys and girls who received them, but to the parents, grandparents, and teachers who screened and purchased those books—and most of them were women. It was logical for publishers to direct the titles and physical features of these books to capture and please perceived female tastes. Like the salting of canned baby food, or the manufacture of dog and cat toys in colors that can be seen only by humans, the look and content of Victorian gift books were skewed by a third-party payer system; what mattered was catching the eye of the person who decided on the purchase. This appeal to adult taste remains the norm for most early children's books today. In the Victorian era, stereotyping of adult women's tastes and domestic roles makes gift books for children lure consumers with magpie bindings that are pretty rather than sturdy. These gift books with flowery decorations may not aim at girls any more than boys, but publishers marketed them almost exclusively to the adult woman selector. As a savvy publisher, Stead knows that "Gift Literature" tries to net women—those practical purchasers and gift wrappers of each Christmas season's books for children. Austen's frequency among prize books and Victorian juvenile series, routinely in editions that neither contract nor alter her text, may already reflect a sexist logic linking women authors closely with juvenile books, because mothers are the book testers and buyers of children's literature.

Even in the early twentieth century, links between literature for children and books for women remained unnervingly prominent—especially with Austen. In 1905, a two-volume gift edition by Thomas Nelson & Sons of the novels of Jane Austen exemplified the mixing of women readers with a juvenile audience (figure 5.1). At first glance, the small-format leather binding version, decorated with telltale gilded hearts, looks like an early instance of Austen being marked as a romance writer to adult women. Nothing could be clearer than the marketing signal sent by those shiny hearts. The two-volume set of all six novels printed on thin India paper was available in a variety of binding styles, with the heart-decorated leather binding topping the charts of luxury.[15] Printed on larger and much thicker paper, in the cheaper volumes of their Famous Books series, Nelson recycled the same settings for *Pride and Prejudice, Sense and Sensibility,* and *Emma* as juvenile titles that sold individually alongside *Little Women, Oliver Twist, Greenmantle, Alice in Wonderland, The Last of the Mohicans, Robin Hood and the Men of Greenwood, Grimm's Fairy Tales, The Water Babies, Black Beauty, Treasure Island,* and *Tom Sawyer.*[16] The same colored frontispiece of Bingley and Jane "dancing together" found in the luxury gift edition for adult women reappeared on the dust wrapper of the cheap hardbound juvenile edition. For Nelson, the romance writer Jane Austen was simultaneously a children's classic—with identical text and fronting image, barring a few cosmetic alterations. No textual emendation was needed. Austen was not alone in this uneasy double life on the romance and nursery shelves. George Eliot, Charlotte and Emily Brontë, and Mrs. Gaskell join her on the list of Nelson's Famous Books, touted on the inside flaps of their jackets as "illustrated editions of masterpieces of literature, ideal for school prizes, for gifts, and for the home library" for a mere 2s.6d.

The category of books for "the home library," then, is what sticks to Austen as she enters the twentieth century. Yes, she is a classic writer, even a romance writer, but her novels, unedited and entire, are suitable for reading by the whole family. This conflation of women and children certainly lacked sophistication, but it also conveyed universal cultural approval.

5.1. At Christmas of 1905, the novels of Jane Austen sold as a boxed gift set of two leather-bound volumes with gilt hearts stamped on front covers and spines (London: Thomas Nelson & Sons, 1903). The reprint of *Pride and Prejudice* in the Famous Books series is a reissue for a juvenile audience. This image shows two copies of the leather-bound sets, with one *Pride and Prejudice* open to show the matching frontispiece. Collection of Sandra Clark.

SOLDIERING JANES

A soldiering Jane soon supplanted the juvenile Jane, when Austen reached troops on active duty through the American Library Association's War Service Library program, which collected donations of used books for the military. Between 1917 and 1920, 100 million secondhand books and magazines were moved to hospitals and encampments. One such volume was the Porter & Coates reprint from the 1880s seen in figure 5.2, a combo of *Pride and Prejudice* and *Northanger Abbey* in the Eastlake design discussed in chapter 4. This example of wartime reading survives in its original publisher's binding with the World War I camp library bookplate, its passport to the front, still pasted inside. Austen was not only entertainment for soldiers but a fitting reminder of the comforts and traditions they were fighting to protect.

The most famous account of World War I soldiers reading Jane Austen is Rudyard Kipling's powerful short story "The Janeites," which describes a front-line artillery unit bonding over her novels. In spite of the many cheap editions for the working poor and middlebrow reader during the latter part of the nineteenth century, Kipling presents Austen as an enduring marker of an elite social class. His story begins with a handful of former soldiers cleaning a Masonic Lodge. As one comment leads to another, a relatively uneducated former "mess-waiter" named Humberstall, a hairdresser twice wounded in the war, narrates his wartime experiences with a secret society of "Janeites." He reminisces about the time when, while repairing screens at the French front, he overhears an exchange between Macklin, the senior mess waiter, and some officers about "this Jane woman." He misinterprets her name as a "password" and their animated debate as "secret society business," since it apparently allows different ranks to mix: "It *was* a password, all right! Then they went at it about Jane—all three, regardless of rank. That made me listen." Envying their classless camaraderie, he pays Macklin "five bob more" for instruction, reading all six of Austen's novels at the camp: "What beat me was there was nothin' *to* 'em nor *in* 'em. Nothin' at all, believe me." In an effort to impress the others, he renames the guns in the artillery unit after Austen's characters. Amused, his fellow "Janeites" reward him with a gift of cigarettes, "about a hundred fags." After their unit is destroyed by heavy enemy fire, Humberstall, the sole survivor, views the destruction through the lens of his newly acquired cultural shorthand: "The Reverend Collins was all right; but Lady Catherine and the General was past prayin' for."[17]

In the end, Jane Austen does provide Humberstall with a magic password. Wounded and dying among many, he criticizes a talkative nurse as an annoying "Miss Bates." His offhand remark spurs the head "Sister," who catches the reference, to put him immediately on a departing train previously regarded as too full for "a louse" like him. The nurse's class prejudices are overcome by an accidental dose of Austen, and Humberstall is miraculously saved. Back at the Masonic Lodge, another former soldier observes, "No denyin' that Jane business was more useful to you than the Roman Eagles or the Star an' Gar-

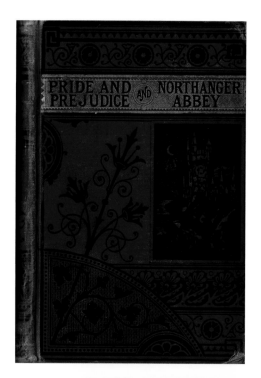

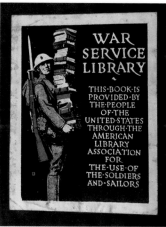

5.2. *Pride and Prejudice-Northanger Abbey* in Eastlake binding circa 1880, published by Porter & Coates of Philadelphia, with original War Service Library label on the inside. Author's collection.

5.3. Rudyard Kipling's story "The Janeites" as it appeared, with illustrations by Harvey Dunn, in *Hearst's International Magazine*, May 1924. Harry Ransom Center, University of Texas at Austin.

ter." "Well," explains Humberstall, "as pore Macklin said, it's a very select Society, an' you've got to be a Janeite in your 'eart, or you won't have any success. An' yet he made *me* a Janeite!" Humberstall's recent rereading of Austen takes him back to his time at the front: "I read all her six books now for pleasure 'tween times in the shop; an' it brings it all back—down to the smell of the glue-paint on the screens. You take it from me, Brethren, there's no one to touch Jane when you're in a tight place. Gawd bless 'er, whoever she was."[18]

In 1924, when the story was published in *Hearst's International Magazine*, the accompanying illustrations by Harvey Dunn showed Humberstall amid the devastation of the artillery barrage (figure 5.3).[19] Rarely are these grim

The Janeites

❦ *I lay there takin' it all in, till I felt cold and looked at myself. I hadn't much on except me boots, and I was the only Janeite left.*

visuals reproduced when Kipling's story is retold as a heart-warming episode in Austen's reception history. And yet, part of the original point seems precisely the gut-wrenching juxtaposition between the modern horrors of war and the orderly Regency atmosphere of Austen's fiction as a badge of the educated elite. To Kipling, Austen is not important as a time capsule to the past but as the cultural cement of the present day. She can fuse different classes, and genders, into a "United Kingdom," assisting the wartime imperative of social cohesion to override the realities of class hierarchy. Even as Kipling insists that she remains the particular literary favorite of the most privileged class, his influential publication added grit to Austen's popular reputation.

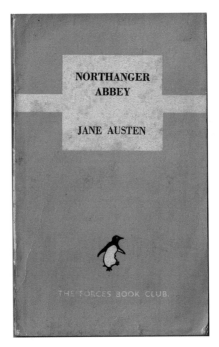

5.4. The Forces Book Club versions of *Northanger Abbey* and *Persuasion* (Penguin Books for the Forces Book Club, 1943) distributed to British troops. Author's collection.

By the 1940s, Jane Austen had been further democratized as official troop reading for the British. During World War II, heavy shipments of used books for camp libraries gave way to lightweight paperbacks designed to fit easily in a soldier's uniform pocket. After the War Office contracted with Penguin to supply cheap books via their Forces Book Club series for servicemen, especially in "remote and inaccessible units," new paperbacks of Austen's novels reached British troops through more official channels. Starting in July 1942, a Penguin Books committee selected ten books a month, for a total of 120 titles, including *Northanger Abbey* in April 1943 and *Persuasion* in June of the same year (figure 5.4). As if intent upon reinforcing the myth and pathos of Kipling's story, Penguin chose Austen twice for those soldiers who were the most cut off from the comforts of home. These specials for British soldiers came with the same unnerving advertisements for toothpaste, dog food, candy bars, and light bulbs that accompanied their civilian counterparts in telltale orange (see figures 1.25 and 1.26). In addition, the hugely popular *Talking of Jane Austen,* praised by W. H. Smith as among their bestsellers of the entire war period, was also reprinted as a Services Edition in 1944, making it the only secondary work on Austen produced for troops on active duty.[20] On the American side, however, the list of books in the Armed Services Editions grew to 1,322 titles (123 million copies) between 1943 and 1946, but contained no Austen at all.[21] That is, the British selection committee picked two of her novels for their narrow inventory, but the mammoth American ASE series ignored her. The publishers making American selections filtered her out not because of a gendered bias but because of perceived differences in popular tastes between Americans and Brits in the 1940s.

Even if Jane Austen remained more popular in Britain than America during the 1940s, combine Dunn's raw illustrations with the complex reception history evidenced by these wartime survivors, then add Sir Winston Churchill's well-known enthusiasm, and you have to ask, "How did this soldiering Jane of the first half of the twentieth century ever become the girly 'chick lit' author hyped at the century's close?" If, for more than a hundred years, her many reprints at a wide range of price points led her to be recruited indiscriminately for schools, for literacy projects directed at the poor, for the nursery, for politics, and for war, how and why did her target audience narrow so definitively by gender over time?

POSTWAR GENDERING

For starters, Austen's legacy of wartime reading had an equally powerful impact upon women serving at the home front. In June 1946, and in spite of continued paper scarcities, a surprising edition of Jane Austen's works appeared from Williams & Norgate of London, presenting the Regency novelist simultaneously through the lenses of war and of gender. Over the course of three years, a firm known for scholarly and scientific books rather than fiction brought out re-edited texts of all six novels, challenging the reigning Oxford University Press edition by R. W. Chapman. Based upon first-edition texts, the Williams & Norgate volumes were free of any explanatory notes that historicized Austen to her own time. Each modest-looking volume cost 8s.6d., a price that reflected postwar inflation and paper scarcity rather than the drab production values and dull dustjackets of army green. The austere outward appearance of this unusual edition may explain why it has received less critical attention than it deserves. Williams & Norgate served up Austen in a contemporary context, capturing women

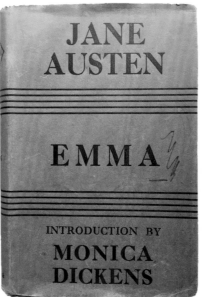
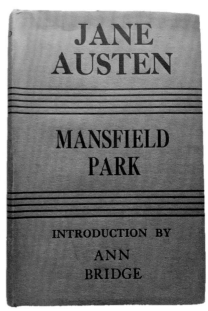

5.5. *Persuasion,* with an introduction by Angela Thirkell; *Emma*, with an introduction by Monica Dickens; and *Mansfield Park*, with an introduction by Ann Bridge (London: Williams & Norgate Ltd., Great Russell Street, 1946, 1947, and 1948, respectively). Author's collection.

readers not with frilly bindings but with introductions by six women novelists. Angela Thirkell (1890–1961) introduced *Persuasion;* Monica Dickens (1915–1992) *Emma;* Ann Bridge (1889–1974) *Mansfield Park;* Elizabeth Bowen (1899–1973) *Pride and Prejudice;* Daphne du Maurier (1907–1989) *Northanger Abbey;* and Naomi Royde-Smith (1875–1964) *Sense and Sensibility* (figures 5.5 and 5.6). The names of the six writers appear in large type on the front of the green book jackets as a powerful selling point. Each had built a reputation writing about the impact of war upon British women and their domestic relationships. Together, these fiction writers reshape Austen as a quiet but staunch wartime feminist.

The first novel in this series was *Persuasion*, an unusual choice as leader, but suitable as a cautionary war novel about false endings. After all, the temporal setting of *Persuasion*, the short peace of the summer of 1814, warned of a false and precarious pause in Napoleonic Wars that would need to be fought for another full year—until the decisive Battle of Waterloo in June 1815. With an introduction by Angela Thirkell dated June 1946, this first installment gestures to the revival of interest, begun by Rudyard Kipling, in the reading of Jane Austen during wartime. Thirkell was a not-too-distant

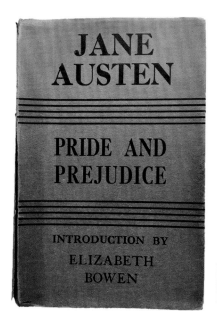

cousin of Kipling's, and the book jacket hints at this family legacy with an invocation of his famous story: "When Macklin was instructing Humberstall in the mysteries and privileges of the Janeites, he taught that *Persuasion* ranked first of the Austen novels, with the others following in a bunch, and *Northanger Abbey* three lengths behind."[22] The line of continuity from Austen to Kipling to Thirkell could not have been drawn more clearly.

As Kipling's relative, Thirkell was already a smart choice for this edition's postwar message, but she also represented a British feminism reshaped and tempered by the home front, where the New Woman had become a Land Girl. A few of Thirkell's own novels, particularly *Cheerfulness Breaks In* (1940) and *Northbridge Rectory* (1941), show British housewives coping with the departure of loved ones and absorbing the deprivations of wartime life with resigned good cheer and a brave chin-up attitude. Thirkell is also known for her "Austen echoes," plot elements and recurring character names that borrow substantially from Austen's works. For example, as Sara Bowen points out, "Thirkell's Crofts are a retired military colonel and his wife, who, like the no-nonsense Admiral and Mrs. Croft in *Persuasion*, have returned to England after defending the Empire."[23] Thirkell knew her

5.6. *Pride and Prejudice,* with an introduction by Elizabeth Bowen; *Northanger Abbey,* with an introduction by Daphne du Maurier; and *Sense and Sensibility,* with an introduction by Naomi Royde-Smith (London: Williams & Norgate Ltd., Great Russell Street, 1948–49). Collections of Sandra Clark and author.

Austen. Predictably enough, in the introduction Thirkell stresses the ambiguous "tax of quick alarm" in *Persuasion*'s wartime ending. She also touches on female camaraderie and shared defiance in the novel, walking the reader through Austen's characters and pausing to observe, "It appears to us that women novelists find women far more interesting than men; as indeed, with the greatest respect for men, they so often are."[24]

In January 1947, Monica Dickens, great-granddaughter of Charles Dickens, introduced *Emma*. Though born into privilege, Dickens entered domestic service, and her experiences as cook and servant shaped her first book, *One Pair of Hands* (1939). Similarly, her work as a wartime nurse and eventually an aircraft factory worker led to *One Pair of Feet* (1942) and *Edward's Fancy* (1943). Dickens exemplified the modern woman who, ironically, was emancipated by wartime labor. She presents *Emma* to "new readers" with a postwar urgency: "After six years of war with its book famine and its gap in adolescent education, many young people have never read *Emma*." Knowing that Austen wrote *Emma* after moving to Chawton, Dickens sketches this "mature" Jane as almost a volunteer war widow who at age 35 donned "the caps which were then the mark of confirmed spinsterhood," in sympathy for her bereaved sister Cassandra, whose fiancé had died.[25] With one biographical detail, Dickens deftly makes Jane Austen, in her spinster cap, grieve alongside all would-be sisters and widows who had recently lost someone they loved.

Ann Bridge carries on this sense of women's solidarity in her introduction to *Mansfield Park*. Ann Bridge was the penname of Mary Ann Dolling Sanders, a great traveler and intrepid mountain climber who wrote novels set in remote locations, including China, Portugal, and Turkey. She and her family fled the German advances via the Trans-Siberian Railroad in 1941 and spent a year in the United States before returning to Turkey. Bridge's novel *Frontier Passage* (1942) allegedly provided British intelligence with information for an anti-German resistance movement in Spain. Given her reputation for informed worldliness, Bridge describes Austen as a keen moralist who shares an interest in "the conflict between right and wrong" with "most of the earlier English women novelists, in a way that the men writers did not." Bridge next lashes out at "the curious dullness and insipidity" of "modern novelists"—by which she clearly means male novelists—for dwelling on impropriety rather than offering a moral compass. She charges

D. H. Lawrence's banned *The Rainbow* (1915) with "dreary promiscuity," dismissing it as "really hardly more interesting than an account of rabbit-breeding." By contrast, Bridge calls Austen as freshly invigorating as "bubbling spring-water after last night's stale cocktails."[26] Even Austen's complaint in *Northanger Abbey* about the dullness of histories written by men lacks the venom reserved by Bridge for her male contemporaries in this introduction.

Elizabeth Bowen's introduction to *Pride and Prejudice*, released next in this series, is appropriately wistful about the youth and vitality of Austen's stories. But Bowen is the only author of the six who refuses to engage directly with the postwar mission of Williams & Norgate's edition. Since hers is also the only introduction left undated and unsigned, I suspect that Bowen's text was recycled or augmented from something with an earlier and different purpose.[27] No preliminary draft survives among her papers, however. Bowen, a literary critic whose radio dramatizations during the war had aligned her with Austen and Burney, was a fitting choice to introduce Austen's best-loved novel.[28] As a recidivist reader of Austen, Bowen also returned to this author again and again in later writings. She does not, however, connect a reading of Austen to the specific wartime experiences of British women. Bowen's airy comments about the "youthful" features and "early-morning sparkle" of *Pride and Prejudice* seem strangely disconnected from Williams & Norgate's patriotic reprinting project.[29] Perhaps she was busy dedicating all her energies to *The Heat of the Day* (1949), a major novel about women in wartime, and unable to also write a brand new essay to spec.[30] All my guesswork is by way of admission that Bowen declines to offer the gendered postwar message found in the other introductions for this series.

Daphne du Maurier, best known for the wildly popular *Rebecca* (1938), is predictably assigned to *Northanger Abbey*, amply compensating for any momentary slackening of the series' purpose. Dating her introduction "April 1948," du Maurier is arguably the most explicit about how Austen can recalibrate postwar values for women. First, she disarms her reader by acknowledging that, of course, there is "nothing world-shaking" in Austen, "yet how the little pinpricks of day-by-day in Bath stab us to feeling."[31] Summarizing Catherine's teenage frustrations in John Thorpe's carriage, du Maurier slides into a justification for the reading of Austen that bumps up against larger frustration about gendered power struggles during wartime, when information can be withheld from women:

> Small Matters, the thoughts and feelings of a very young woman in the Bath of long ago, but how we yearn to them, in retrospect. That France, and the Reign of Terror, blistered the map of Europe, mattered very little to Catherine Morland and other young ladies of her day. Women did not have to know about these things. Gentlemen discussed them, of course, and it was all very dreadful. But they did not interfere with a winter in Bath. To-day, when the whole of Europe is a seething scab, there is not much to be said for a winter anywhere. But at least, when we read Jane Austen, we can keep a sense of proportion.[32]

Here du Maurier deftly mimics Austen's style, ventriloquizing her habits of free indirect discourse to convey a suppressed frustration: "Women did not have to know about these things." She communicates, in spite of explicit statements to the contrary, a shared sense of postwar despair from which the reading of Austen brings only temporary relief. She imagines Jane Austen "today," asking whether "she would have become effected [*sic*] by two world-wars." She writes, "No doubt as a parson's daughter she would have been a useful and efficient member of her local W.V.S. (perish the thought!), she would have packed parcels for German prisoners, and possibly organized a village Comforts fund." But none of this, she argues, would have altered her stories: "Her curates would still have been pompous, her elderly gentlemen still afraid of draughts." Austen would not have allowed herself to be changed by the dutiful toils and horrors of war, because the "essence of Jane Austen's art" was unmoved by local influences and instead "written for all time." It is as if du Maurier, hoping that the recent war has not scarred or dated her own fiction, clings to Austen in "the swirling current" of political upheaval.[33]

The closing installment in the William & Norgate edition comes with *Sense and Sensibility*, introduced by Naomi Royde-Smith, novelist and first woman editor of the *Westminster Gazette*. Her introduction's precise date, "August 18th, 1948," marked the eighth anniversary of the start of the Battle of Britain, air battles known simply as the Hardest Day. Royde-Smith was already specifically associated with wartime coverage of German air raids, having published *Outside Information: A Diary of Rumour* (1941), a novel that began as a serialized account of the limited information available to civilians and ended as a published memoir of the Blitz. In her introduction, Royde-Smith starts off with a breezy defense of *Sense and Sensibility* against accusations of immaturity by pointing to sardonic passages, but she ends by observing that it is "Miss Austen's metropolitan novel."[34] For her, the activities that "take place in London" give "*Sense and Sensibility* a more positive actuality than we find in the invented scenery of the other tales." The local habitations of her characters resonate with war-torn Londoners, in particular:

> We cannot visit Netherfield, or Randalls, or Mansfield Park, but we can still walk past Stratford Place and into Portman Square, and, on a moonlight night, a hundred and fifty years after Lucy Steele waited for Robert Ferrars to call on her in Bartlett's Buildings, two of Miss Austen's devotees stood amid the rubble and firewood that mark the site of Thavies Inn at Holborn Circus, and looked up to the curved parapet, topping all that is left of the cliff-like edifice from which the Misses Steele set out "to present themselves before the more grand relations in Conduit and Berkeley Streets."[35]

This startling image reminds readers that Jane Austen's world also suffered from German air raids, because her London was just as devastated by the recent bombings. Like Kipling, who brought suffering soldiers together through Austen, Royde-Smith links the suffering home front, where the loss of many of London's landmark buildings by bombings triggered universal interest in the history cut short there. In the latter half of the nineteenth century, Norgate & Williams had originally occupied number 14 Henrietta Street, next door to the bank and residence of Jane Austen's brother Henry. Perhaps the firm's own historical connections to Austen by means of London's pockmarked geography prompted this too-little-known reprinting project, an edition suffused with a sense of wartime loss.

It is impossible to isolate the impact of any one edition upon Austen's midcentury reputation. There are numerous surviving copies of the Williams & Norgate volumes, priced just high enough when postwar books were scarce to prompt their preservation. And at the time of publication, the

5.7. *In center: Más fuerte que el orgullo* in La Novela Rosa series (Barcelona: R. Plana, n.d. [1945]). On either side are romances from the same Spanish paperback series. Author's collection.

prominent status of the women writers who penned the introductions would have boosted visibility and popular sales. These introductions take forceful possession of Austen as a writer about and for women, eagerly aligning her biography and work with a shared war-torn purpose. And yet, one edition cannot prove that Jane Austen was starting to shift incontrovertibly toward a readership of women. In addition, the impulse behind this edition was more inclusive than exclusive, merging women with men in the wartime reading of an Austen who healed. This differs from the postwar "pinking" that dramatically shifted Austen's popular audience exclusively toward women. That phenomenon may well have begun in the 1940s in Spain, a country ravaged by back-to-back civil and world wars, where women turned for comfort to the *novela rosa*.

LA NOVELA ROSA

In Spanish, the colloquial term for cheap romantic fiction is "*novela rosa*," or pink novel. The "pink" usefully distinguishes the modern type of romance novel, or *novela romántica*, from fiction dating to the period of romanticism. *Novela rosa* has come to mean a trashy romance novel, cheap in every sense of the word, akin to the way *dime novel* or *pulp* denotes lowbrow fiction. In other words, while in English my questions about the "pinking" of Austen rely on a literal reading of her packaging, in Spanish, popular romances are already referred to as metaphorically pinked fictions—especially when the production values are low. In 1945, at the close of World War II, Austen joined the pink fiction of Spain when she was selected for a cheap paperback series called La Novela Rosa, where *Pride and Prejudice* appeared as number 121, priced at four pesetas and tightly printed on bad paper in dual columns, amid a burst of popular escapist romances published under the dictatorship of Generalissimo Franco (figure 5.7).[36] Wartime inflation in Spain makes it impossible for me to give an accurate conversion of the original price into today's buying power in euros. But this *novela rosa* series, printed on cheap paper and roughly glued into mawkish covers worthy only of Mills & Boon, was priced at the bottom end of the Spanish book market. In a series marketed exclusively to adult women, Austen was therefore pinked in both senses—cover and content. But this pinking was not mere twaddle. For the women of Francoist Spain, the lowbrow genre of the *novela rosa* may well have served a powerful double role, as both solace and mild defiance.

The translator of this *Pride and Prejudice* edition from 1945 remains unknown, and the translation is viewed as a "curious" outlier among Spanish translations. The novel had circulated under the straightforward title *Orgullo y prejuicio* ever since 1924, in a well-regarded translation by José J. de Urríes y Azara.[37] The choice of *Más fuerte que el orgullo* (stronger than pride) nods instead to the Hollywood film, released under that title in 1945; the book's cover also adapts the escutcheon, or ornate framed badge, of the movie posters. More powerful than the titular nod to the film version is the way Austen's new series companions reshape her novel by association, turning the cultural cement of classic literature into the frothy syllabub of historical romance. At first, the packaging seems to demote Austen's status. Whereas in 1919 the first-ever translation of Jane Austen into Spanish stressed her canonicity by including her among Los Grandes Novelistas, this *novela rosa* edition of 1945 surrounds Austen with popular romances.[38] These include a reprint of *En pos de la ilusión* (1940), by María Mercedes Ortoll, a pen name associated with seventy *novelas rosa* published in Spanish between 1930 and 1963, and a translation of a romance by Berta Ruck, or Amy Roberta Ruck (1878–1978), a British writer credited with more than eighty romance novels. With all due respect to the prolific Ortoll and Ruck, Austen appears in their company as a writer of formulaic romances, churned out and reprinted in bulk under the Franco regime.

It is widely acknowledged that authoritarian regimes such as that of Francoist Spain stimulated the popularity of escapist literature, from the detective story to the *novela rosa*.[39] Popular literature often thrives under oppressive dictatorships, even under the eyes of Generalissimo Franco's conservative censors, because innocuous stories with happy endings provide a useful coping mechanism. "Of all the forms of popular literature by far the best-selling was the *novela rosa*," confirms Patricia O'Byrne; this was also "the only form specifically aimed at women."[40] Scholars of Spanish postwar literature and feminist historians therefore assign the *novela rosa* a tragic "soporific capacity," calculated to "consolidate resignation and acceptance of personal, social and political circumstances."[41] This, then, looks like a Jane Austen who functions as a mask on political upheaval and violence, peddled cheaply to housewives as a popular balm for the wounds of fascist oppression.

When judged, in 1945, solely by the telltale packaging and new companions of the *novela rosa*, Austen's reputation as a keen observer of social injustices in the Regency era threatens to disappear. The rosy Jane of this paperback is not the proud Jane held high on banners by London suffragettes in 1908, nor does she look anything like the soldiering Jane sent to two world wars. Packaged as a formulaic *novela rosa*, the story of Isabel Bennet—some names are adjusted to Spanish equivalents—looks like yet another reassuringly predictable plot where the virtuous and chaste heroine is "rewarded with the love of and marriage to the most sought after hero."[42] Isabel's struggle to fend off genteel poverty overlaps neatly with the two dominant formulas for the *novela rosa* in the 1940s: an aristocratic heroine whose coming out encounters temporary obstacles, and a young virtuous heroine who falls victim to temporary deprivation. Austen's plot need not change in order for the interpretation to narrow. "Lidia" and her improprieties need not vanish from the novel, since these transgressions are frowned upon and set right by marriage to Wickham. This Spanish translation follows the original plot in its entirety—in Protestant *Inglaterra*, complete with references to Brighton and London. But the context of Francoist Spain, assisted by the *novela rosa* genre, looks to insist upon a formulaic reading, reducing Austen's nuanced story to the mere reward of virtue and the punishment of vice.

But looks can be deceiving. Franco's conservative censors seem to have largely ignored *novelas rosa*, whose telltale packaging and reputation for predictable stories shielded them from censors seeking to curb deviations from Catholic hierarchy.[43] Foreign books usually received close scrutiny by censors, but not the translations found among these popular *novelas rosa*. Sonia Núñez Puente warns that literary studies may underestimate the complex escapist mechanisms of the popular *novela rosa* during the time of Franco, missing its mildly subversive cultural impact. She points out that while this genre did traffic in limiting clichés about women, in the many stories where foreign female protagonists struggled with independence outside of Francoist Spain, they may also have provided Spanish women with alternative, if conservative, role models.[44] A great number of the "pink" novels written and published between 1940 and 1970 had sympathetic female leads who showed gumption and heart under duress, offering a modest prototype of the female agency denied under the fascist regime. All this is in addition to wider arguments made decades ago by Janice Radway, who contradicted demeaning myths about romance reading in an American context.[45]

It is possible, therefore, that *Pride and Prejudice* is meaningfully reprinted in 1945 "under cover" of the *novela rosa*, allowing a British classic to hide in plain sight among contemporary escapist romances. The bold resistance of the pert Isabel to the old-fashioned wishes of Lady Catalina de Bourgh, a scene whose verbal fireworks burn as brightly in Spanish as in English, apparently went unnoticed by censors. I cannot discover anything about the publishing firm, or even whether Austen's presence was a one-off or rare insertion of a British classic into this particular series. All I can assess is the tenor of this anonymous translation, unique to this edition and not a model of literary sophistication or academic correctness at four pesetas in paperback.[46] The translator does not, however, tinker with or edit Austen's plot to assist a dull formulaic reading but retains its edginess and subversive humor—albeit in a workmanlike way. The translator deviates from strict equivalencies in ways that drop the original register of Austen's language, although such colloquial liberties never endanger her characterizations. For example, where Austen writes, "Mrs. Bennet all amazement, though flattered by having a guest of such high importance, received her with the utmost politeness," the *novela rosa* translates this into "*La señora Bennet pasmadísima aunque muy ufana al ver en su casa a persona tan encumbrada, la recibió con la mayor cortesía.*"[47] Google's translation of "all amazement" would render the phrase coldly as "*todo asombro,*" but the translator's choice in 1945 to opt for "*pasmadísima*" enhances, as in the exaggerated likeness of a Rowlandson cartoon, Mrs. Bennet's dramatic astonishment in the face of a visit from Lady Catherine. Also, Google blandly equates the words "such high importance" with "*de tanta importancia,*" whereas "*encumbrada*" dials up Lady Catalina's implied grandeur and exalted status—allowing her sense of self-importance to come through with a possible hint of Austen's free indirect discourse. Admittedly, these small choices cannot fully reconstruct the translator's intentions, but across the text, many similar local choices add up to a profound fidelity to Austen's subversive comedy.

Some local deviations take liberties with wording but not with wider meaning or plot.[48] The translator is faithful to the point of adding an explanatory footnote when Mrs. Bennet exclaims near the novel's close that Elizabeth must be immediately married to Darcy by "*licencia especial,*" or "special license." The translator's note reads: "*Los miembros the la Corte de Inglaterra, necesitan licencia del rey para casarse. (N. Del T.).*"[49] It certainly jars to see Elizabeth and Darcy misidentified as members of the English "Court" and invoking a king's permission. Perhaps this false note, conspicuous as the only editorial interruption in the book, was a closing nod to fascist authority. In spite of being genuinely faithful to Austen's story, not every aspect of this translation is correct. But I sense that the heart of this *novela rosa* was in the right place. Certainly, in 1945, the context for the gendered packaging of this cheap reprint should prevent the dismissing of the pinking of Jane Austen as derivative stereotyping, or as uniformly misguided attempts to demote her. Instead, the *novela rosa* edition of *Pride and Prejudice* shows how political and social purposes shape the packaging and reception of Austen.

After learning all this, I came upon two further Spanish-language Austens in this same "pinked" format from the war-torn 1940s (figure 5.8). Both paperbacks are published by Editorial Molino in the series Colleccion Violéta—a shade darker than pink but still aiming at an exclusively female audience. The translator of the 1944 *Orgullo y prejuicio* is identified evasively as "E. Molino," implying an in-house workmanlike translation by

5.8. Two Spanish translations from the Colleccion Violéta series: *Orgullo y prejuicio* (Barcelona: Editorial Molino, 1944) and *Persuasion,* translated by Enriqueta S. Albanella (Buenos Aires: Editorial Molino, 1943). Author's collection.

the Editorial Molino firm. At 190 pages, again in double columns, this story is also complete, but now wrapped in an illustration by Joan Pau Bocquet (1904–1966) that conjures a scene from the 1940 MGM film by copying a promotional still. Molino also produced *Persuasion*, dated 1943, for the Colleccion Violéta series. This additional fragile survivor suggests that the sly packaging of Austen as escapist romance was not limited to *Pride and Prejudice* and also traveled to other parts of the Spanish-speaking world. This *Persuasion* was printed and sold in Buenos Aires in October 1943, hard on the heels of the famous Argentine coup d'état that ended the so-called Infamous Decade.[50] The refracted Hollywood glamour of both Molino products, each promising a distraction from oppressive politics, is unmistakably gendered female. It seems that Spanish-language reprints during the 1940s pinked Austen in distant countries. Location aside, the fact that *Persuasion*, the author's most explicit wartime novel with arguably her most nonconformist heroine, received the same radically gendered treatment as *Pride and Prejudice*, extends Austen's twin function as comfort and defiance for women during turbulent times.

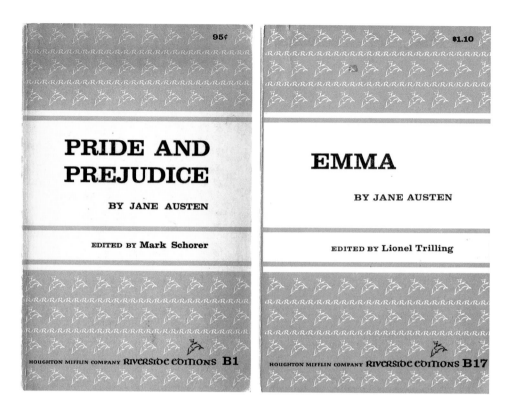

5.9. First-generation paperback Riverside Editions of Jane Austen for use in university classrooms, starting in the 1950s. Author's collection.

IN THE PINK WITH PAPERBACKS

From war-torn Spain to England and the States, unique conditions allowed the paperback format to flourish in the 1950s and 1960s. The paperback had met with public appeal during the first century of publishers' experiments with this format (see chapter 1), but in the middle of the twentieth century, the success of Penguin, Pocket Books, and all their hangers-on gave it new momentum. Paperbacks of every sort soon were everywhere, prompting creative experimentation with cover design and aggressive niche marketing on both sides of the Atlantic. The American college classroom proved a particularly fertile ground for paperbacks after 1944, when Congress passed the Servicemen's Readjustment Act, better known as the GI Bill. Benefits included dedicated payments of tuition and living expenses to attend high school, college, or vocational/technical training. By 1956, roughly 8.8 million veterans had taken advantage of GI benefits, with 2.2 million attending colleges or universities. Many GIs were first-generation college students.

The expansion of the traditional college classroom with students from a greater-than-ever range of cultural and economic backgrounds coincided with the introduction of women into the same classrooms, for this era also saw enormous strides in coeducation. Every publisher craved a piece of the classroom action when it came to this dual expansion of the market. Austen was served up as fit food to the heady mix of college students, becoming every publisher's go-to leader of cheap reprint series of established works.

Starting in the 1950s, student editions of Austen appeared for the first time in paperback, with textual emendations and introductions by prominent academics. In 1957, Lionel Trilling supplemented R. W. Chapman's edited text of *Emma* (first published in 1923 in hardback) with a twenty-page introduction plus a "Biographical Sketch," fashioned by Houghton Mifflin Company in a larger and more imposing size than the increasingly common paperback format sold to general readers (figure 5.9). These first-generation Riverside Editions cost around $1, or about three times the price of a Cardinal Edition from Pocket Books, which by 1952 had started its own slightly upmarket line of classics, or "books of outstanding merit," for the

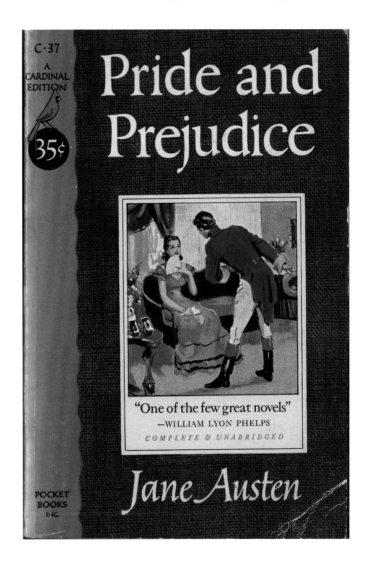

university market. The Cardinal Edition of *Pride and Prejudice*, priced at 35 cents in paperback, was wrapped in a cover more traditional than any used by Pocket Books on its first twenty-one printings of the novel (figure 5.10). For some, however, the scholarly paperback remained a contradiction in terms, including Oxford University Press, which instead opted to miniaturize its hardback "pocket edition" of the World's Classics series to resemble the new generation of paperbacks—with pastel-colored pictorial dust jack-

5.10. Cardinal Edition paperback of *Pride and Prejudice* (New York: Pocket Books, 1953). Author's collection.

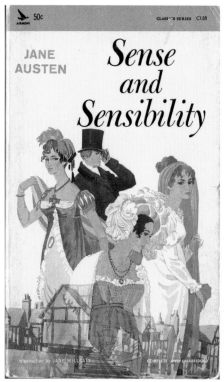
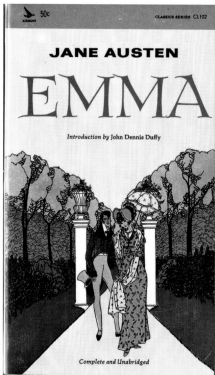
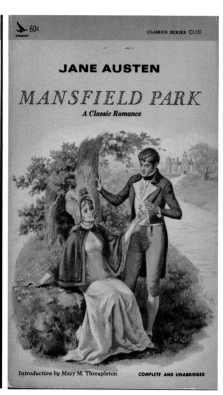

5.11. Airmont Classics paperbacks of *Sense and Sensibility, Emma,* and *Mansfield Park* (New York: Airmont, 1966-67). Author's collection.

ets to mimic the rainbow of competing covers. For a long time, Oxford held out in smaller hardbacks; not until 1980 did they shift their World's Classics imprint to paperback.

During the 1960s, less fastidious operators in the student market celebrated Austen in paperbacks by Airmont, Everyman, Harper & Row, Fawcet, Pan, Scholastic, Signet, and many more. In 1966, with Austens in paperback priced around 50 to 70 cents in the States, the song "Paperback Writer" by the *Beatles* remained the number one hit single for two consecutive weeks. At that cultural moment, bookstores displayed so many Janes that there was a look to suit every reader. For those troubled by political upheaval and antiwar demonstrations about the Vietnam War, Airmont offered conservatively packaged Austens with illustrations showing characters in period dress (figure 5.11). Their 1967 paperback of *Mansfield Park*, priced at 60 cents, is subtitled "A Classic Romance" and carries a back

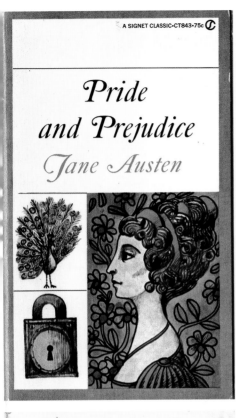

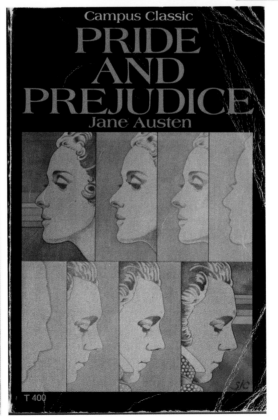

5.12. *Top:* Signet Classic reprints of *Pride and Prejudice* and *Sense and Sensibility* (New York: New American Library, 1961) and an Everyman's Library paperback reprint of *Emma* (London and New York: Dent and Dutton, 1963). *Bottom:* Perennial Classic paperback of *Sense and Sensibility* (New York: Harper & Row, 1961) and Campus Classic paperback of *Pride and Prejudice* (New York: Scholastic Magazines, 1962). Author's collection.

Jane Austen
Sense and Sensibility

An Everyman
Paperback

Bede Masterman

E L

An
EVERYMAN
Paperback

JANE AUSTEN

Northanger Abbey
and Persuasion

6s
net

Faith Jaques

50c

AIRMONT

CLASSICS SERIES, CL107

JANE AUSTEN
Persuasion

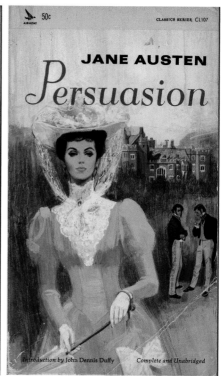

Introduction by John Dennis Duffy   Complete and Unabridged

PAN
X689 books   *Bestsellers of Literature*

PRIDE AND
PREJUDICE
Jane Austen

E L

An
EVERYMAN
Paperback

JANE AUSTEN

Sense and
Sensibility

6s
net

GM

W·151   45c

SENSE
AND
SENSIBILITY
Jane Austen
Author of *Pride and Prejudice*

A novel of love and manners

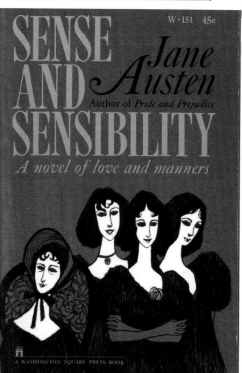

A WASHINGTON SQUARE PRESS BOOK

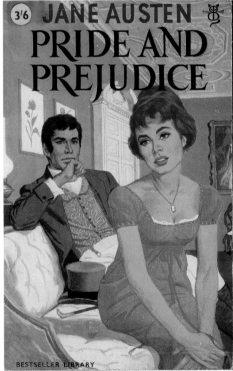

5.13. Examples of pinked paperback editions from the 1960s. Author's collection.

5.14. The Campus Classic paperback edition of *Emma,* with an introduction by Mary Stolz (New York: Scholastic Book Services, 1967). Author's collection.

blurb explaining that Austen "defends the decency and integrity of the 'Establishment,' represented by Mansfield itself, against the urbanity and shallowness of the Crawfords' world."[51] The blurb quotes Lionel Trilling: "No other work of genius has ever spoken . . . so insistently for cautiousness and constraint, even for dullness." In tumultuous times, dullness becomes a selling point. Austen also leans to the right in other Airmont paperbacks, reassuring potential buyers by means of period costume and deft summaries of the novel's quiet solace. Tilting radically left, however, were psychedelic Janes capturing the attention of hipster students who preferred book covers to resemble contemporary LPs (figure 5.12).[52] Both right- and left-leaning Janes during the 1960s occasionally carried introductions or afterwords by women.

As the number of women college students increased, more publishers of paperbacks matching student budgets sought to make their classic reprints appeal to women specifically. At Harvard, for example, Jane Austen had been on literary syllabi since the 1880s, as Looser discusses.[53] But not until the 1960s was she taught there to women who shared the classrooms with men.[54] Reprinters of classic titles in paperback responded to this new visibility of women students by contriving ways to capture a share of the expanding market. The history of the color pink may be complex, but by the 1960s it was a dominant and transparent consumer signal to women, appearing upon everything from clothes to appliances. Publishers responded by buying pink ink in bulk, making the "pinked" paperback Austens for college campuses that would irrevocably gender her literary reputation (figure 5.13)

No equivalent pink army of covers for any other single woman writer can be mustered, probably because Austen was already so favored on college syllabi when publishers looked around for candidates to pink. As in Nabokov's literary classroom and the Appleby do-it-yourself box, Austen had appeared on many traditional reading lists as the first, or only, woman writer. "First" among women writers, she therefore became the first to be thoroughly pinked among the dominantly male population of authors taught at universities. Pink worked astonishingly well as a gendered sig-

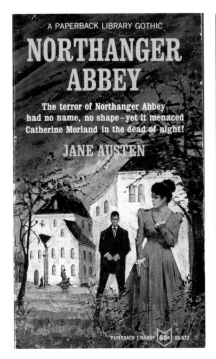
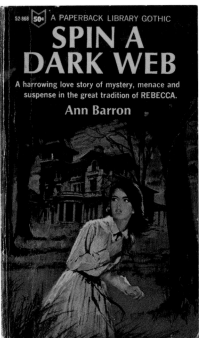

nal to women students that these new books acknowledged their aesthetics and their interests. Even publishers such as Oxford University Press and Thomas Nelson, when staunchly resisting the paperback format as low-brow, dialed up the pink to appeal to women readers when making dust covers for hardback editions of Austen. The extraordinary success of an expanding market for cheap books aimed at female readers left a visible mark on Austen's public image.

Of course, the color pink did not accomplish all of the feverishly gendered marketing of Austen all by itself. On the cover of the Campus Classic paperback edition of *Emma* in 1967, published by Scholastic with an introduction by Mary Stolz, a woman sported a beehive hairdo whose silhouette made half of a heart shape—a variation of the Nelson edition's not-so-subtle marketing signal of 1905 (figure 5.14). In 1965, a short-lived romance series called Paperback Library Gothic reprinted Jane Austen, at 60 cents, as part a series of gothic romances of various qualities and heritages. Covers showed young women running away from menacing buildings, usually in

5.15. Three examples of reprints from the Paperback Library Gothic series (New York: Paperback Library, 1965). Author's collection.

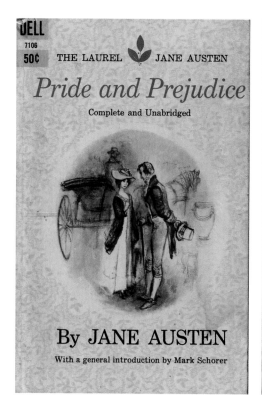 

5.16. Laurel Series paperbacks of *Pride and Prejudice* and *Sense and Sensibility* (New York: Dell, 1964 and 1967, respectively). Author's collection.

the dark and rain (figure 5.15). Starting in the 1960s, professors in the English Department of my own university taught many books in Dell's Laurel Series, 50-cent classics for the large student market, often with introductions by established literary critics. English Professor Mark Schorer provided Dell with introductions for the Laurel reprints of Jane Austen, which were aggressively gendered with pale cameo-style designs that prefigure the look of Harlequin's line of popular romances (figure 5.16).

If you feel this transformation of Austen into chick lit risks demeaning her as a serious author, you are by no means alone. In 2006, when Headline Books relaunched Jane Austen in a series of Dell look-alike covers, one reviewer hissed that it was tantamount to declaring Austen "a romantic novelist in the style of Danielle Steel and Dame Barbara Cartland." Such saccharine packaging, he warned, would appeal only to the timid and ignorant: "glossy, pastel covers designed to appeal to women put off by the idea of

reading a 19th century writer."[55] Harriet Evans, editor of the Headline series, in turn, accused leading publishers of literary classics such as Penguin
and Oxford of treating Austen as a "dry, academic author" and of "reaching
only a tiny fraction of her potential audience." Such overt battles over Austen, between the popular and the elite versions of her books, had been fought
continually since Henry James sneered at the frivolities of Austen in popular
gift editions. Evans damned her with faint praise: "Jane Austen is the fairy
godmother of women's fiction and we want to take her back to her romantic
roots." Endorsed by celebrities, Headline's books had no distracting notes
but contained lists of questions for book clubs instead of students. In spite
of all this seething and sneering from various positions along the cultural
parapet, Penguin Books immediately selected from its black-jacketed line
of literary classics anything that might qualify as romantic and created a
brand new line of Penguin Red Classic reprints that were stripped of footnotes and dressed in pastel covers mimicking Headline Books. If a pinked or
chocolate-box Austen sold better, why maintain the high ground?

Viewed after the latest waves of feminism, including the fashion for unisex clothing and the popularity of a gender-free shade termed "millennial
pink," some or all of this early, bright, Barbie-style pinking and romantic
tweaking may resemble bad feminism—an appeal to the crudest stereotypes about women as girls.[56] And yet, just as in 1945 the Novela Rosa
series awarded Austen a free pass from Franco's censors, her recruitability
for various causes—and her capacity to both rally and mollify—proved
a boon to her popularity among readers of all stripes. For publishers, the
gendered marketing of Austen is simply a no-brainer, for better and worse.
Niche marketing remains risky. Publishers from Routledge to Dicks and
Clarke to Appleby wedged a space for their own editions of Austen into a
crowded book market—not always successfully. In the 1960s, publishers of
cheap paperbacks could suddenly hope to reach half the population at once.
Pinked books sold more Austen. Judging by the numbers of publishers who
joined the initial pinking of Austen in the 1960s, plus those who have copied it since, this color-coded marketing "technique" amounts to the most
successful Jane Austen packaging of all time. The legacy of this pinked
success, however, remains problematic for her reputation.

V.VII.1. Annie Munro's copy of *Northanger Abbey* (Glasgow: Blackie & Sons, n.d.), awarded to her as an attendance prize in 1911 from her school in Forfar, Scotland. Author's collection.

Vignette VII
Annie's Prized Gift

About 1910, Blackie & Sons of Glasgow published *Northanger Abbey* in a gift series that joined the book to dozens of juvenile titles bound in similar cloth casings of popping bright colors, each stamped with the same eye-catching design that featured the Mackintosh Rose, the hallmark of Scottish art nouveaux. In this juvenile series, once popular as school prizes but never as collection material for serious libraries, Austen kept company with *Dog Crusoe, Hans Brinker, Swiss Family Robinson, Little Women,* and *The Wide, Wide World.*

The bookplate in this copy identifies it as a school attendance prize for 1910–11 (figure V.VII.1). A century ago, the book's colors would have been even brighter than today and it must have made a stunning prize for Annie Munro, named as the proud recipient. The name of another girl, presumably her sister, is written opposite, in a childish hand at the top of the free endpaper:

Florence Munro
4 Market Street
Feofar
Scotland

Since the official bookplate belongs to the Burgh School Board in Forfar, the town's name has been slightly misspelled in the inscription. Even after an awkward self-correction, the result is wrong, with the spelling as well as the hand shaky and immature.

The specific street address and two full names made finding the Munros at 4 Market Street easy. In the census for 1911, the year Annie received this book as a prize, the Munro family consisted of two working-class parents in their early 40s, Bain and Annie Munro, plus their six daughters, ranging in age from 19 to 2.[1] Bain Munro, age 42, worked as "mechanical engineer" in an "Iron Foundry." Their eldest daughter, Norah (19), was a weaver of linen and jute, while Florence (16) is listed as "dressmaker." In other words, the older Munro girls were already wage earners. Annie (12) was in school, along with Helen (7). The littlest Munros, Alice (4) and Jessie (2), remained at home with their mum. From the mere fact that the book was awarded as an "Attendance Prize," Annie must have liked school and her parents must have valued and supported her education.

Since the handwriting of the inscription opposite the award label looks more childish than that of a 16-year-old, Florence's name and address were probably penned by someone else. Annie Munro, a full four years younger, seems the likeliest person to have made her own prize over to an older sister. As someone intimately familiar with the complexities of barter economics among siblings, I first hazarded that Annie, perhaps with great ceremony, traded her fancy school prize with her older sister in exchange for something she preferred over Austen. Perhaps Annie liked a book that Florence owned far better? Or, I thought, perhaps Annie was, to paraphrase Elizabeth Bennet, *not* a great reader and had pleasure in other things? *Northanger Abbey*, with a 15-year-old heroine, does seem more apt reading for 16-year-old Florence than for 12-year-old Annie. But my guesses were innocent of Annie's true circumstances.

Sadly, Annie's death occurred less than six months after receiving her end-of-year school prize. On December 5, 1911, at age 13, she died of diphtheria and toxemia in the local hospital.[2] More than likely, Annie valued her shiny, bright prize book so much that she gave it to her sister Florence just before her death, solemnly bequeathing it with that shaky inscription of her sister's name and their home address. Perhaps Annie's colorful prize book was brought to her in the hospital so that a family member might read it aloud to her. Only ten days later, on December 15, little Alice Munro, age 5, also succumbed to diphtheria.[3] There must have been a widespread diphtheria outbreak, for the entry before the record of Alice's death mentions an 8-year-old boy who died of the same disease four days earlier. Effective worldwide inoculation against diphtheria did not begin until the 1920s, and just before World War I, among the overcrowded homes of the Scottish working classes, many such outbreaks ravaged not just families but whole towns. At that time, there was an exodus of Scotland's working poor to countries such as the United States and Australia.

Eventually, Florence also went to America. In 1915 an outward-bound passenger list gives her occupation as "dressmaker."[4] The highest level of education reported for Florence Munro (1894–95 to 1946) on her immigration papers to the United States was "elementary." Florence married Michael Mowers (1893–1968), a carpenter in road construction from New York, and they had two daughters. Florence, who became a naturalized American citizen, was buried in Madison County, New York. Leaving school by age 15 did not prevent her from building a productive life. In the context of these working-class patterns of girlhood, book prizes must have had a far different currency from the perfunctory role they often serve in today's schools. At a time when girls turned into wage-earning women at 14 or 15, a book of one's own was not, as now, a passport to further study, but often the end of childhood and book learning. In Annie's case, this copy of *Northanger Abbey* may have been, quite literally and brutally, her very last book.

I need to confess that the history behind Annie's prize copy took the wind out of my research sails. Surviving Blackie volumes from this popular children's series remain ubiquitous on retail sites selling secondhand books, and I had long and naively associated their colorful covers with rosy-cheeked children reading after their release for school holidays. A few years ago, I scanned the art nouveaux cover of Annie's book, so bright and sunny, in order to design large fridge magnets for bookish friends. The brightness of the cover, and the idea of one girl gifting her Jane Austen prize to her sister, had charmed me so utterly that I failed to consider the visceral reality of the working-class schoolkids who received these books, until I came face to face with their census records and death registers. Then I saw it as bizarre that I, and a handful of friends, had copies of Annie's prize book cover, life-sized, on the well-stocked refrigerators of our middle-class houses.

CODA
A CALL TO ACTION

After I gave a recent talk about some of the research for this book, one audience member introduced herself in the most gratifying manner: "I've been collecting Jane Austen for forty years, and yet so many of the books in your slides I've never seen before." Her approval mixed surprise with excitement. For me, her generous comments amounted to welcome validation from an independent expert. Here was a dedicated collector who had relied for decades upon the established bibliographies of Jane Austen to hunt for her copies. She had been thorough and methodical, which is precisely why she had missed the unrecorded reprints that tell the story of Austen's dispersal among the working and lower middle classes. In the digital age, you cannot find what you cannot name in a search box.

The books highlighted here do indeed demonstrate how gobsmackingly incomplete the historical record of one of the best-known English authors remains. Our current sense of Jane Austen's audience is startlingly elitist and selective. I sincerely hope my examples have surprised and excited the readers of this book. My project, however, is not intended as an alternative bibliography. I also wish to caution against the inevitable complacency that the "lost" books I have chronicled are now safe simply because I was able to show them to you in my illustrations or describe them in my text. These pages are an initial plea to incite action, rather than a rescue mission's self-satisfied reportage. The lost books of Jane Austen are, for the most part, still lost and out of sight. Let's not get too comfortable too soon.

In addition to unrecorded reprints that my own search algorithms have surely missed, many of the copies shown in my illustrations are not known outside of the collections mentioned in the accompanying captions. Most of their brethren were pulped or destroyed long ago. That makes the information that lone copies might yield vulnerable to further loss. One large private Austen collection on the coast of Texas was nearly wiped out by hurricane Harvey during the writing of this book. At the time, I felt guilty about worrying about the possible loss of low-value books when scores of people were deprived of their homes and livelihoods. But it is my job to worry about books. And the rest of the Jane Austen community was then blissfully unaware of how close it came to the gut-wrenching irony of losing so many of the lost books newly recounted here. Someone had to lie awake at night to appease the gods.

And even if additional copies do survive on dispersed private shelves, scholars cannot currently find or study them. What is needed is for rare-book libraries to change their collecting practices to accommodate these cheap reprints, allowing posterity to lock in a more complete reception history for Austen—and perhaps for other major authors for whom established scholarly interest can stand as guarantor of such investment. But institutional space is limited, and while mine is, I hope, a compelling case for Jane Austen, it may not suffice to disrupt long-standing curatorial habits. To shift institutional practices, more private collectors need to help. Actually, private collectors have always shifted the sands of scholarship: Chester W. Topp's collection of yellowbacks at Emory University is a case in point close to my heart. The bulk of institutional holdings began life as private collections, eventually gifted or sold to a major rare-book library. For only in such libraries will books be examined by scholars whose professional practices train the expert's gaze upon the collections of major institutions. And only such libraries offer resident fellowships with well-established brands that augment curriculum vitae. For this project, for example, I was unable to apply for any resident library fellowship, since the material I sought to study was not yet inside the building. The status quo remains a Catch-22 for the creation of new knowledge—and the retention of the old.

As I scan today's offerings on eBay and AbeBooks, I see that prices have climbed significantly since my own curious collecting of the unwanted began in 2011. Books by Jane Austen are no longer being thrown out or sold for a pittance, no matter how tatty or inauthentic the version of her work. In 1912, the Bodleian did not own even a first edition of *Pride and Prejudice*. Not until later in the twentieth century did Austen's famous firsts find forever homes in many institutional libraries. Since then, the institutional capture of Austen's most coveted firsts has forced private fans and collectors to increasingly satisfy their thirst for Austen books with versions and reprints of the lower orders. Now, Austen is so "collectable" that anything bearing her name sells, no matter how insignificant. This is good for the preservation cause, although, as we saw, a certain misplaced fervor can lead to make-over follies and radical rehousing. But even the survivors safeguarded by thoughtful private hands will remain invisible if atomized across disparate collections and households.

I hope that seeing what these books can tell us when arranged side by side will spur private owners to want to join forces. The books shown here, which survive in scattered private and, for a few, institutional hands, give us powerful data *only* when they can be compared with one another. Only when physical evidence allows us to arrange undated books in chronological order can multiple runs of the same title reveal the handovers from one publisher to another (as in Routledge to Lever to Miles & Miles or the dizzying series of handoffs from Bunce & Brother to Henry T. Coates). Throughout my research, I was taken aback by the need to examine and reexamine the physical copies to slowly make sense of their origins. Many B-grade publishing houses have not left behind their papers or business records, so the battered and often undated copies they produced are the only record we have of certain professional swaps and of specific individual readers. Scholars and students of book history need access to physical exemplars.

Some exemplars do remain out there. At this moment, as my book goes to press, George Bayntun of Bath (along with other booksellers) is offering piecemeal a large collection amassed over decades by John Jordan, the friend of David Gilson's who, after the publication of the 1982 *Bibliography,* "formed a collection of editions and issues 'not in Gilson'" that, in turn, contributed to the modest list of missed books at the front of the 1997 reprint.[1] But Jordan appears to have kept on searching, assembling a formidable Jane Austen collection of well over a thousand volumes, with many reprints on the low end. It is frustrating to see a collection, one that has been put together over decades and with the potential to add so much to the historical record, broken up and, yet again, disbanded—and before its intellectual value can be fully mined. But until rare-book libraries alter their approach, a collection that is not filled with precious firsts but instead traces the messy reception and inglorious history of an author in a deep way, well, such a collection does not yet have an obvious destination.

My role as self-appointed Pied Piper of tatty Jane Austen reprints, leading the dispersed vermin of bibliography to one central location to benefit a larger community of scholars and fans, may prove a fairytale vision. Perhaps a responsible, crowd-sourced, digital site—one where a reprint's cover styles, imprint information, current location, and key sample pages can be recorded by private owners—can serve as an interim safeguard and capture a little of the lost knowledge. But I hope that private collectors will want to enhance the scholarly value of their books by reuniting them in, ideally, one institutional location. The books in question have little value in financial terms. Most of my own eBay finds cost me as much in postage as in purchase. Unlike Jane Austen's coveted firsts, which fetch tens of thousands of dollars at auction, these dregs of the book trade, even though they boast the name of Austen, are unlikely to alter the financial futures of my descendants.

Meanwhile, I hope that this volume raises awareness of the impact that unsung paperbacks, neglected school editions, and motley reprints have had upon Jane Austen's animated and inclusive reception history. Only cheap books make authors immortal.

ACKNOWLEDGMENTS

The path to researching and writing this book differed from the one I walked in previous projects, and it generated fresh debts owed to new guides. This time I had to locate books that libraries do not tend to preserve and that bibliographers do not always record. I needed to find private collectors with unorthodox tastes who might help a researcher they did not yet know. My project gained traction only after John Spiers offered access to his collection of nineteenth-century publishers' bindings and when Sandra Clark invited me to make use of her editions of Jane Austen. Without the generosities of John and Sandra, who each shared knowledge gained over decades of collecting, this project would have stalled. Their energies for my queries seemed inexhaustible. When geography proved tricky to negotiate, John drove a carload of examples from his collection to Oxford, where I was teaching for the summer. When a foot injury resulted in months of bedrest and my virtual captivity at home in Austin, Sandra arranged for Texan friends and relatives to periodically make miraculous "book drops" from her collection. Both John and Sandra read sections of the project, providing feedback that inevitably led to further offers of books, articles, or expertise. I cannot thank them enough.

In addition, hard-to-find items needed to be photographed or tracked down on the shelves of far-flung collectors, booksellers, and—on a few occasions—rare-book libraries. I did not spare the shelves of generous colleagues and friends, including Deborah Barnum, Susan Jaret McKinstry, Devoney Looser, Elizabeth Steele, Rosemary Stevens, Elizabeth Wilson, and Jennifer Winski. For the taking of photographs and digital sharing of books, I also want to thank the following strangers, with whom I now feel a special bond: Alastair Jollans, Beth Dominianni (Mark Twain Library), Greg Matthews and Doug Lambeth (Washington State University Libraries), Lady Martine J. Roberts, Emma Lea, Felicity McColl (the University of Tasmania), Courtney Chartier (Emory University), and Anne Holloway and Zachary Kendal (Matheson Library, Monash University). I also thank the Robert Frew Antiquarian Bookshop in London, George Bayntun in Bath, the John G. White and Special Collections Department at the Cleveland Public Library, and Paul Frecker, whose collection of Victorian photographs offered a glimpse into the world of one lost reader. I owe debts to the archivists, librarians, and scholars who helped track items, correspondence, or information during the research process. In particular, I benefited from the sleuthing skills of Darren Bevin at Chawton House, Chris Latimer at Stoke-on-Trent City Archives, Aaron Pratt at the Harry Ransom Center, and Molly Schwartzburg at the University of Virginia.

To Kristina Straub and Jocelyn Harris I owe special thanks. Kristina was my cocurator on the "Will & Jane" exhibition in 2016 at the Folger Shakespeare Library, where we road-tested several ideas now extended here. Jocelyn kindly took her pen to the final draft, straightening out baroque prose habits with an experienced hand. Many other colleagues, near and far, guided me through unfamiliar ground: Lance Bertelsen ventriloquized Captain Baird; Douglas Bruster brainstormed concepts; Magda Novoa and Aída Díaz Bild took on a Spanish translation; Allan Hepburn and Stefania Porcelli responded to questions about Bowen; K. C. Hysmith helped with things pink; Andrew King was a resource on John Dicks; Kenneth Larsen improved my religious vocabulary; Devoney Looser and Michael Gamer both suggested more books; Douglas Murray interpreted a musical fragment; Chris Peirson revealed old meanings of peacocks; Shef Rogers and Peter Sabor steadied wobbly drafts; Elizabeth Scala voiced my book's subconscious while supplying parallels in medieval studies; Mark Weiner conjured up shillings and pence; Joanne Wilkes made room for me in her seminar in Auckland; and Michael Winship shared knowledge of nineteenth-century America. Few academic authors benefit from an editor as engaged as mine: Matthew R. McAdam at Johns Hopkins University Press encouraged the out-of-the-box book bios and then periodically steered me "out of the weeds."

There were many new teachers. In 2010 the sixth-grade teacher at the Girls' School of Austin, Miss Liberty Heise, reached out about a particular student edition of *Pride and Prejudice*, setting off a chain of events. In 2011, I was able to study "Publishers' Bookbindings, 1830–1910" at Rare Book School under the great Sue Allen, for whom that summer's class proved her last. Almost completely blind by then, Sue effortlessly showed our class just how to look at books. Then four years as jury member on SHARP's De Long Prize offered a panoptic view of the field of book history. From studies on incunabula to modernism, the hundreds of volumes vetted for that prize enriched my thinking about how books are made, marketed, bought, and read. I also learned much from the audiences at academic gatherings, clubs, bookstores, colleges, universities, and high schools where I had the honor of giving a talk or lecture while working on this project. In particular, the members of the Jane Austen Society of North America (JASNA) have been princely in hosting me at regional and Annual General meetings—and bighearted in nurturing my fledgling ideas. Among JASNA royalty, Claire Bellanti and Cheryl Kinney deserve extra thanks for heroics on behalf of this project and its author. My students in the classrooms at the University of Texas at Austin have also, if sometimes unwittingly, served as important beta-testers, teaching the teacher.

Artist Mike Stilkey, who has a new way with old books, enthusiastically made a Jane Austen book sculpture for use on this book's cover. Two Humanities Research Awards from the College of Liberal Arts (COLA) at the University of Texas at Austin aided with research trips and expenses; further funds from the office of the Vice President for Research, the Dean's Office in COLA, and the English Department helped to subvent the illustrations in this book. A version of one chapter appeared previously in *Book History* ("Sense, Sensibility, and Soap: An Unexpected Case Study for Digital Resources in Book History," 2013). In addition, some ideas initially made their way into the *New York Times*, the JHU Press Blog, and the exhibition hall of the Folger Shakespeare Library in Washington, DC. I am grateful to the publishers, anonymous reviewers, readers, and gallery visitors for early encouragements and corrigenda.

Finally, my family put up with a lot during the writing of this book and the prolonged collecting phase that preceded it. They made room on the family shelves for a seemingly endless torrent of the same six books—often in conditions that compromised immune systems. I know that the sixteen months of nonbipedalism that proved a boon to the manuscript was hard on those who had to walk the dog and do the chores. Thank you, Isaac and Madison. I also owe Madison a big thank you (and probably some cash) for patiently serving as my official photographer and unofficial assistant.

NOTES

PREFACE

1. Such assaults on Victorian books are fiercely recounted by Nicholson Baker in *Double Fold: Libraries and the Assault on Paper* (orig. 2001; New York: Vintage, 2002).

2. "Books in Millions: An Interview with Mr. Edmund Routledge," *Pall Mall Gazette* (London), December 4, 1888, accessed via database *British Library Newspapers: Part I, 1800–1900*.

3. Jonathan Rose, *The Intellectual Life of the British Working Classes*, 2nd ed. (New Haven, CT: Yale University Press, 2010).

4. Rose, 135.

5. Rose, 230.

Vignette I

1. Isaac Slater, printer publisher, *Slater's Directory of Berkshire, Cornwall, and Devon* (1852–53), 118, University of Leicester, Special Collections online, http://specialcollections.le.ac.uk/digital/collection/p16445coll4/id/64260.

2. *Census Returns of England and Wales, 1851*, Kew, Surrey, England, in National Archives of the UK, class *HO107*, piece *1879*, folio *597*, page 52, GSU roll *221027–221028*, accessed via Ancestry.com.

3. *England and Wales Civil Registration Indexes*, General Register Office, year: April–June 1852, vol. 5b, page 198. Quoted from "Will of James Wallace, Commander in the Royal Navy of Plymouth, Devon," on record with National Archives of the UK (PROB 11/2157/24). Probate occurred on April 5, 1852.

4. Quoted from the "Besley's Hand Book Advertiser" section bound with [Henry Besley], *The Route Book of Cornwall: A Guide for the Stranger and Tourist* (Exeter: Henry Besley, [1853]). As the advertisement indicates, by then the shop of W. H. Luke had shifted to number 16 Bedford Street.

5. *Census Returns of England and Wales, 1861*, Kew, Surrey, England, in National Archives of the UK, class *RG9*, piece *1672*, folio *80*, page *30*, GSU roll *542849*.

6. *Census Returns of England and Wales, 1871*, Kew, Surrey, England, in National Archives of the UK, class *RG10*, piece *2459*, folio *57*, page *43*, GSU roll *835188*.

INTRODUCTION

1. See advertisements in the *Morning Chronicle*, February 1, 1833; and the *Examiner*, January 13 and February 24, 1833.

2. Bentley purchased from Thomas Egerton and the Austen family the copyrights to *Pride and Prejudice, Sense and Sensibility*, and *Mansfield Park* for twenty-eight years from initial publication, plus the copyrights to *Emma* and *Northanger Abbey–Persuasion* for forty-two years. His access to the first three novels expired in 1839, 1841, and 1842, respectively, while his hold over the last three novels lapsed in 1857 and 1860. These expiration dates explain why Bentley's competitors pounced on reprinting some novels earlier than others, although, as I will show, not all publishers waited politely for copyrights to terminate, cutting short Bentley's presumed exclusivity. See David Gilson, *A Bibliography of Jane Austen* (New Castle, DE: Oak Knoll Press, orig. 1982; rev. ed., 1997), at 211. Gilson assigns "Editions Published by Richard Bentley" their own substantial section in his bibliography, complete with illustrations in the 1982 edition (211–34). He remains deferential to Bentley's elegant books in "Later Publishing History with Illustrations," in *Jane Austen in Context*, ed. Janet Todd (Cambridge: Cambridge University Press, 2005), 121–59, at 128: "From 1833 to 1892 Bentley may be said to lead the field."

3. Before the advent of publisher's cloth bindings, bound books were often sold in stiff paper cardboard covers. This temporary binding "in boards" could be replaced by a binder with a more permanent leather covering if the owner deemed the book worthy of that extra investment. The oak boards of medieval manuscript volumes are the likely origin of this term.

4. Only when John Murray remaindered unsold copies did the price of Austen's novels drop, briefly, to 2s. 6d. In January 1821, Murray remaindered a substantial number of copies after interest at the standard price stalled: 498 copies of the second edition of *Mansfield Part* at 2s. 6d., 529 copies of *Emma* at 2s., and 282 copies of *Northanger Abbey* and *Persuasion* at 3s. 1d. See David Gilson, "Jane Austen's Text: A Survey of Editions," *Review of English Studies*, n.s., 53.209 (2002): 61–85, at 66.

5. For estimated first-edition runs, see Gilson, *Bibliography*, at 8 and 69.

6. On October 26, 1833, the *Athenaeum* advertised all six Austen novels as a "set" in five volumes for 30s., "elegantly printed and embellished, neatly bound for the library." *Northanger Abbey* and *Persuasion* shared a volume. For a description of the four distinct binding styles recorded by Michael Sadlier, see his *XIX Century Fiction: A Bibliographical Record Based on His Own Collection*, 2 vols. (London: Constable, 1951), at 2:96. Optional leather bindings sold at a higher price.

7. Royal A. Gettmann, *A Victorian Publisher: A Study of the Bentley Papers* (Cambridge: Cambridge University Press, 1960), 51. See also Gilson, *Bibliography*, at 214.

8. "Cheap Books and Their Readers: An Interview with Mr. Routledge," *Pall Mall Gazette* (London), November 19, 1885.

9. The first novel sold at this price was Sir Walter Scott's *Kenilworth* in 1821. See Simon Eliot and Andrew Nash, "Mass Markets: Literature," in *Cambridge History of the Book in Britain*, vol. 6, *1830–1914*, ed. David McKitterick (Cambridge: Cambridge University Press, 2009), 416–42, at 419.

10. According to Dale H. Porter, *The Thames Embankment: Environment, Technology, and Society in Victorian London* (Akron, OH: University of Akron Press, 1997), workers in London received these wages for a ten-hour day and six-day week during the mid-1860s: common laborers, 3s.9d.; bricklayers, carpenters, masons, smiths, 6s.6d.; engineers, 7s.6d. Other sources estimate higher weekly wages, with clerks earning 10s., laborers 20s., and artisans up to 36s.

11. George Routledge in 1885, as quoted in "Cheap Books."

12. See Gilson, *Bibliography*, 227. He records seeing copies in original bindings with prices stamped on the spines "2/6" and "3/6" dated 1846 and 1851, respectively, to which I can add a similar copy dated 1848 (and already marked "3/6"), with advertisements on the endpapers listing all Standard Novels for 3s.6d., including Austen.

13. Lady Molesworth's rebound set of Bentley's reprints of Austen contain the bookbinder's ticket of Westley's & Co., London. Bentley's top-end middle-class prices resemble those of Charles Mudie (1818–1890), famous as the founder of high-end Victorian lending and subscription libraries where readers could also purchase a selection of books in handsome bindings. In 1878, Mudie's Barton Arcade branch in Manchester advertised all of Austen's novels for purchase in ornamental bindings of "Half Morocco" for 6s.7d. each, suitable as "birthday presents and bridal gifts." British Library, RB.23.a.21392(6). The British Library's website, when displaying a few of Mudie's catalog pages, glosses 6s.7d. as "equivalent to a week's rent on a three-bedroomed terraced townhouse."

14. For a broad reception history of Shakespeare that takes into account popular versions of all stripes, see Lawrence W. Levine, *Highbrow/Lowbrow: The Emergence of Cultural Hierarchy in America* (Cambridge, MA: Harvard University Press, 1986).

15. Henry James, "The Lessons of Balzac" (1905), quoted in Brian Southam, *Jane Austen: The Critical Heritage, Volume 2, 1870–1940* (London: Routledge & Kegan Paul, 1987), 230.

16. Margaret Sullivan, *Jane Austen Cover to Cover: 200 Years of Classic Covers* (Philadelphia: Quirk Books, 2014), provides images of just some of this variety, emphasizing the twentieth century.

17. For accounts of the Cult of Jane, see Claire Harman, *Jane's Fame: How Jane Austen Conquered the World* (Edinburgh: Canongate, 2009); Claudia Johnson, *Jane Austen's Cults and Cultures* (Chicago: University of Chicago Press, 2012); Devoney Looser, *The Making of Jane Austen* (Baltimore: Johns Hopkins University Press, 2017); Juliet Wells, *Everybody's Jane: Austen in the Popular Imagination* (London: Bloomsbury, 2011); and Deborah Yaffe, *Among the Janeites: A Journey through the World of Jane Austen Fandom* (Boston: Mariner Books, 2013).

18. Brian Southam collected the published responses into two volumes, *Jane Austen: The Critical Heritage* and *Jane Austen: The Critical Heritage, Volume 2, 1870–1940* (London: Routledge & Kegan Paul, 1969 and 1987, respectively).

19. Annika Bautz, "'In perfect volume form, Price Sixpence': Illustrating *Pride and Prejudice* for a Late-Victorian Mass-Market," in *Romantic Adaptations: Essays in Mediation and Remediation*, ed. Cian Duffy, Peter Howell, and Caroline Ruddell (London: Routledge, 2013), 101–24.

20. See Juliette Wells, *Reading Austen in America* (London: Bloomsbury Academic, 2017).

21. Wells, *Reading Austen in America*, 3. I discuss the prolonged flatlining of American interest in Austen during the 1860s and 1870s in chapter 4.

22. See Kathryn Sutherland, *Jane Austen's Textual Lives: From Aeschylus to Bollywood* (Oxford: Oxford University Press, 2005), particularly chapter 1, "The Making of England's Jane."

23. See my article "Why K. M. Metcalfe (Mrs. Chapman) Is 'really the originator in the editing of Jane Austen,'" *RES: Review of English Studies* 68.285 (June 1, 2017): 583–611. Katharine Marion Metcalfe (1887–1978) was editor of an unassum-

ing "school" edition of *Pride and Prejudice* published by Oxford in 1912. Her modest edition was the first to rescue Austen's text from almost a century of careless reprintings, eleven years before Chapman published his much-lauded edition of the novels in 1923, which mimics Metcalfe's earlier volume in virtually every detail. The facts that Katharine Metcalfe became, in 1913, Mrs. R. W. Chapman, and that she allowed her husband to take over the editing project she began have masked her role as innovator.

24. Geoffrey Keynes, *Jane Austen: A Bibliography* (London: Nonesuch, 1929); and Gilson, *Bibliography*.

25. Her extra-annotated copy, almost handled to pieces from heavy use, is part of the Alberta and Henry Burke collection at Goucher College Special Collections, Baltimore (Z8048 .K44 1968).

26. Wells discusses this friendship appreciatively in *Reading Austen in America*, 185–207.

27. For example, a generation earlier the famous collecting couple Henry and Emily Folger proceeded in exactly the same manner. Their heavily annotated copy of James Orchard Halliwell-Phillips (1820–1889), *A Calendar of the Shakespearean Rarities*, 2nd ed., ed. Ernest E. Baker (London: Longmans, Green, 1891), shaped their collections for the Folger Shakespeare Library (W.a.199).

28. K[aren]. E. Attar, "Jane Austen at King's College Cambridge," *Book Collector* 51.2 (2002): 197–221, quoted at 205 and 206.

29. In 1997 Gilson published a facsimile reprint of his 1982 bibliography, with a new introduction and only a modest list of corrections and additions. He continued to collect books even beyond 1997, since a few items in the collection remain listed as "unseen" even in the amended bibliography. Before 1997, Gilson was assisted by his "friend Mr. John Jordan," who had "formed a collection of editions and issues 'not in Gilson'" (1997 ed., xxxvi). Sadly, John Jordan's extensive collection of books not in Gilson is currently being sold, piecemeal, by a bookseller in Bath as my own book goes to press.

30. Attar, 206–7.

31. "The real power and value of stereotyping, which had been widely regarded with such suspicion in the 1810s and 1820s, was proved when stereotypes and the harder electrotypes were worked to their limits in order to meet demands from a reading public used to the idea of cheap books." David McKitterick, ed. *Cambridge History of the Book in Britain*, vol. 6, *1830–1914* (Cambridge: Cambridge University Press, 2009), 86. For a description of the technology and its influence

in America, see Michael Winship, "Printing with Plates in the Nineteenth-Century United States," *Printing History* 5.2 (1983): 15–26. American professional habits and storage practices differed from British ones, but stereotyping lowered book prices on both sides of the Atlantic.

32. See William St. Clair, "Following up *The Reading Nation*," chapter 20 in McKitterick, 704–35, quoted at 719. St. Clair admits that true capacity was hard to calculate, noting that even the plates could be reproduced—but only before they became worn, since further duplication cannot sharpen the type.

33. See Gilson, *Bibliography*, at E12: "Sense and Sensibility. London: George Routledge and Co., Soho Square, 1849."

34. See Gilson, *Bibliography*, at E41: "187_. Sense and Sensibility. London: Routledge. (Ruby Series)," which he identifies as "A reprint of E12."

35. All seven of these undated versions identify the publisher as "London / George Routledge and Sons / The Broadway, Ludgate / New York: 416 Broome Street," imprint wording that dates them to at least 1866. The reason is that in 1865 the firm moved to new premises at 7 Broadway in Ludgate, becoming ". . . and Sons" only after Edward Routledge joined his brother Robert as a partner in 1866. See James J. Barnes and Patience Barnes, "George Routledge (1812–1888), publisher," in *Oxford Dictionary of National Biography* (2004).

36. See Keynes, entry 52. Gilson notes that the Boston Public Library has an undated copy, cataloged as 1874, with the expanded imprint quoted above, allowing—at the very least—for a variant. By 2005, when Gilson published his article, he had found at least the one Ruby copy with a frontispiece. David Gilson, "Later Publishing History with Illustrations," in *Jane Austen in Context*, edited by Janet Todd (Cambridge: Cambridge University Press, 2005), 121–59, at 130 and 132.

37. See definition of "edition," in John Carter and Nicolas Barker, *ABC for Book Collectors*, 8th ed. (New Castle, DE: Oak Knoll Press; London: British Library, 2006).

38. See advertisement in *Notes and Queries*, March 26, 1870, insert following 334. Gilson dates Bentley's launch of this new edition to December 13, 1869.

39. See Gilson, *Bibliography*, E34, E35, E37-39. Gilson does not record the half-crown cloth versions in Chapman & Hall's Select Library of Fiction series. See also Sampson Low, *The English Catalogue of Books*, Vol. 2 for 1863–1872 (London: Low and Searle, 1873), 18, accessed via Hathi Trust Digital Library.

40. Advertisement in the *Athenaeum* 2215 (April 9, 1870): 474.

41. See Low, 18. "Fancy covers" usually referred to colored paper wrappers.

42. I traced the inscription "*Pavey/Mansfield*" to Reverend Alfred Pavey, who in 1873 became vicar of Mansfield Parish Church in Nottinghamshire. Although contemporary, the inscription does not help date the edition definitively.

43. This Routledge design also appears on a reprint of *Emma* in green cloth, suggesting that consumers could choose among casings of different colors.

44. In the illustration, Elinor and Marianne sit on a bed. Gilson describes this image in an undated Boston Public Library copy. *Bibliography*, at E41.

45. See Marc Flandreau, *Anthropologists in the Stock Exchange: A Financial History of Victorian Science* (Chicago: University of Chicago Press, 2016), 23, and corresponding note 15 on 311.

46. *Census Returns of England and Wales, 1871*, in the National Archives of the UK, class *RG10*, piece *114*, folio *60*, page *28*, GSU roll *838766*, accessed via Ancestry.com.

47. *Census Returns of England and Wales, 1891*, in the National Archives of the UK, class *RG12*, piece *71*, folio *125*, page *30*, GSU roll *6095181*, accessed via Ancestry.com.

48. Quoted in Joshua Rothman, "The History of Loving to Read," *New Yorker*, February 2, 2015. Gilbert Ryle wrote an essay entitled "Jane Austen and the Moralists" in the *Oxford Review* 1 (1966), complimenting Austen with the term he himself coined, calling her "a moralist in a thick sense."

49. The abbreviation "aff^te" stands for "affectionate." The inserted advertisement also lists Routledge's "Jane Austen's Novels. In 5 vols. Fcap. 8vo, cloth, price 10s. 6d." None of these examples, however, fit this ad's description of an enlarged edition.

50. The final page of the handlist identifies the printer as "J. Ogden and Co. Printers, 172, St. John Street, B. C."

51. Low's *The English Catalogue of Books*, vol. 3 for 1872–80 (London: Low, Searle & Rivington, 1882), 23; quoted at 555.

52. The older Ruby copy in blue cloth is inscribed with the name "*Hitching Lion.*"

53. In *How to Do Things with Books in Victorian Britain* (Princeton, NJ: Princeton University Press, 2012), historian Leah Price looks to everything from crumbs, pennings, pressings, and stains as she considers the things readers do with books besides reading them.

54. See Wellesley College, *Wellesley College Record, 1875–1900* (Wellesley, MA, 1900). A brother's obituary provides family context: "Aaron C. Thayer Dies; Lawyer Here 30 Years," *New York Times*, December 17, 1933, 37. Aaron was a Harvard graduate and "grand nephew of H. B. Claflin, Dry Goods Merchant."

55. *Mansfield Park* (London: George Routledge and Sons, Limited / Broadway, Ludgate Hill / Glasgow, Manchester, and New York, n.d.). The final page of text, 443, gives the name of the printer as "Woodfall & Kinder, Printers, 70 to 76 Long Acre, London, W.C," an address used after 1889.

56. Low's *The English Catalogue of Books*, vol. 4 for 1881–89 (London: Sampson Low, Marston & Co., 1892). records up to the first twenty-seven titles of the *Pansy Books*. Since the Thayer copy ad for this series matches that list, adding only three further titles printed in 1890, the advertisement dates this copy to sometime in 1890.

57. For Gilson's account of the illustration in the edition of 1883, see his *Bibliography*, E62.

58. See Alan Gribben, *Mark Twain's Library: A Reconstruction*, 2 vols. (Boston: G. K. Hall, 1980), 1:32–34, at 34.

59. All of Twain's remarks quoted from Gribben, 32–33.

60. Alan Gribben records a Clemens copy of *Mansfield Park* (Leipzig: Bernhard Tauchnitz, 1867), noting that the Mark Twain Library's accession list shows that Clara Clemens donated it in 1910. When I enquired in June 2017, the staff was unable to locate it in the collection and presumed it lost. Gribben does not describe the binding.

61. William Shakespeare, *As You Like It* (Leipzig: Bernhard Tauchnitz, 1868), part of Joyce Trieste Library, Harry Ransom Center, University of Texas–Austin (PR 2803 A2 D9 1868 JJT).

62. Jane Austen, *Mansfield Park*, The Parlour Library (London: Simms and M'Intyre, Paternoster Row; and Donegall Street, Belfast, 1851). See Gilson, *Bibliography*, E18: "no copy in original binding seen."

63. Quoted from "Kennedy v. George," National Archives of the UK, reference C 17/3/128. Ellen Martha Horwood was baptized on January 12, 1825, in the Parish of Islington, Middlesex. In that parish record, her mother's name is "Martha Capiern" and her father, Samuel Horwood, appears as "Butcher." London Metropolitan Archives.

64. See entry in the Parish Registry of St. Mary, Hornsey, in the County of Middlesex, February 24, 1854. London Metropolitan Archives. The marriage was not an altogether happy one. Ellen bore her husband six children before he abandoned her on December 13, 1869. In 1870 she sued him in divorce

court for "protection of earnings" to safeguard the property she had amassed since his desertion by her own industry, still as a seller of meat. Her petition was refused. National Archives of the UK, *England & Wales, Civil Divorce Records, 1858–1916*.

65. Edward Mogg, *Mogg's New Picture of London and Visitors' Guide to Its Sights* (London: E. Mogg, 1844), 41.

66. For a full inventory of the Woolfs' Austens, see Julia King and Laila Miletic-Vejzovic, *The Library of Leonard and Virginia Woolf: A Short Title Catalog* (Pullman: Washington State University Press, 2003). The Woolf collection now at Washington State University represents a substantial portion—four thousand strong—of the books that the Woolfs inherited, bought, were given, and published.

67. *Pride and Prejudice*, Everyman's Library series (London, New York: Dent and Dutton, 1906); and *Pride and Prejudice*, 3rd ed., 2 vols. (London: Thomas Egerton, 1817), the Library of Leonard and Virginia Woolf collection at MASC, Washington State University (MASC PR4034.P7 1906 and MASC PR4034 .P7 1817). On the front free endpaper of the first volume, John Maynard Keynes wrote: "Virginia from JMK, Christmas 1932." For Christmas 1936, Woolf gave him a copy of *Orlando Furioso* signed on its flyleaf by Jane Austen. Woolf acquired it from the Austen-Leigh family. In her turn, Woolf inscribed it to Keynes. That marvel of accumulated provenance resides in Special Collections at King's College, Cambridge.

68. Virginia Woolf to Lytton Strachey, May 26, 1919, quoted in *Virginia Woolf: The Critical Heritage*, ed. Robin Majumdar and Allen McLaurin (London: Routledge, 1975, reprint 2003), 227.

69. *Sense & Sensibility* and *Emma*, Everyman's Library series (London and New York: Dent and Dutton, 1906), the Library of Leonard and Virginia Woolf collection at MASC, Washington State University (MASC PR4034.S4 1906 and MASC PR4034.E5 1906). See Gilson, *Bibliography*, E107 and 110.

70. For insights into the financial attitudes and chaotic domestic arrangements of the Woolf household, see Alison Light, *Mrs. Woolf and the Servants* (New York: Bloomsbury; reprint, 2009).

71. Virginia Woolf, *Orlando: A Biography*, Oxford World's Classics series (Oxford: Oxford University Press, 2008), 165.

72. Virginia Woolf, "Jane Austen," *Common Reader*, 1925, quoted in Southam, *Jane Austen: The Critical Heritage, Volume 2*, 281.

73. Anne Olivier Bell, ed., *The Diary of Virginia Woolf* (London: Hogarth Press, 1984), Sunday, March 31, 1940, p. 277, accessed through the UK's *Reading Experience Database, 1450–1935* (*RED*), www.open.ac.uk/Arts/reading/UK/, Record Number 19026. Crowdsourced by volunteers and housed by the English Department of the Open University, The *RED* holds more than thirty thousand records of reading experiences by British subjects—both famous and not. The database is open access: www.open.ac.uk/Arts/reading/UK/.

74. Jane Austen, *Northanger Abbey–Persuasion*, illust. by Hugh Thomson and intro. by Austin Dobson (London, 1897). From the library of H. G. Wells, Harry Ransom Center (Temp Au747 no 1897). Amy Catherine Wells, née Robbins, was his second wife and a former student.

Vignette II

1. *Emma* (London: G. Routledge and Co., Farrington Street; and 18, Beekman Street, New York, 1857). See Gilson, *Bibliography*, E25.

2. Obituary, *Gentleman's Magazine* 215 (July 1863): 111. Her middle name is mistakenly given as Emily.

3. See *Fowler's Commercial Directory of the Lower Ward of Renfrewshire for 1836–37* (Paisley: Fowler, 1837), 246.

4. *Ayrshire OS Name Books, 1855–57*, OS1/3/42/136, https://scotlandsplaces.gov.uk.

5. *Fowler's Commercial Directory*, 248.

6. See the mezzotint by John Le Conte, *Major Morris, Moorburn, Largs*, in the British Museum, (2010,7081.4473).

CHAPTER 1

1. William St. Clair, "Following up *The Reading Nation*," chapter 20 in McKitterick, 715.

2. Gilson, *Bibliography*, A3, p. 24.

3. Rose, 49.

4. The difference in length between the Simms & M'Intyre Parlour Library edition of *Mansfield Park* in 1847 and that of 1851 amounts to a reduction by 44 pages of a 332-page book, a significant cost savings.

5. See Gilson, *Bibliography*, E15, where he mentions being unable to locate a copy in original paper boards.

6. Gilson surmises, "Presumably Simms & M'Intyre had come to some arrangement with Bentley." *Bibliography*, 244.

7. See John Carter, ed., *New Paths in Book Collecting: Essays by Various Hands* (Freeport, NY: Constable, 1934; reprint, 1967). In this collection, Michael Sadleir offers a working definition: "'Yellow-back' was the nickname given to the particular type of cheap edition evolved about the middle of last century for display and sale on railway bookstalls. It was usually (but not always) a cheap edition of fiction; it usually (but not always) cost two shillings; its basic colouring was usually (but not always) yellow—to which last characteristic, not surprisingly, it owed its *soubriquet*" (127).

8. For an unsurpassed account of the immense competition in this book format, see Chester W. Topp, *Victorian Yellowbacks & Paperbacks, 1849–1905*, 9 vols. (Denver: Hermitage Antiquarian Bookshop, 1995).

9. See Gilson, *Bibliography*, at E23 and E25. On the basis of uncanny similarities, Gilson astutely observes that Routledge's yellowback of *Mansfield Park* in 1857 was set from the Simms & M'Intyre version of 1851. Similarly, Routledge set its yellowback of *Emma* in 1857, the year Bentley's copyright to this text officially expired, from a Simms & M'Intyre copy dated 1849.

10. Gilson includes this image in black and white in "Later Publishing History," 136.

11. While the threat of falling into the ha-ha is a double entendre that may not need much explaining, for other instances of erotic humor in the Sotherton scene, see Jill Heydt-Stevenson, *Austen's Unbecoming Conjunctions: Subversive Laughter, Embodied History* (New York: Palgrave Macmillan, 2005). The Bodleian Library has made the entire text of its 1857 copy of Routledge's Railway Library edition of *Mansfield Park* available for viewing online, including the original boards: http://dbooks.bodleian.ox.ac.uk/books/PDFs/600069550.pdf. Gilson inspected this copy (see *Bibliography*, E23).

12. Growing interest in all things Austen has prompted the Bodleian Library to also put their 1883 copy of this Routledge *Pride and Prejudice* online: http://dbooks.bodleian.ox.ac.uk/books/PDFs/600070025.pdf.

13. See Elizabeth James, "Sale of the Standard Novels: An Unobserved Episode in the History of the House of Bentley," *Library*, 5th series, 33 (1978): 58–62. The sale took place on February 28, 1856, and announcements in *The Athenaeum* of the impending auction mentioned Austen's works specifically. The short account of the auction in the *American Publishers' Circular* of March 1, 1856, notes that the Austen plates sold, as a set of five, for a mere £70, while "the whole sale of copyright and stock of the Standard Novels is said to have realized upwards of £10,000" (192).

14. Gilson suspects that Bentley himself purchased the Austen plates for later use. Gilson, *Bibliography*, 230.

15. Devoney Looser's deference to Bentley follows Gilson's lead: "With Bentley's firm hold on Austen's copyright, with regular reprinting, and with her slow if steady growth in readership over the course of the nineteenth century, these illustrations enjoyed a virtual visual monopoly for nearly four decades" (20).

16. The series was best documented by William Todd and Ann Bowden in a monumental bibliography covering all the English-language editions published by Tauchnitz. See William B. Todd and Ann Bowden, *Tauchnitz International Editions in English 1841–1955: A Bibliographical History* (New York: Bibliographical Society of America, 1988). The Harry Ransom Center, University of Texas at Austin, holds their working collection of copies.

17. See Michele K. Troy, *Strange Bird: The Albatross Press and the Third Reich* (New Haven, CT: Yale University Press, 2017).

18. Anthony Mandal and Brian Southam, eds., *The Reception of Jane Austen in Europe* (London: Continuum, 2007), 3.

19. Tauchnitz added *Sense and Sensibility* as title 735; *Emma* was the last of the Austen novels to join, at number 1645.

20. See Todd and Bowden, 46.

21. The inscription found in her *Pride and Prejudice* reads: "*Eveline Fane./Rome. February 1885.*" At some point, she added a bookplate to each volume. Decades later, Eveline added "*To Violet Fane/From Eve*" in a more mature hand. She signed over each of the volumes in the set to Violet, sometimes adding the date 1904. The copies of Heman Burr and Eveline Hamlyn Fane are in Sandra Clark's collection.

22. Quoted from Record Number 27531 in the *Reading Experience Database, 1450–1945* maintained by the Open University UK, accessed July 13, 2017, www.open.ac.uk/Arts/reading/UK/.

23. See Southam, *Critical Heritage*, 122–23.

24. Bautz, 115.

25. Sutherland, 6; and Gilson, "Later Publishing History," 128.

26. Gilson, *Bibliography*, E61 and E75.

27. Gilson, *Bibliography*, E65 and E66. Gilson identifies the *Pride and Prejudice* image as Mr. Collin's proposal. His estimate of 1884 for the first Routledge sixpenny version does not match the dates of 6d. print runs found by Bautz in the Routledge ledgers.

28. The colophons name different printers: "Butler and Tanner, The Selwood Printing Works" printed the edition with the woodcut of Darcy giving Elizabeth his letter, and "Ballantyne, Hanson and Co." printed the versions with the proposal scene on the cover. These names cannot help pinpoint dates, since both firms were of long duration, but whereas Ballantyne had a history of literary printing, Butler and Tanner gained a reputation for religious texts.

29. Guy Dicks, *The John Dicks Press* (printed by the author, 2006), 32.

30. Anne Humphreys, "John Dicks's Cheap Reprint Series, 1850–1890s: Reading Advertisements," in *Media and Print Culture Consumption in Nineteenth-Century Britain*, ed. Paul Raphael Rooney and Anna Gasperini (London: Palgrave/Macmillan, 2016), 93–110, at 97.

31. See Alan R. Young, *Steam-Driven Shakespeare* (New Castle, DE: Oak Knoll Press, 2017), 178–79.

32. Gilson, *Bibliography*, E72. Bautz, who located two copies of *Pride and Prejudice*, one in the British Library and another in a private collection, reproduces in her article some of the internal illustrations by John Proctor (1836–1914). A battered copy of the 1901 reprint survives among the Alberta and Henry Burke books at Goucher College, Baltimore (RARE PR4034. P7 1887). See figure 1.12.

33. Low's *English Catalogue of Books for 1901* (London: Sampson Lowe, Marston, 1902) gives the republication date of this title by Dicks, priced at 6d., as August 1901.

34. Quoted in Neil Genzlinger, "New 'Room' Arrives, with a Different View," *New York Times*, April 11, 2008. Harry Evans may or may not be the "H. Evans" who gets the barest of mentions in Simon Houfe, *The Dictionary of British Book Illustrators and Caricaturists, 1800–1914* (Woodbridge, Suffolk: Antique Collectors' Club, 1978): "black and white artist, contributing to The Rambler, 1897" (297).

35. The best of Harry Evans's internal illustrations include Willoughby's windy rescue of Marianne, his cutting off of her hair lock, his refusal to acknowledge her at the London gathering, and his confession to Elinor. Two further images—of characters stepping into a generic carriage and of the backs of Lucy and Elinor before a bland Edward—are drab.

36. For an assessment of the eight *Mansfield Park* illustra-tions by Victorian illustrator Frederick Gilbert (1827–1902), see Looser, at 46–47. The illustrations for the installments of *Sense and Sensibility* are by W. A. Cranston, although Dicks's sixpence edition was illustrated by Harry Evans.

37. Gilson, *Bibliography*, records the Dicks serializations at E68 and E69 but does not indicate prices or multiple formats. This information was supplied by Andrew King, at University of Greenwich, whose research into publisher John Dicks is available on his website, https://blogs.gre.ac.uk/andrew king/2013/08/25/john-dicks-publisher-and-dicks-english-library-of-standard-works/.

38. Anne Humphreys, "Dicks, John Thomas (bap. 1818, d.1881), publisher," in *Oxford Dictionary of National Biography* (online 2004).

39. *Bow Bells*, March 2, 1881, quoted in Humphreys's *ODNB* entry "Dicks, John Thomas."

40. See Gilson, *Bibliography*, E4. The two confirmed titles are *Elizabeth Bennet; or Pride and Prejudice* and *Mansfield Park* (Philadelphia: Carey and Hart, 1845). Both were offered for 25 cents each, announced as "Complete in one volume" and produced by "T.K. & P.G. Collins, Printers" in tight double columns as 100 and 115 pages of text, respectively. As physical objects, these cheap productions anticipate the size and look of the later sixpenny editions sold in Britain.

41. Thanks to Sophie Reynolds at Jane Austen's House Museum, I was able to inspect the copy in person and so quote from the bound advertisement within.

42. For the 1833 retail price, see Orville A. Roorbach, *Bibliotheca Americana*, 4 vols. (New York: P. Smith, 1939), 1:35, accessed via Hathi Digital Trust Library. Roorbach, whose catalog of American publications includes reprints and original works from 1820 to 1852, records the publisher as Carey, Lea & Blanchard.

43. Unrecorded by Gilson, one copy survives in the Cleveland Public Library (824.74 L128).

44. See Gilson, *Bibliography*, E50, E51, E52, E56, E56a, E59, and F1. Gilson records seeing copies of these magazine-style editions in the Library of Congress, but some of them appear to now be lost. The Austen titles in the Seaside Library series may have remained in print through 1894, the year *Emma*, *Lady Susan*, *Mansfield Park*, *Northanger Abbey*, *Pride and Prejudice*, and *Sense and Sensibility* appear in Warren E. Price, *Paper-Covered Books: A Catalogue* (San Francisco: W. E. Price, 1894), a trade catalog of in-print paperbacks, accessed via Hathi Digital Trust Library.

45. WorldCat (OCLC) records only two surviving copies of *Pride and Prejudice* in the Franklin Library series (New

York: Harper & Brothers, 1880), one of which survives in the Harry Ransom Center, trimmed and bound with other issues (-Q- 808.8 F854 v.2 no.5). Numbers in this bound copy are trimmed down to 8 x 11 inches, whereas loose, untrimmed survivors of non-Austen numbers suggest the original size was closer to 9 x 13 inches.

46. Testimonial by *Aberdeen Free Press*, quoted in advertisement pages of a Manchester Library copy of Elizabeth Gaskell's *Mary Barton* (London and Manchester: W. H. White & Co., 1892), in the collection of Sandra Clark.

47. Gilson constructed his initial entry for this title, E77, without seeing a copy, although by 1997 he reports having found one but gives no further details. *Bibliography*, xxxvii. That copy was donated to Kings College as part of his collection (Gilson.A.Se.1892) and is bound in the same manner as the copy of his friend John Jordan, which was described in a 2018 catalog by George Bayntun, a bookseller in Bath.

48. From advertisement in Manchester Library copy of *Mary Barton* in the collection of Sandra Clark.

49. Full-page advertisement signed George Newnes, Ltd., in *The Bookseller*, January 14, 1896, 76.

50. See the entries for "New Journalism" and "Newnes, George (1851–1910)" in *The Dictionary of Nineteenth-Century Journalism in Great Britain and Ireland*, ed. Laurel Brake and Marysa Demoor (Gent, Belgium: Àcademia Press; London: British Library, 2009), 443 and 448.

51. Advertisement in *The Bookseller*, January 14, 1896, 76.

52. On July 6, 1885, Stead published the first installment of *The Maiden Tribute of Modern Babylon* in the *Pall Mall Gazette* (London).

53. [W. T. Stead], "How to Get the Millions to Read: Why Not Penny Popular Novels?" *Review of Reviews* 12 (December 1895): 543.

54. [W. T. Stead], "Wanted, A Reading Revival: Some Practical Suggestions for Reading Revivalists," *Review of Reviews* 13 (January–June 1896): 461–68.

55. [Stead], "Wanted," 466.

56. [W. T. Stead], "Our Penny Publications" *Review of Reviews* 14 (July–December 1896): 85–86, at 85.

57. [Stead], "Our Penny Publications," 86.

58. Joseph O. Baylen, "Stead's Penny 'Masterpiece Library,'" *Journal of Popular Culture* 9.3 (Winter 1975): 710–25, at 719.

59. WorldCat (OCLC) records a total of four copies.

60. Advertisement in *Journal of Education* (October 1904): 695. Also, Gilson, *Bibliography*, E146.

61. *Publishers' Circular and Booksellers' Record* (May 20, 1922): 509.

62. W. H. D. Rouse, introduction to *Emma*, by Jane Austen (London: Blackie & Son, 1921), 3–4, at 4.

63. Rouse, 3.

64. For a colorful account of this publisher's revolutionary series, see R. Alton Lee, *Publisher for the Masses: Emanuel Haldeman-Julius* (Lincoln: University of Nebraska Press, 2017).

65. In order of appearance, the women who follow Austen: Madame de Staël, Charlotte Brontë, Elizabeth B. Browning, George Sand, George Eliot, Christina G. Rossetti, and Mrs. Humphrey Ward. This same collection of quotations was also published as Little Blue Book No. 304, entitled *What Great Women Learned About Men* (Girard, KS: Haldeman-Julius, 1922).

66. Jane Austen, *Pride and Prejudice*, sixpenny version shown in figure 1.10 (London: George Routledge and Sons, Limited, n.d.), 27.

67. Founded in 1922, *Reader's Digest* flourished in the 1930s. The monthly circulation in 1930 was 250,000, and it grew to 4 million by the end of the decade.

68. The Book-of-the-Month Club was founded in 1926 and the Literary Guild in 1927, although both institutions had their biggest impact upon publishing in the 1930s.

69. The series title University Classics may sound familiar, because it was also used by the University Publishing Company of Lincoln, Nebraska, producer of educational books and materials from 1898 to 1962. That company published their University Classics series from 1924 to 1935, with just over a dozen clothbound titles in dust jackets, complete with introductions, explanatory notes, and study questions for use in the classroom. The same series title was wielded a third time by Packard and Company of Chicago, between 1941 and 1947.

70. As little is known about the short-lived publishing house of Appleby & Company, here is the eclectic list of their additional titles: *Autobiography of Benjamin Franklin; Autocrat of the Breakfast Table*, by Oliver Wendell Holmes; *Christmas Stories*, by Charles Dickens; *Frankenstein*, by Mary Shelley; *Gulliver's Travels*, by Jonathan Swift; *Kidnapped*, by Robert Louis Stevenson; *The Little Minister*, by James M. Barrie; *Manon Lescaut*, by Antoine Francois Prevost; *Père Goriot*, by Honoré de Balzac; *Picture of Dorian Gray*, by Oscar

Wilde; *Silas Marner*, by George Eliot; *Short Stories*, by Fiodor Dostoievski; *Treasure Island*, by Robert Louis Stevenson; *Two Years before the Mast*, by Richard Dana; *The Vicar of Wakefield*, by Oliver Goldsmith; and *Wuthering Heights*, by Emily Brontë.

71. On December 16 and 30 in 1939, *Publishers' Weekly* lists *Short Stories*, by Fiodor Dostoievski, as containing 248 pages and costing 10 cents.

72. Some titles were also sold individually in curious lightweight bindings of embossed paper over boards that similarly lacked frills, although these were issued in both green and red. From a distance, the embossed paper pattern on these boards mimics leather, with a printed border that imitates gilt.

73. Thomas Carlyle, "The Hero as Man of Letters: Johnson, Rousseau, Burns," lecture 5 in *Sartor Sartorus* (Boston: Dana Estes and Charles E. Lauriat, 1884), 377–416, at 385.

74. Some Appleby editions still circulate plentifully on retail sites as "vintage paperbacks." However, WorldCat lists a mere fifteen titles held in libraries around the world, and only in single-digit quantities. Gilson does not record either of the Austen reprints by Appleby.

75. See Gilson, *Bibliography*, E191, E202, and E203.

76. Jane Austen, *Pride and Prejudice* (London: Everybody's Books, 1946). Quotations are from the front and back covers.

77. *Publishers' Weekly*, November 18, 1939, p. 1925.

78. *New York Times*, June 19, 1939, 34. Endorsements came from Nicholas Murray Butler, Hendrik Willem Van Loon, Christopher Morley, Lowell Thomas, Clifton Fadiman, Will Durant, and Dale Carnegie. Pocket Books's first ten titles were *Lost Horizon*, by James Hilton; *Wake Up and Live!*, by Dorothea Brande; *Five Great Tragedies*, by William Shakespeare; *Topper*, by Thorne Smith; *Murder of Roger Ackroyd*, by Agatha Christie; *Enough Rope*, by Dorothy Parker; *Wuthering Heights*, by Emily Brontë; *The Way of All Flesh*, by Samuel Butler; *The Bridge of San Luis Rey*, by Thornton Wilder; and *Bambi*, by Felix Salten.

79. See Albert N. Greco, Jim Milliot, and Robert M Wharton, *The Book Publishing Industry*, 3rd ed. (New York: Routledge, 2014).

80. For the numbers, see Louis Menand, "Pulp's Big Moment: How Emily Brontë met Mickey Spillane," *New Yorker*, January 15, 2015, online.

81. For a fuller discussion of the swagger and impact of pulps, see Paula Rabinowitz, *American Pulp: How Paperbacks Brought Modernism to Main Street* (Princeton, NJ: Princeton University Press, 2014).

82. On the inside, pages 403–5 do provide information "About the Author" that dispels such misapprehension.

Vignette III

1. William R. O'Byrne, *Naval Biographical Dictionary: Comprising the Life and Services of Every Living Officer in Her Majesty's Navy* (London: John Murray, 1849), 35.

2. Service Record for Captain Andrew Baird, National Archives of the UK, ADM 196/3/190.

3. "My dear Cassandra, Frank is made.—He was yesterday raised to the rank of Commander, & appointed to the Petterel Sloop, now at Gibraltar." Jane Austen to her sister Cassandra, December 28, 1798, in Deirdre Le Faye, ed., *Jane Austen's Letters*, 4th ed. (Oxford: Oxford University Press, 2011), 33.

4. For the naval careers of Francis and Charles Austen, see J. H. Hubback and Edith C. Hubback, *Jane Austen's Sailor Brothers* (London: John Lane, 1906). For a great book that applies this naval context to Austen's fictions, see Brian Southam, *Jane Austen and the Navy* (London: Hambledon and London, 2000).

5. Jane Austen, *Mansfield Park*, Captain Baird's copy (Belfast and London: Simms & M'Intyre and W. S. Orr & Co., 1846), 266.

6. As testimony to the professional mythology of heroic beginnings on a sloop, Patrick O'Brian's *Master and Commander* (1969) opens with Lt. Jack Aubrey receiving a letter promoting him into the sloop *Sophie* as commander. By the novel's end, Jack in the *Sophie* takes the fictional 32-gun frigate *Cacafuego*, a feat that puts to shame even Wentworth's triumph. Jack's victory is based on Thomas Cochrane's taking of the 32-gun *El Gamo*, so famous that it was the subject of a painting.

CHAPTER 2

1. William Thomas Stead, "Where Britons Are Holding Their Own: The Story of Pears' Soap," *Review of Reviews* 24 (July–December 1901): 437–45, at 445.

2. Stead, "Pears' Soap," 443.

3. Morgen Witzel, *Management History: Text and Cases* (Abingdon, UK: Routledge, 2009), 123.

4. See Gilson, *Bibliography*, E60. The Bodleian Library's copy of the yellowback version of Routledge's 1883 *Sense and*

Sensibility can be viewed online at http://dbooks.bodleian.ox-.ac.uk/books/PDFs/600070026.pdf. Compare its first page to figure 2.3.

5. Exceptional among book historians, Thomas Tanselle and Sue Allen have been calling attention to nineteenth-century publishers' bindings as a lacuna in bibliographies for decades. In 1967 Tanselle argued for more systematized descriptions of bindings in nineteenth-century cloths, outlining how subjectivity in descriptions of color creates ambiguity. See his article, "A System of Color Identification for Bibliographical Description," *Studies in Bibliography* 20 (1967): 203–34. The problems so eloquently outlined by Tanselle may have found a partial solution in digital imaging.

6. In my copy, ownership marks may have been removed, as meticulous yellow endpapers allow for the possibility of a repair in even this cheap book. A watermark of the front of the free endpaper of my copy reads "Desmond Bond."

7. See Edward Hubbard and Michael Shippobottom, *A Guide to Port Sunlight Village* (Liverpool: Liverpool University Press, 2005); Adam Macqueen, *The King of Sunlight* (London: Corgi, 2004), 125.

8. A similar advertising list was bound with a Lily Series copy of E. P. Roe's *Opening of a Chestnut Burr* (London, New York, and Melbourne: Ward, Lock, and Co., n.d.) inscribed "*To Jack with Grandma's love./Xmas 1890.*" That inventory only goes up to number 91 of the Lily Series, however, whereas Austen's *Emma* is listed as number 121 in a similar inventory of the Lily titles attached to *Ben-Hur* in the Pansy series. Handlists and inscriptions can narrow dates for undated reprint series.

9. The New York Public Library catalog estimates the date of its Ward & Lock *Emma* to be 1889, listing it as No. 164 in a "Select Library of Fiction" series, with 435 pages, the same page count as my Lily Series copy. The NYPL also lists a copy of *Sense and Sensibility* as No. 163 in that same series, with 331 pages, as well as copies of *Pride and Prejudice* (340 pages) and *Northanger Abbey–Persuasion* (440 pages). Gilson notes the first two NYPL copies in entries for Ward & Lock 1881 editions of *Sense and Sensibility* and *Emma* (E53 and E57). In both cases he assumes that the later Ward & Lock books were reprints, reasoning that "the series numbering seems not to have been constant." He duly admits, "No copy seen," with "(details derived from E57 and from assumption)." *Bibliography*, 256. Thus, while Gilson nowhere mentions a Lily Series, he does allow for the existence of differently packaged Ward & Lock reprints.

10. See volume two, devoted to "Ward & Lock," in Topp.

11. Macqueen, 124.

12. Macqueen, 44–45.

13. The Lever novel reprinted under the Lever Bros. label in the 1890s is *The O'Donoghue: A Tale of Ireland Fifty Years Ago.*

14. An advertisement in the *Review of Reviews* in 1893 promises the following monthly giveaways during 1894 in each of eight districts: 200 books at 5s., 300 at 3s. 6d., 400 at 2s. 6d., 500 at 2s., and 1,000 at 1s. That makes for a total of 2,400 winners of books per month in each of the eight districts that year, or 230,400 books as giveaways for 1894 alone.

15. Gilson, *Bibliography*, E71, quoted at 262. My copy of the Cassell edition in their hallmark red cloth lacks the ad, but it does record one reader's actual response to *Sense and Sensibility*. The copy is inscribed to "*O: Parkin/Jan 1st 1888*," and, at the back, a penciled annotation in an elegant hand roughly contemporary with the date of the inscription reads, "*I have read this book not entirely, but far enough to make me feel bored enough to get angry at myself for reading so much of it, and thereby laying me open to the same fault with which I charge it, viz. extremely stupid.*" The last two words are doubly underlined for emphasis.

16. Early versions of the Pears' Soap optical illusion (one extant copy is inscribed in pencil "*Jubilee year 1884*") featured two large "strobic circles" and the nearby directive "Please place this in your Scrap Book." Soon, the advertisement increased the circles from two to seven, as in figure 2.11.

17. See Price, *Books in Victorian Britain.*

18. Obituary, "Thomas J. Barratt Dead: Chairman of the Firm of A. & F. Pears an Advertising Genius," *New York Times*, April 27, 1914, 11.

19. Simon Stokes, *Art and Copyright* (Oxford, UK: Hart, 2001), 167. See also "Jane Austen Trade Mark" in *Reports of Patent, Design, and Trade Mark Cases* 117.23 (2000): 879–92.

20. Since there are no library copies listed in WorldCat (OCLC), I would like to again thank Emma Lea and Lady Martine J. Roberts for reaching out to me about their copies.

21. Because some readers may wish to check whether their go-to authors and books, too, circulated as Lever giveaways, here is a list of the additional titles that appear only on the earlier Lever list (in the order of their appearance): *Leila, Zanomi, The Caxtons, Falkland, Lucretia, Coming Race, Kenelm Chillingley, Pausanias, What Will He Do With It?* (2 vols.), *The Parisians*

(2 vols.), *My Novel* (2 vols.), *A Strange Story, Sketches by Boz, Lancashire Witches, Rockwood, Rob Faithful, Poor Jack, Settlers in Canada, Bunyan's Pilgrim's Progress, Rory O'More, Sceptres and Crowns, Old Helmet, Barry Lyndon, Bret Harte's Tales, Macaria, Inez, Ingoldsby Legends, Roderick Random,* and *Frank Farleigh.*

22. Jane Austen, *Sense and Sensibility* (London: Miles & Miles, Foresters' Hall Place, Clerkenwell Road, E.C., n.d.).

23. Jane Austen, *Sense and Sensibility* (London: Miles & Miles, 3 Leicester Place, Little Saffron Hill, E.C., n.d.). I suspect this location is later than the one on Clerkenwell Road, based upon inscriptions in other Miles & Miles copies with this imprint address.

24. According to WorldCat (OCLC), a lone copy of *Melbourne House* survives from the Miles & Miles undated Marguerite Series at the Bibliothèque Nationale de France. OCLC: 458868629.

25. Jane Austen, *Mansfield Park* (London: Miles & Miles, [1900]). The British Library derives this date "from presentation bookplate in copy." The bookplate reads: "Cleveland Rd: Girls' School Ilford 1899–1900. Awarded to Lilian Hill for perfect attendance. [signed by Head Teacher]." OCLC: 558097031. Since books used as school prizes tended to be new, this date seems a sensible estimate.

26. Jane Austen, *Sense and Sensibility* (London: Standard Authors Publishing Company, 59, 60 & 61, Hatton Garden, E.C., n.d.).

27. Jane Austen, *Sense and Sensibility* (London: Londoner Press, 13 Clerkenwell Road, E.C., n.d.).

28. This Miles & Miles *Pride and Prejudice* measures 21 centimeters in height, instead of the Marguerite Series format of 19 centimeters. This is the same larger size as reported by the British Library for their circa 1900 Miles & Miles edition of *Mansfield Park.*

29. There are only two recorded survivors of the Miles & Miles Sundial Series in WorldCat (OCLC), a copy of *Robinson Crusoe* at the New York Public Library and another of *Home Influence: A Tale for Mothers and Daughters* at the Bodleian. The latter copy bears a handwritten inscription with the date 1897. *Sense and Sensibility* was also offered in this binding style.

30. See Gilson, *Bibliography,* E62. While I was unable to inspect the British Library's copy of the Miles & Miles *Mansfield Park,* I did inspect another copy of the same version in private hands and confirmed that it, too, was printed from the 1883 Routledge plates.

31. The genetic chain that I trace here leaves out many other shoddy reprints of Austen that went unrecorded and uncollected when stereotype plates traveled through multiple hands. For example, at the dawn of the twentieth century, publishers still trafficked in cheap Austens made from Bentley's old 1833 plates, after many decades of use by Chapman & Hall and Ward & Lock.

32. John Spiers, *Books for the Million: Popular Book Publishing in Late-Victorian and Edwardian Britain* (Brighton, UK: Edward Everett Root, 2018), 3.

Vignette IV

1. See *The Royal Court Guide, and Fashionable Directory,* 1842 (London: George Virtue, 1842), 40, GoogleBooks online.

2. *Census Returns of England and Wales, 1851,* Kew, Surrey, England, in National Archives of the UK, Public Record Office, 1851, class HO107, piece 1489, folio 520, page 4, GSU roll 87816, accessed via Ancestry.com.

3. *England, Church of England Marriages and Banns, 1754–1932,* in London Metropolitan Archives, London, England, reference number p89/mry2/070, accessed via Ancestry.com. See also the exceptionally well-documented Wikipedia entry for Edward Henry Cooper.

4. *Census Returns of England and Wales, 1861,* Kew, Surrey, England, in National Archives of the UK, Public Record Office, 1861, class RG9, piece 45, folio 105, page 10, GSU roll 542562, accessed via Ancestry.com.

5. Jane Austen, *Northanger Abbey* and *Persuasion* (London: Simms and M'Intyre, Paternoster Row; and Donegall Street, Belfast, 1850), 47.

6. *Memoirs of the Royal Astronomical Society,* vol. 20 (London: Royal Society, 1851), 218, GoogleBooks online.

CHAPTER 3

1. Jane Austen, *Pride and Prejudice,* 2nd ed., 3 vols. (London: Printed for T. Egerton, 1813), in Harry Ransom Center, University of Texas–Austin (An Au74pr 1813a). It bears the ownership signature of "Frances Morgan," wife of financier J. Pierpont Morgan (1837–1913) and appears to have been her personal reading copy.

2. Ezekiel Blomfield, *The Life of Jesus Christ, with the History of the First Propagation of the Christian Religion, and the Lives of the Most Eminent Persons in New Testament.* In 1813 it appeared twice, both times with a Bungay imprint, one for "Brightly and Childs" and another for "T. Kinnersley." The imprint infor-

mation is missing from the scraps reused to bind the Austen. Comparisons of the layout against copies of both imprints could determine which one was repurposed. Information gleaned through such binding accidents can reveal networks in the print trade, supplying the stuff of bibliographical detection.

3. Peter Knox-Shaw, *Jane Austen and the Enlightenment* (Cambridge: Cambridge University Press, 2009), 9.

4. John Henry Newman to Mrs. John Mozley in 1837, quoted in *Jane Austen, Emma: A Casebook*, ed. David Lodge (Nashville, TN: Aurora, 1969), 49.

5. William Dean Howells, *Criticism and Fiction* (New York: Harper, 1891), 73. In 1769, David Garrick (1717–1779) had turned Shakespeare's own line from *Romeo and Juliet* into the public deification of its author in his "Ode" at Stratford.

6. Hallam Tennyson Baron Tennyson, *Alfred Lord Tennyson: A Memoir by His Son* (New York: McMillan, 1905), 47, entry for August 23, 1867.

7. Constance Hill, *Jane Austen: Her Homes and Her Friends* (London: John Lane, 1902), v. The book's illustrations were provided by Ellen G. Hill. For a fuller discussion of this work in the locus of Austen fandom, see Looser, 8–10.

8. *Nation*, February 27, 1902, 177.

9. See Irene Collins, *Jane Austen and the Clergy* (New York: Hambledon and London, 2002); Michael Giffin, *Jane Austen and Religion* (New York: Palgrave, 2002); and Laura Mooneyham White, *Jane Austen's Anglicanism* (Burlington, VT: Ashgate, 2011).

10. *Sense and Sensibility*, 2 vols. (London: H. G. Clarke and Co., 66, Old Bailey, 1844). No. 21 in Clarke's Cabinet Series.

11. *The English Maiden: Her Moral and Domestic Duties*, 5th ed. (London: H. G. Clarke and Co., 278 Strand, 1849), quoted from "Advertisement to the First Reader" in the preliminaries. Since, in 1841, the advertisement is signed "H. G. C.," Clarke himself is the probable author.

12. H. G. Clarke's Gothic flyer bears the imprint "Vizetelly Brothers and Co., Printers and Engravers, Peterborough Court, 135 Fleet Street." In Morgan Library, Gordon Ray Box 13. The Vizetelly Brothers specialized in color printing.

13. *Manchester Times*, October 19, 1844. *The Amber Witch* was a German literary hoax of 1838 purporting to document a genuine seventeenth-century witchcraft trial. Incidentally, it was a favorite of young Oscar Wilde's. Frances Anne Butler was the pen name of actress Fanny Kemble (1809–1893), Sarah Siddons's niece.

14. Gilson, *Bibliography*, E2 and E3.

15. Looser, 164.

16. See *London Gazette* 1 (1846): 303. James Hayward and David Adam carried on the business at 66 Old Bailey.

17. The notice to the trade in the *Publishers' Circular* on June 1, 1848, announces the upcoming "sale of the remaining stock of Clarke's Cabinet Series of new and popular works," scheduled for June 3. The fact that the notice lists many titles "in morocco elegant, cloth and quires" confirms that the fancy morocco bindings were part of the publisher's ready stock.

18. The earliest record of Clarke at this address is in the *Post Office London Directory* of 1843 (London: Kelly & Co.), accessed via Hathi Trust Digital Library.

19. Some attribute this anonymous work to H. G. Clarke and others to Artemas Bowers Mussey. The positive review in the *Northern Star* (London), October 16, 1841, 3, gives no hint of the author's identity, other than presuming that he is a man.

20. On July 18, 1843, Henry Green Clarke married Ann Briggs Sissison (1817–1861), the daughter of a "commercial traveler," at St. Marylbone, Middlesex. The register lists Henry's father's name as "George Clarke, Surgeon." On April 5, 1862, he married again, this time to Elizabeth Hannah Grayburn, "spinster" daughter of a shipowner. See London Metropolitan Archives; *Church of England Parish Registers, 1754–1931* (p89/mry1/214) and West Yorkshire Archive Service; *Yorkshire Parish Records* (RDP44/15/1), all three sources accessed via Ancestry.com.

21. "Henry Green Clark (sued as H. G. Clarke), formerly of no. 34 Granville-Square, Bagnigge-wells-road, Middlesex, and of No. 66, Old Bailey, London, Bookseller, Publisher, and Printer, for a short period in copartnership in same business with James Hayward and David Adam, of No. 18½, Paternoster-row, London, then lodging at Dulwich-common, Dulwich, Surrey, formerly Clerk to said Messrs. Hayward and Adam and latterly Reader to a Printer, and late of No. 87 Cornwall-street, Stamford-street, Blackfriars-road, Surrey, not in business or employment." *London Gazette* 1 (1847): 44.

22. Guidebooks and maps remained the staple of H. G. Clarke's business. In 1855 he sold his handbook to the British Museum and popular guides to London at 252 Strand. His guides and modeling kits appear on a bibliography prepared for the tercentenary of Shakespeare's birth in 1864, including *The Little Modeller, or How to Make Shakspeare's Birth-place* (London: H. G. Clarke and Co.). Lest my reader think such printed kits were Clarke's invention, see Suzanne Karr Schmidt, *Interactive and Sculptural Printmaking in the Renaissance* (Leiden: Brill, 2017).

23. At the Oxford Bible Depository, at 106 High Street,

pocket Bibles sold in a variety of styles at escalating price points: "common sheep binding, embossed roan, illuminated binding, strong grained binding, and turkey morocco." *Jackson's Oxford Journal*, February 12, 1848. I found only one non-Bible instance of "illuminated binding" in advertising, which was for a small, elite, series of children's titles, including *Puss in Boots* and *Cinderella*, published by William S. Orr of Paternoster Row and advertised as "Books for Christmas Parties." See *Examiner* (London), December 16, 1843.

24. Motivations of early collectors are not always transparent: in the "Books Wanted to Purchase" section of the *Publishers' Circular* on September 1, 1869, S. and T. Gilbert inquire about "History of Prostitution. An American work" alongside "Amber Witch. Imp. 32mo. In Clarke's Cabinet Series."

25. Gilson, *Bibliography*, E2, 239. Gilson's friend Dorothy Warren owned an unhoused copy of Clarke's *Sense and Sensibility* with only its illuminated title page as the presumed "wrapper." This copy, which joined Gilson's own books at King's College circa 1990, may have been a fragile survivor of the remaindered "quires" mentioned in the 1848 sale (see note 17). Karen Attar, 220, offers an image of Warren's copy.

26. In some copies, a variant imprint includes the firm's address, "108 Hatton Garden." One of two original advertisement posters for the series, held by the Morgan Library, New York City, bears this same firm's full imprint: "Gregory, Collins and Reynolds, 108 Hatton Garden."

27. *Bent's Monthly Literary Advertiser*, June 1844.

28. Sweden's first women's rights organization, established in 1884, bears her name: the Fredrika Bremer Organization.

29. Anonymous review of a New York edition of *The Magic Goblet, or the Consecration of the Church of Hammarby*, in *North American Review* (April 1845): 492–93, quoted at 492.

30. The Sunday School Union was founded in 1803. See William Henry Watson, *The Sunday School Union: Its History and Work* (London: Sunday School Union, 1869).

31. Gilson does not have an entry for the Blackie's Crown Library edition of *Northanger Abbey*, although his description of an 1895 edition by Blackie for an earlier series matches the page divisions of text and anonymous introduction. Gilson, *Bibliography*, E81. This may, indeed, be Blackie's repackaging of Austen from their earlier series, with a frontispiece by Paul Hardy.

32. Jane Austen, *Northanger Abbey*, Crown Library series (London, Glasgow, and Bombay: Blackie and Son Limited, n.d.), v–vi, vi, v. Quoted from Winnie Valentine's copy.

33. See M. H. Spielmann and Walter Jerrold, *Hugh Thomson:*

His Art, His Letters, and His Charm (London: A. &. C. Black, 1931), at 2.

34. See *Slater's Royal National Directory of Scotland*, part 1 (1903), 283.

35. For a glimpse of Victorian pub life on Sundays, see Graham Hill, "Bar and Saloon London," in *Living London*, ed. George R. Sims, 2 vols. (London: Cassell, 1902), 2:286–92. Some pubs did have six-day licenses, but even in London the notion of Sunday closings, "though rigorously paraded, is rarely strictly observed" (290). Instead, "the greater number of publicans are entitled to open on Sundays between the hours of one and three in the afternoon and from six to eleven in the evening" (291).

36. Jennifer Davies, *Oxford Dictionary of National Biography* entry for "John Blackham (1834–1923), founder of the Pleasant Sunday Afternoon movement" (October 3, 2013).

37. See The Local History of Stoke-on-Trent, England, www.thepotteries.org, for an index of pottery jobs.

38. The membership number was reported in an article in the *Staffordshire Advertiser* in 1890 and reprinted in the same paper on October 26, 1940, in the "50 Years Ago" section, p. 3.

39. Quoted in Davies, *Oxford Dictionary of National Biography*.

40. See J. Haddon, *Review of the Churches* 6 (1894): 173.

41. For a brief history of the PSA movement in the context of adult Sunday schools, see William Dwight Porter Bliss and Rudoph M. Binder, eds., *The New Encyclopedia of Social Reform* (London: Funk and Wagnalls, 1909), 510.

42. William McIlroy himself seems to have funded the building of a Congregationalist church in his resident town of Reading, a fact repeated in historical accounts of that church. In January 1901, Mrs. Clarke McIlroy laid the foundation stone of Tabernacle Mission on Union Street in Hanley, the advertised location in 1907 of PSA meetings (Sunday afternoons "at 3:15"). See "Business Reference Guide to the Potteries, Newcastle & District," in the *Staffordshire Sentinel* guide for 1907, under listings for religious houses. Mrs. Clarke McIlroy's name is carved into the building's foundation stone, along with the date.

43. Gary Kelly, "Religion and politics," in *Cambridge Companion to Jane Austen*, ed. Edward Copeland and Juliet McMaster (Cambridge: Cambridge University Press, 1997), 149–69, at 156.

44. Jane Austen, *Mansfield Park* (Hanley: McIlroy's Pleasant Sunday Afternoon Depôt, n.d.), 436.

45. Jane Austen to Cassandra Austen, January 24, 1809,

quoted from Le Faye, 177. Hannah More had a strong reputation as a religious writer. See Collins, 145–47. Collins also writes of Jane's distaste for evangelical preaching (216–17), making an inventory of her disagreements with evangelicalism(186–88).

46. Jane Austen to Fanny Knight, November 18–20, 1814, in Le Faye, 292.

47. See John R. Turner, "Title-Pages Produced by the Walter Scott Publishing Co. Ltd.," *Studies in Bibliography* 44 (1991): 323–31.

48. John R. Turner, *The Walter Scott Publishing Company: A Bibliography* (Pittsburgh: University of Pittsburgh Press, 1997), xv.

49. Rose, 131.

50. Turner, "Title-Pages," 323.

51. See Turner, *Bibliography*, 158–59. *Mansfield Park* was the only Jane Austen title published by Scott's printing house. I own a copy dated 1892, with the imprint "Walter Scott / London: 24 Warwick Lane, Paternoster Row 1892." That text block is identical to the PSA edition and printed from the same plates, but the copy is bound with a frontispiece illustration not in the PSA survivor. Gilson, *Bibliography*, lists the Scott reprint at E74. According to Turner, it was reissued in 1904.

52. Turner, "Title-Pages," 324.

53. All three were available from the same British seller on eBay in separate listings during April 2017. According to Turner, *Bibliography*, the *Pickwick Papers* was first reprinted by the Scott firm in 1884 and *The Heart of Midlothian* between 1887 and 1892, while *Old Mortality* is listed as "Published but not seen" with no date estimated (590).

54. In May 2017, a British bookseller advertised on AbeBooks a copy of J. G. Edgar's *How I Won My Spurs* (Ward & Lock, 1900), complete with "a Pleasant Sunday Afternoon Society Prize label" dated 1901. At the same time, eBay offered a copy of J. Arthur Baine's *Life and Explorations of Fridtjof Nansen* (Walter Scott, 1897), containing a "Pleasant Sunday Afternoon" prize label from the Motherwell chapter, made out to Robert Mack for "25 attendances during the Term ending March 1898."

55. Turner, "Title-Pages," 331.

56. Rose, 250.

57. Sidney E. Berger, *The Dictionary of the Book: A Glossary for Book Collectors, Booksellers, Librarians, and Others* (Lanham, MD: Rowman & Littlefield, 2016), 289.

58. The binding is signed "OJ."

59. *Publishers' Weekly* 1826 (January 26, 1907): 189.

60. e. e. cummings owned both volumes of the Nelson set, although not in a yapped binding. Both volumes are part of the extensive Cummings Library at the Harry Ransom Center (PZ A93 PR4 and PZ A93 Se 1907).

61. Around this time, McMillan and Company reprinted their popular 1895 edition of *Sense and Sensibility*, illustrated by Hugh Thomson and introduced by Austin Dobson, in a smaller format, on thin paper, and in red limp leather (see Gilson, *Bibliography*, E113). The title page has thin red borders, and the edges of the cover, although drooping, do not yapp. As a result, the McMillan packaging is not as overtly "religious" as the Nelson. All extant McMillan copies I examined date from 1912 and are in terrible condition, perhaps proving librarians right.

62. See Gilson, *Bibliography*, E95, for a description of the Methuen edition.

63. For anecdotal information about life in the Taft Hotel, see Stephen Lewis, *Hotel Kid: A Times Square Childhood* (Paul Dry Books, 2002). In 1931 Lewis, at 18 months, moved into the hotel, where his father was manager. He does not mention reading the Taft editions as a boy, presumably because it was only during the hotel's startup years that the books were promotional giveaways.

64. Sample Taft titles include James Matthew Barrie's *The Little Minister;* Arthur Conan Doyle's *Sherlock Holmes Detective Stories;* Robert Louis Stevenson's *Treasure Island,* *The Dynamiter,* and *Dr. Jekyll and Mr. Hyde,* bound with *Kidnapped;* Rudyard Kipling's *Soldiers Three and Other Stories;* and Jonathan Swift's *Gulliver's Travels.* WorldCat lists a baker's dozen of the Taft titles, but no copies survive in libraries of Austen, likely the series's sole female author.

65. George L. Gray, *Shakespeare Boiled Down* (Chicago: New Home Sewing Machine Co., 1890s), at Folger Shakespeare Library, Washington, DC (Sh. Misc. 267-792q).

66. C. Allan Gilbert (1873–1929), artist, *Horlick's Malted Milk Shakespearean Calendar 1908* (United States: Horlick's Malted Milk Co., 1907), Folger Shakespeare Library, ART Inv. 1145.

67. *An Album of Celebrities of British History* (London: Carreras Limited, ca. 1935), in author's collection.

68. Spielmann and Jerrold, 2. In Ireland, where Thomson spent his early years, the peacock was even more ubiquitous as a well-known Catholic symbol. One biographer assumes that Thomson's childhood was Catholic, explaining that London editor Comyns Carr gave young Thomson a chance because Carr "was also a discerning and Catholic-minded critic." Hep-

worth Dixon, "Hugh Thomson, Illustrator," *International Studio* 61.241–44 (March–June 1917): 120–29, quoted at 122.

69. See figure 2.4. Evelyn Waugh Collection, Harry Ransom Center (PR 4034 P7 1894 WAU).

Vignette V

1. *Harvard College, Class of 1877, Secretary's Report, No. IV, 1890* (Cambridge, MA: Riverside Press, 1890), 11, Google-Books online.

2. *Harvard College Report*, 11.

3. See Heman M. Burr's US passport application of 1895, in National Archives and Records Administration, roll 36, volume 065: "Germany," accessed via Ancestry.com.

CHAPTER 4

1. See Phil Baines, *Penguin by Design: A Cover Story, 1935–2005* (London: Allen Lane, 2007).

2. *Publishers' Weekly* 1714 (December 3, 1904): 1550.

3. Among the books discussed thus far, the onlay technique appears on the 1870s Routledge gift book with the oval image of a mother and daughter at prayer, figure I.6, in the introduction.

4. I found the wrapper on a copy of *Emma* with the name of Winston on the spine as publisher, even though the imprint is that of Coates, proving that Winston sold existing paper stock run off by Coates after taking over the business. He may have maintained the series for only as long as it took him to deplete existing stock.

5. For the fascinating lost history of the publisher's wrapper and jacket, see Mark Godburn, *Nineteenth-Century Dust Jackets* (New Castle, DE: Oak Knoll Press, 2016); and G. Thomas Tanselle, *Book Jackets: Their History, Forms, and Use* (Charlottesville, VA: Bibliographical Society of the University of Virginia, 2011).

6. George Romney's portrait is *Mrs. Tickell*, painted circa 1795. For description and provenance, see Julius Bryan, *Kenwood: Paintings in the Iveagh Bequest* (New Haven, CT: Yale University Press, 2003), 394–97. *Lady Bridges*, by Francis Cotes, painted before 1769, was engraved by James Watson and sold as a popular print. See the catalogue raisonné by Edward Mead Johnson, *Francis Cotes: Complete Edition with a Critical Essay and a Catalogue* (Oxford: Phaidon, 1976), 93, entry 254. Reynolds's portrait is *Mrs. Jane Braddyll* (1788), currently in the Wallace Collection. See David Mannings, *Sir Joshua Reynolds:*

A Complete Catalogue of His Paintings (New Haven, CT: Yale University Press, 2000), entry 238.

7. Cotes's painting is of Lady Fanny Bridges (1747–1825), the wife of Sir Brook Bridges (1733–1791), 3rd Baronet of Goodnestone Park in Kent. Her brood of eleven children included Elizabeth Bridges (1773–1808), wife of Jane Austen's brother Edward Knight. For more information on the connection between the Bridges family and Jane Austen, see the biographical index in Le Faye's edition of the *Letters*, 500–501.

8. See the announcement of the Laurel Library as being "in preparation." *Publishers' Weekly* 1326 (June 26, 1897): 1014.

9. The firm announced their New Alta Series in *Publishers' Weekly* 487 (May 14, 1881): 534.

10. Full-page announcement in the *Ladies Home Journal* 5.12 (November 1888): 26, signed "Cyrus H. K. Curtis, Publisher, 435 Arch Street, Philadelphia, PA."

11. Porter & Coates advertisement in *Publishers' Weekly* 448 (August 14, 1880): 178.

12. Eastlake's *Hints on Household Taste* (1868) soon revolutionized all manner of design, including the casings of books. The rich black scrollwork on this Porter & Coates cover typifies the style of the 1870s and early 1880s.

13. The Williamsburg Library Association accession records for 1876–1912 are now available online. On page 19 of the original ledger, this copy—No. 391 according to the label it still retains on the inside cover—was cataloged on April 6, 1877, along with "Philadelphia" copies of all of Austen's other novels. https://archive.org/details/accessionreco18761912will /page/19. The Celtic design in black contains the initials "PC" on the top board. It was printed by "Caxton Press of Sherman & Co., Philadelphia." The text on the spine, "Miss Austen's Novels," suggests a set.

14. This copy, bought from a Portland bookstore and now in my possession, was for many years in the library of Alfred Powers (1888–1984), author and historian of Oregon literature. The binding is green cloth with blind stamping on front and back and gilt lettering on the spine: "Miss Austen's Novels / Sense / and / Sensibility / Persuasion." The cover's decorative blind stamp is yet another recycled element, for it is the same as used by Ticknor & Fields, but with the firm's telltale initials removed from the central oval.

15. See Leslie Carol Ulven's pamphlet *The Story of Hubbard, Oregon* (Hubbard, OR, 1991), [6]. Since Ulven does not mention any trading post, and Hubbard's city hall, which does not license businesses, keeps no records of local establishments,

it's hard to narrow the "Trading Post" stamp to a specific date. By the time the *Salem Daily Capital Journal* reports a robbery in Hubbard on February 26, 1898, the town's main retail store is called "General Merchandise store of Geo. W. Beebe." The stamp may date nearer to the book's publication in 1875, before Hubbard's main store carried the name of an owner, but it could just as easily be a throwback nomenclature for a twentieth-century retailer of used books.

16. See Osgood's advertisement in *Publishers' Weekly*, March 4, 1876, 271. Without seeing any copies, Gilson tentatively lists only Osgood's *Pride and Prejudice* (1875) and *Mansfield Park* (1876). In WorldCat, however, further editions of *Emma* and *Mansfield Park* appear under the aegis of "Fields, Osgood & Co." in 1870, as well as Osgood's solo reprints of *Sense and Sensibility* in 1871 and 1873. WorldCat records only nine known copies in total of the five inventoried Osgood reprintings of Austen.

17. For the price paid for these plates, see *Publishers' Weekly*, April 1, 1876, 438. Osgood's retail price was $1.75 per volume.

18. See the account of day six of "The Book Trade-Sales," *New York Times*, September 22, 1870.

19. For statistics confirming the radical shrinking of the publishing trade in wartime, even in the North, see Michael Winship, "The American Book Trade and the Civil War," in *A History of American Civil War Literature*, ed. C. Hutchison (Cambridge: Cambridge University Press, 2015), 17–32.

20. See "Cost book, fair" (C: Jan. 1857-Apr. 1863. MS AM 2030.2 [16]), in Houghton Mifflin Company records, 1832–1944, Houghton Library, Harvard University. The digitized fair copy of the cost book has entries for "Jane Austen's Novels," starting on page 318, with cross-references, https://iiif.lib.harvard.edu/manifests/view/drs:52478795$176i. The cost-book entry for the first run of *Pride and Prejudice* in 1863 falls on the same page (324) as an identical order for 500 copies of *Uncle Tom's Cabin*. This accidental juxtaposition is entirely misleading as it does not reflect identical demand. Public fervor for Stowe's novel, which in 1852 sold 300,000 copies during its first year, had indeed slowed to a crawl just before the war. Ticknor & Fields, after buying both plates and copyright, was strategically rekindling public interest in Stowe's work with a steady supply of small batches of reprintings. See the essay posted by Michael Winship, "*Uncle Tom's Cabin*: History of the Book in the 19th-Century United States" (2007) on the University of Virginia's multimedia archive, http://utc.iath.virginia.edu/interpret/exhibits/winship/winship.html.

21. The official Sheet Stock Book, not digitized, records a total of 2,030 copies of *Pride and Prejudice–Northanger Abbey*, 1,609 of *Mansfield Park*, 1,528 of *Emma*, and 1,529 of *Sense and Sensibility–Persuasion*. The firm did not run the four titles off at once or in equal numbers; entries appear for the different titles in 1863, 1866, 1869, 1870, 1871, 1872, 1875, and 1876. Starting in 1871, the runs become smaller, as low at 96 for *Emma* in 1876. With the generous help of Michael Winship, I accessed the information in the Sheet Stock Book via microfilm (see especially pages 4 and 134).

22. See Jeffrey Gross, "Courtesy of the Trade," in *History of the Book in America*, vol. 3, *The Industrial Book, 1840–1880*, ed. Scott E. Casper, Jeffrey D. Groves, Stephen W. Nissenbaum, and Michael Winship (Chapel Hill: University of North Carolina Press, 2007), 139–48.

23. In his *Bibliography*, Gilson devotes a separate section to the "First American Editions" by Carey & Lea, 95–132, and enters the 1838 reprinting by Carey, Lea, & Blanchard as E1. See also David Kaser, ed., *The Cost Book of Carey & Lea, 1825–1838* (Philadelphia: University of Pennsylvania Press, 1963).

24. Wells, *Reading Austen in America*, 5 and 136.

25. David Gilson, "The Early American Editions of Jane Austen," *Book Collector* 18 (1969): 340–52, at 349.

26. See Emily Schultheis's article about the canonizing force of the early Carey & Lea editions: "Philadelphia and the Making of Jane Austen in the United States, 1816–1838," *Women's Writing* 25, special issue, "Bicentennial Essays on Jane Austen's Afterlives," ed. Annika Bautz and Sarah Wootton (October 2018): 454–67.

27. Wells, *Reading Austen in America*, 138. Eliza Susan Quincy (1798–1884) and Anna Cabot Lowell Quincy Waterston (1812–1899) of Boston were huge Austen fans who left behind letters and papers attesting to their fervor. As early as 1969, Gilson invokes the enthusiastic Quincy sisters, making them a veritable synecdoche for Austen's presumed American readership.

28. See entry for October 1862 in the Ticknor & Fields cost book for "Jan 1857–April 1863" (MS AM 2030.2 [16]), in Houghton Mifflin Company records, 1832–1944, Houghton Library, Harvard University. See also Obituary for George Ayres Leavitt, *Publishers' Weekly* 882 (December 22, 1888): 977–78, online. As auctioneer, Leavitt ran many trade sales, including the fall Regular New York Trade Sale on September 18, 1862 (the catalog of that trade sale is in the New York Public Library).

29. *American Publishers' Circular and Literary Gazette*, November 1, 1862.

30. The steel illustrations appear on engraved extra title pages and in no way resemble the frontispieces made subsequently for Porter & Coates. Instead, the engraved Derby & Jackson illustrations mimic the fronting images found in Richard Bentley's London editions. The engraved title in my copy of an 1861 reprint of *Sense and Sensibility* from Derby & Jackson's Standard Female Novelists is a serviceable counterfeit of an engraved Bentley title page—complete with similar fonts and layout—but for the name of the New York firm at the bottom. The American publisher evidently intended for his edition to follow in Bentley's footsteps and not those of his cheaper competitors.

31. See advertisement in *American Publishers' Circular and Literary Gazette*, July 25, 1857, 480.

32. See Gilson on the Derby & Jackson editions, *Bibliography*, E21, E22, E24, and E26. I quote from the original advertisement pages at the back of a Derby & Jackson copy of *Sense and Sensibility–Persuasion* in my own possession, dated 1857, in brown cloth with blind stamping on front and back boards.

33. See advertisements in *American Publishers' Circular and Literary Gazette*, September 1, 1855, and January 26, 1856, 11 and 56. See also Gilson, *Bibliography*, E19 and E20.

34. In 1849 George W. Briggs of Boston printed *Pride and Prejudice*, apparently from plates first used by Wilkins, Carter & Co. in 1848. See Gilson, *Bibliography*, E14 and E11.

35. At the fall 1856 New York trade sale, an Edward Stephens is listed as Bunce & Brother's successor. See advertisement in *American Publishers' Circular and Literary Gazette*, August 30, 1856, 531.

36. The Ticknor & Fields cost book records a payment of $14 on December 30, 1862, for repairs to the Austen stereotype plates: "Work: Examining & Repg." On November 15, the firm spent another $5 for electros of four fresh title pages and one advertisement. For an additional $14.25, Ticknor & Fields also purchased thirty-eight boxes, exclusively for the storing of these Austen stereotype plates. The large number of boxes indicates both the amount of metal involved and the storage habits of American publishers.

37. See Kevin H. O'Rourke and Jeffrey G. Williamson, *Globalization and History: The Evolution of a Nineteenth-Century Atlantic Economy* (Cambridge, MA: MIT Press, 1999).

38. See Gilson, *Bibliography*, E28, E29, and E30.

39. Michael Winship, "Manufacturing and Book Production" in *History of the Book in America*, vol. 3, *The Industrial Book, 1840–1880*, ed. Scott E. Casper, Jeffrey D. Groves, Stephen W. Nissenbaum, and Michael Winship (Chapel Hill: University of North Carolina Press, 2007), 40–69, at 59.

40. For a sumptuous visual history of the elegant American book from the Golden Age, see Richard Minsky, *The Art of American Book Covers, 1875–1930* (New York: George Braziller, 2010).

41. Baines, 46. William Grimmond drew the roundel of a sailing ship for the cover of Homer.

42. Vladimir Nabokov, *Lectures on Literature*, ed. Fredson Bowers (San Diego: Harcourt, 1980), 179. In the 1980s, the entire lecture, including the rant about the Pocket Book cover, was reprinted as an introduction to the Signet Classics paperback of Stevenson's novel.

43. *Emma*, SAS series, No. 25 (Torino: Editrice S.A.I.E., 1959), paperback, 189 pages. The translator is unnamed, but Gilson attributes a 1953 edition (at 214 pages by the same publisher) to Francesco Dall'Orso. Gilson, *Bibliography*, C128. The Goucher copy of the earlier hardback sports the same cover image.

44. With grateful thanks to Will Pritchard. Other movie images suggested by colleagues include posters of *Mutiny on the Bounty* (1962) and *That Hamilton Woman* (1941), duplicating the same man-woman-ship composition and the necessary naval uniform. A specific allusion may not have been intended, since the formulaic book cover is instantly recognizable as a generic movie moment.

45. See the advertisement in *Publishers' Weekly* 174.11 (September 15, 1958), 44.

46. "Bantam to Launch Low-Cost Classics Line," *Publishers' Weekly*, May 19, 1958, 30.

47. Five-star customer review, dated May 30, 2016, accessed on Amazon.com on June 29, 2017.

48. See Steven K. Galbraith, *Edges of Books: Specimens of Edge Decoration from Rit Cary Graphic Arts Collection* (Rochester, NY: Rit Cary Graphic Arts Collection, 2012). Goffered edges are crimped with heated irons; resulting patterns of indentation often resemble lacework.

49. Christopher Jobson, "New Paintings on Salvaged Books by Mike Stilkey," a blog review on *This Is Colossal*, July 10, 2014, www.thisiscolossal.com/2014/07/new-paintings-on-salvaged-books-by-mike-stilkey/.

50. Jenna Krajeski, "Mike Stilkey's Library," *New Yorker*, November 13, 2009, accessed online at https://www.newyorker.com/books/page-turner/mike-stilkeys-library.

Vignette VI

1. On the inside cover of volume 1, the bookseller appears to have noted in pencil that this copy is "very poor," along with the reduced price of £250. After 1854, someone made home repairs to many of the book's torn pages (e.g., in volume 1, pages 249, 250, and 295; and volume 2, page 217), using strips of the perforated tear-aways from sheets of penny postage stamps: one remnant reads, "Price 1ᵈ Per." Perforation on postage stamps became standard practice only in 1854.

2. Ernest Philip Alphonse Law, "List of Occupants of Private Apartments," in *History of Hampton Court Palace* (1891), 459. See also "Births, Marriages, and Deaths" notice in *Belfast Newsletter*, September 4, 1875. In the census of 1861, her occupation is given as "Right Honorable," while in the census of 1871 it is "Duke's Daughter."

3. In volume 2, one leaf (pages 199 and 200) is completely missing and has been replaced with two leaves of handwritten text, neatly bound into the repaired book. The handwriting here does not match Lady Isabella's.

4. Working backward from her comments in the final volume, I assume all the corrections in the same color of ink to be hers. She crosses out "an" in "The little visitor meanwhile was as an unhappy as possible" (1:22); she alters an initial description of Lady Bertram, "of little use and no beauty," to read "of little beauty and no use" (1:37); and she removes the "sweet" from "sweet wood" (1:195). Some underlinings of unknown origin survive in pencil. For example, repetition of phrasing in one of Julia's comments is underlined in pencil, and Edmund's long defense of the clergyman's role is similarly marked for special notice in the margin with pencil (1:126, 190–93).

5. I do not know what led to the de-attribution. From the mid-1830s through the early 1850s, newspapers announced a handful of publications by Lady Isabella St. John, including *Augustus Courtenay, and Other Tales*, 2 vols. (London: Shoberl, 1852). Some copies are now erroneously cataloged as by "Isabella Annie Fitzmaurice," who was born in 1863 and married to Frederick Robert St. John in 1882. Annie cannot therefore be the author of these earlier works. Lady Isabella St. John does not appear in the *Oxford Dictionary of National Biography*, and I hope others will discover more about the woman who wrote such formulaic Victorian romances.

6. *Athenaeum*, January 30, 1836, 86.

CHAPTER 5

1. Literary critic George Saintsbury (1845–1933) coined the term in his introduction to the Peacock Edition of *Pride and Prejudice* in 1894. In May 1924, Kipling's "The Janeites" appeared in *Story-Teller*, *MacLean's*, and *Hearst's International* magazines. A few years later, it was also included in *Debits and Credits* (1926), with minor cuts and alterations.

2. Looser, 164.

3. Quoted in Anna Broadway, "Pink Wasn't Always Girly: A Short History of a Complex Color," *Atlantic Monthly*, August 12, 2013, accessed at https://www.theatlantic.com/sexes/archive/2013/08/pink-wasnt-always-girly/278535/.

4. Jo B. Paoletti, *Pink and Blue: Telling Boys from Girls in America* (Bloomington: Indiana University Press, 2012), 85.

5. F. Scott Fitzgerald, *The Great Gatsby* (New York: Scribner, 2004), 122. In the 1920s, elite American fashion houses tried to shed the old working-class connotations associated with seersucker fabric. Steam engine workers, oil derrick men, and farm laborers wore seersucker suits in both pink and blue.

6. Paoletti, 91.

7. Paoletti, 92.

8. See Barbara Nemitz, ed., *Pink: The Exposed Color in Contemporary Art and Culture* (Ostfildern, Germany: Hatje Cantz Verlag, 2006).

9. Quoted from bound advertisement at the front of Jane Austen, *Sense and Sensibility* (New York: Bunce & Brother, 1856).

10. *Putnam's Monthly Magazine of American Literature Science and Art* 5 (May 1855): 554.

11. Full-page announcement in the *Ladies Home Journal* 5.12 (November 1888): 26.

12. See the advertisement in *Publishers' Weekly* 1286–87 (September 26, 1896): 547.

13. W.T. Stead, "Gift Literature: A First Batch of Christmas Books," *Review of Reviews* 8 (July–December 1893): 556.

14. Stead, "Gift Literature," 556.

15. The New Century Library edition, first issued by Thomas Nelson and Sons in 1903 (Gilson, *Bibliography*, E103), contained all six novels in two compact volumes: *Pride and Prejudice*, *Mansfield Park*, and *Northanger Abbey* in the first volume; *Sense and Sensibility*, *Emma*, and *Persuasion* in the second. They were later offered as "Two volume sets in special bindings." The heart-stamped binding style sold as a boxed

set, with the volumes dated 1905 and 1904, respectively, and the set may have been a special season's gift edition in 1906. In America, the per volume price for Austen in this edition differed according to "style of binding" ($1, $1.25, or $1.50). See the advertisements in *Publishers' Weekly* 1635 (May 30, 1903): 1299; and 1805 (September 1, 1906): 492. The first advertisement contains a picture that suggests the standard prices applied to editions without gilded hearts.

16. Nelson's children's version of the same setting of *Pride and Prejudice* sold in Britain for 2s. 6d. as part of the Famous Books series.

17. Rudyard Kipling, "The Janeites," in *Debits and Credits* (Kelly Bray, Cornwall: House of Stratus, 2009), 121–42.

18. Kipling, "Janeites," in *Debits and Credits*, 121–42.

19. Rudyard Kipling, "The Janeites," *Hearst's International Magazine*, May 1924, n.p.

20. See Annette M. LeClair, "In and Out of the Foxholes: Talking of Jane Austen during and after World War II," *Persuasions* 39 (2017): 100–111, esp. 100.

21. For an animated account of the ASE series, see Molly Guptill Manning, *When Books Went to War: The Stories That Helped Us Win World War II* (Boston: Mariner Books, 2014).

22. Jane Austen, *Persuasion*, with an introduction by Angela Thirkell (London: Williams & Norgate Ltd., Great Russell Street, 1946), dust jacket.

23. Sarah Bowen, "Angela Thirkell and 'Miss Austen,'" *Persuasions* 39 (2017): 112–25, at 119 and 121.

24. Angela Thirkell, introduction to *Persuasion*, by Jane Austen (London: Williams & Norgate Ltd., Great Russell Street, 1946), xiv, xii.

25. Monica Dickens, introduction to *Emma*, by Jane Austen (London: Williams & Norgate Ltd., Great Russell Street, 1947), ix, x.

26. Ann Bridge, introduction to *Mansfield Park*, by Jane Austen (London: Williams & Norgate Ltd., Great Russell Street, 1948), viii.

27. Editor Allan Hepburn reprints Bowen's introduction directly from the Williams & Norgate edition in *People, Places, Things: Essays by Elizabeth Bowen* (Edinburgh: Edinburgh University Press, 2008), 217–24.

28. In 1942, Bowen dramatized sections of Austen and Burney as radio broadcasts by the BBC; they were rebroadcast in 1948.

29. Elizabeth Bowen, introduction to *Pride and Prejudice*, by Jane Austen (London: Williams & Norgate Ltd., Great Russell Street, 1948), ix and viii.

30. In 1946, "a postponement was found necessary" in the production of Bowen's biography *Antony Trollope: A New Judgement*, a delay that adds to the impression of multiple postwar commitments. See "Notes and Queries," *Trollopian* 1.3 (September 1946): 55.

31. Daphne du Maurier, introduction to *Northanger Abbey*, by Jane Austen (London: Williams & Norgate Ltd., Great Russell Street, 1948), xiii.

32. Du Maurier, xiii–xiv.

33. Du Maurier, xiv.

34. Naomi Royde-Smith, introduction to *Sense and Sensibility*, by Jane Austen (London: Williams & Norgate Ltd., Great Russell Street, 1949), xiii.

35. Royde-Smith, xiii. An air raid followed by fire on April 16, 1941, rather than on August 18, 1940, destroyed Thavies Inn at Holborn Circus.

36. Jane Austen, *Más fuerte que el orgullo*, La Novela Rosa series (Barcelona: R. Plana, n.d. [1945]). Gilson, *Bibliography*, records this edition as C199.

37. For Austen's Spanish translations, see Aída Díaz Bild, "Still the Great Forgotten? The Reception of Jane Austen in Spain," in *The Reception of Jane Austen in Europe*, ed. Anthony Mandal and Brian Southam (London: Bloomsbury Academic, 2007), 189–205, quoted at 191.

38. Jane Austen, *Persuasión*, trans. M. Ortega y Gasset, Los Grandes Novelistas series (Madrid: Calpe, 1919). This small-format edition was also cheap, priced at 2½ pesetas.

39. See Sonia Núñez Puente, "La novela rosa como mascarada de la muerte de lo social: Concha Linares Becerra y María Mercedes Ortoll," in *Asparkia: Investigació feminista*, 19 (2008): 105–122.

40. Patricia O'Byrne, *Post-War Spanish Women Novelists and the Recuperation of Historical Memory* (Woodbridge, UK: Tamesis, 2014), 90.

41. Translation of historian Fernando Martínez de la Hidalga, quoted at Patricia O'Byrne, 90.

42. Patricia O'Byrne, 90.

43. See Patricia O'Byrne, 92.

44. Sonia Núñez Puente terms this ulterior function of the *novela rosa* "a sort of conservative modernity." See her article

"The Romance Novel and Popular Culture during the Early Franco Regime in Spain: Towards the Construction of Other Discourses of Femininity," *Journal of Gender Studies* 17.3 (September 2008): 225–36, at 226. I am grateful to Magdalena Novoa for directing me to this article.

45. Janice A. Radway, *Reading the Romance: Women, Patriarchy, and Popular Literature* (Chapel Hill: University of North Carolina Press, orig. 1984; reprint, 1991).

46. Magdalena Novoa gave invaluable help in assessing this translation. I would also like to thank Aída Díaz Bild, who confirmed the low quality of the 1945 translation.

47. Jane Austen, *Pride and Prejudice*, ed. Vivien Jones (London: Penguin Books, 2003), 332–33, and Austen, *Más fuerte que el orgullo*, La Novela Rosa series (Plana), 130.

48. Take, for example, the insertion of a gratuitous Spanish idiom into the lead-up to Mr. Collins's proposal: "On finding Mrs. Bennet, Elizabeth, and one of the younger girls together, soon after breakfast, he addressed the mother in these words." Austen, *Pride and Prejudice* (Penguin, 2003), 102. The translator tosses in a Spanish expression to stress the exquisite nature of Mr. Collins's timing: "*Ni cortó ni perezoso.*" Austen's sentence then translates into two: "*Poco después del almuerzo encontró juntas a la señora Bennet, a Isabel y a una de las hijas menores. Ni cortó ni perezoso le espetó a la primera.*" Austen, *Más fuerte*, 42. The result, though oddly colloquial, diminishes neither the integrity of Austen's plot nor her characters. Above all, nothing in the translation mutes or censors a scene that anticipates a young woman's radical refusal of parental authority and male desire. Instead, Mr. Collins's implied calculations may urge sympathy for Isabel's unrehearsed candor.

49. Austen, *Más fuerte*, 140.

50. The advertisement on the back cover shows the price in the Argentine peso (which used the $ sign) rather than in the peseta, used in Spain.

51. In the Airmont *Mansfield Park*, the designer of the cover image of a couple in period dress, by a tree, is identified only as "Edrien."

52. Artist Saul Lambert (1928–2009) designed the cover of the Perennial Classic of *Sense and Sensibility*.

53. See Looser, 182 and 185–88.

54. In 1963 Harvard first began awarding its degrees to Radcliffe students.

55. Joel Rickett, "Jane Austen Dives between the Chick Lit Covers," *Telegraph* (London), January 14, 2006, www.telegraph.co.uk/news/uknews/1507778/Jane-Austen-dives-between-the-chick-lit-covers.html.

56. See Lauren Schwartzberg, "Why Millennial Pink Refuses to Go Away" (March 19, 2017), in Cut, https://www.thecut.com/2017/03/why-millennial-pink-refuses-to-go-away.html.

Vignette VII

1. 1911 Census (288/A23/4). National Records of Scotland, accessed via Scotland's People website.

2. Statutory Registers Deaths 288/A 190. National Records of Scotland, accessed via Scotland's People website.

3. Statutory Registers Deaths 288/A 194. National Records of Scotland, accessed via Scotland's People website.

4. *UK, Outward Passenger Lists, 1890–1960*, May 28, 1915, Port of Departure, Glasgow, Scotland, accessed via Ancestry.com.

CODA

1. Gilson, *Bibliography* (1997 ed.), xxxvi.

SELECTED WORKS CITED

This is a selected list of contextual histories, academic books, and critical articles to assist further reading on wider subjects and enable scholarly consultation or verification. Other sources—such as specific editions or reprintings of Jane Austen's works, manuscripts in archives, advertisements, dictionary entries, census records, isolated collection items, directories, reference works, and newspapers—are cited in the notes and in the captions to the figures.

Attar, K[aren] E. "Jane Austen at King's College Cambridge." *Book Collector* 51.2 (2002): 197–221.

Baines, Phil. *Penguin by Design: A Cover Story, 1935–2005*. London: Allen Lane, 2007.

Baker, Nicholson. *Double Fold: Libraries and the Assault on Paper*. Original 2001; reprint, New York: Vintage, 2002.

Barchas, Janine. "Why K. M. Metcalfe (Mrs. Chapman) Is 'really the originator in the editing of Jane Austen.'" *RES: Review of English Studies* 68.285 (June 1, 2017): 583–611.

Bautz, Annika. "'In perfect volume form, Price Sixpence': Illustrating *Pride and Prejudice* for a Late-Victorian Mass-Market." In *Romantic Adaptations: Essays in Mediation and Remediation*, edited by Cian Duffy, Peter Howell, and Caroline Ruddell, 101–24. London: Routledge, 2013.

Baylen, Joseph O. "Stead's Penny 'Masterpiece Library.'" *Journal of Popular Culture* 9.3 (Winter 1975): 710–25.

Bliss, William Dwight Porter, and Rudoph M. Binder, eds. *The New Encyclopedia of Social Reform*. London: Funk and Wagnalls, 1909.

"Books in Millions: An Interview with Mr. Edmund Routledge." *Pall Mall Gazette*, December 4, 1888. Accessed via *British Library Newspapers: Part I, 1800–1900* database.

Bowen, Elizabeth. Introduction to *Pride and Prejudice*, by Jane Austen. London: Williams & Norgate, 1948.

Bowen, Sarah. "Angela Thirkell and 'Miss Austen.'" *Persuasions* 39 (2017): 112–25.

Brake, Laurel, and Marysa Demoor, eds. *The Dictionary of Nineteenth-Century Journalism in Great Britain and Ireland*. Gent, Belgium: Academia Press; London: British Library, 2009.

Bridge, Ann. Introduction to *Mansfield Park*, by Jane Austen. London: Williams & Norgate, 1948.

Broadway, Anna. "Pink Wasn't Always Girly: A Short History of a Complex Color." *Atlantic Monthly*, August 12, 2013. Accessed at https://www.theatlantic.com/sexes/archive/2013/08/pink-wasnt-always-girly/278535/.

Bryan, Julius. *Kenwood: Paintings in the Iveagh Bequest*. New Haven, CT: Yale University Press, 2003.

Carlyle, Thomas. "The Hero as Man of Letters: Johnson, Rousseau, Burns." Lecture 5 in *Sartor Sartorus*, 377–416. Boston: Dana Estes and Charles E. Lauriat, 1884.

Carter, John, ed. *New Paths in Book Collecting: Essays by Various Hands*. Freeport, NY: Constable, 1934. Reprint, 1967. Page references are to the 1967 edition.

Carter, John, and Nicolas Barker. *ABC for Book Collectors*. 8th ed. New Castle, DE: Oak Knoll Press; London: British Library, 2006.

"Cheap Books and Their Readers: An Interview with Mr. Routledge," *Pall Mall Gazette* (London), November 19, 1885. Accessed via database *British Library Newspapers: Part I, 1800–1900*.

Collins, Irene. *Jane Austen and the Clergy*. New York: Hambledon and London, 2002.

Díaz Bild, Aída. "Still the Great Forgotten? The Reception of Jane Austen in Spain." In *The Reception of Jane Austen in Europe*, edited by Anthony Mandal and Brian Southam, 189–205. London: Bloomsbury Academic, 2007.

Dickens, Monica. Introduction to *Emma*, by Jane Austen. London: Williams & Norgate, 1947.

Dicks, Guy. *The John Dicks Press*. Printed by the author, 2006.

Du Maurier, Daphne. Introduction to *Northanger Abbey*, by Jane Austen. London: Williams & Norgate, 1948.

Eliot, Simon, and Andrew Nash. "Mass Markets: Literature." In *Cambridge History of the Book in Britain*, vol. 6, *1830–1914*, edited by David McKitterick, 416–42. Cambridge: Cambridge University Press, 2009.

Flandreau, Marc. *Anthropologists in the Stock Exchange: A Financial History of Victorian Science*. Chicago: University of Chicago Press, 2016.

Galbraith, Steven K. *Edges of Books: Specimens of Edge Decoration from Rit Cary Graphic Arts Collection*. Rochester, NY: Rit Cary Graphic Arts Collection, 2012.

Genzlinger, Neil. "New 'Room' Arrives, with a Different View." *New York Times*, April 11, 2008.

Gettmann, Royal A. *A Victorian Publisher: A Study of the Bentley Papers*. Cambridge: Cambridge University Press, 1960.

Giffin, Michael. *Jane Austen and Religion*. New York: Palgrave, 2002.

Gilson, David. *A Bibliography of Jane Austen*. New Castle, DE: Oak Knoll Press, 1982. Rev. ed., 1997. Page references are to the 1997 edition unless otherwise indicated.

———. "The Early American Editions of Jane Austen." *Book Collector* 18 (1969): 340–52.

———. "Jane Austen's Text: A Survey of Editions." *Review of English Studies*, n.s., 53.209 (2002): 61–85.

———. "Later Publishing History with Illustrations." In *Jane Austen in Context*, edited by Janet Todd, 121–59. Cambridge: Cambridge University Press, 2005.

Godburn, Mark. *Nineteenth-Century Dust Jackets*. New Castle, DE: Oak Knoll Press, 2016.

Gray, George L. *Shakespeare Boiled Down*. Chicago: New Home Sewing Machine Co., 1890s.

Greco, Albert N., Jim Milliot, and Robert M. Wharton. *The Book Publishing Industry*. 3rd ed. New York: Routledge, 2014.

Greenfield, Susan Celia, and Audrey Bilger. "*Pride and Prejudice* Forever." *Los Angeles Review of Books*, January 27, 2013. https://lareviewofbooks.org/essay/pride-prejudice-forever.

Gribben, Alan. *Mark Twain's Library: A Reconstruction*. 2 vols. Boston: G. K. Hall, 1980.

Gross, Jeffrey. "Courtesy of the Trade." In *History of the Book in America*, vol. 3, *The Industrial Book, 1840–1880*, edited by Scott E. Casper, Jeffrey D. Groves, Stephen W. Nissenbaum, and Michael Winship, 139–48. Chapel Hill: University of North Carolina Press, 2007.

Haldeman-Julius, Emanuel, ed. *What Great Women Have Said about Men*. Girard, KS: Haldeman-Julius, 1922.

Halliwell-Phillips, James Orchard. *A Calendar of the Shakespearean Rarities*. 2nd ed. Edited by Ernest E. Baker. London: Longmans, Green, 1891.

Harman, Claire. *Jane's Fame: How Jane Austen Conquered the World*. Edinburgh: Canongate, 2009.

Heydt-Stevenson, Jill. *Austen's Unbecoming Conjunctions: Subversive Laughter, Embodied History*. New York: Palgrave Macmillan, 2005.

Hill, Constance. *Jane Austen: Her Homes and Her Friends*. London: John Lane, 1902.

Houfe, Simon. *The Dictionary of British Book Illustrators and Caricaturists, 1800–1914*. Woodbridge, UK: Antique Collectors' Club, 1978.

Howells, William Dean. *Criticism and Fiction*. New York: Harper, 1891.

Hubback, J. H., and Edith C. Hubback. *Jane Austen's Sailor Brothers*. London: John Lane, 1906.

Hubbard, Edward, and Michael Shippobottom. *A Guide to Port Sunlight Village*. Liverpool: Liverpool University Press, 2005.

Humpherys, Anne. "John Dicks's Cheap Reprint Series, 1850-1890s: Reading Advertisements." In *Media and Print Culture Consumption in Nineteenth-Century Britain*, edited by Paul Raphael Rooney and Anna Gasperini, 93–110. London: Palgrave/Macmillan, 2016.

James, Elizabeth. "Sale of the Standard Novels: An Unobserved Episode in the History of the House of Bentley." *Library*, 5th series, 33 (1978): 58–62.

Jobson, Christopher. "New Paintings on Salvaged Books by Mike Stilkey." Review on *This Is Colossal* blog, July 10, 2014. www.thisiscolossal.com/2014/07/new-paintings-on-salvaged-books-by-mike-stilkey/.

Johnson, Claudia. *Jane Austen's Cults and Cultures*. Chicago: University of Chicago Press, 2012.

Johnson, Edward Mead. *Francis Cotes: Complete Edition with a Critical Essay and a Catalogue*. Oxford: Phaidon, 1976.

Kaser, David, ed. *The Cost Book of Carey & Lea, 1825–1838*. Philadelphia: University of Pennsylvania Press, 1963.

Kelly, Gary. "Religion and Politics." In *Cambridge Companion to Jane Austen*, edited by Edward Copeland and Juliet McMaster, 149–69. Cambridge: Cambridge University Press, 1997.

Keynes, Geoffrey. *Jane Austen: A Bibliography*. London: Nonesuch, 1929.

King, Julia, and Laila Miletic-Vejzovic. *The Library of Leonard and Virginia Woolf: A Short Title Catalog*. Pullman: Washington State University Press, 2003.

Kipling, Rudyard. "The Janeites." *Hearst's International*, May 1924, n.p.

Knox-Shaw, Peter. *Jane Austen and the Enlightenment*. Cambridge: Cambridge University Press, 2009.

Krajeski, Jenna. "Mike Stilkey's Library." *New Yorker*, November 13, 2009. https://www.newyorker.com/books/page-turner/mike-stilkeys-library.

LeClair, Annette M. "In and Out of the Foxholes: Talking of Jane Austen during and after World War II." *Persuasions* 39 (2017): 100–111.

Lee, R. Alton. *Publisher for the Masses: Emanuel Haldeman-Julius*. Lincoln: University of Nebraska Press, 2017.

Le Faye, Deirdre, ed. *Jane Austen's Letters*. 4th ed. Oxford: Oxford University Press, 2011.

Levine, Lawrence W. *Highbrow/Lowbrow: The Emergence of Cultural Hierarchy in America*. Cambridge, MA: Harvard University Press, 1986.

Lewis, Stephen. *Hotel Kid: A Times Square Childhood*. Paul Dry Books, 2002.

Light, Alison. *Mrs. Woolf and the Servants*. New York: Bloomsbury. Reprint, 2009.

Lodge, David, ed. *Jane Austen, Emma: A Casebook*. Nashville, TN: Aurora, 1969.

Looser, Devoney. *The Making of Jane Austen*. Baltimore: Johns Hopkins University Press, 2017.

Macqueen, Adam. *The King of Sunlight*. London: Corgi, 2004.

Majumdar, Robin, and Allen McLaurin, eds. *Virginia Woolf: The Critical Heritage*. London: Routledge, 1975. Reprint, 2003. Page references are to the 2003 edition.

Mandal, Anthony, and Brian Southam, eds. *The Reception of Jane Austen in Europe*. London: Continuum, 2007.

Mannings, David. *Sir Joshua Reynolds: A Complete Catalogue of His Paintings*. New Haven, CT: Yale University Press, 2000.

McKitterick, David, ed. *Cambridge History of the Book in Britain*. Vol. 6, *1830–1914*. Cambridge: Cambridge University Press, 2009.

Menand, Louis. "Pulp's Big Moment: How Emily Brontë Met Mickey Spillane." *New Yorker*, January 15, 2015. Accessed online.

Minsky, Richard. *The Art of the American Book Covers, 1875–1930*. New York: George Braziller, 2010.

Mogg, Edward. *Mogg's New Picture of London and Visitors' Guide to Its Sights*. London: E. Mogg, 1844.

Nabokov, Vladimir. *Lectures on Literature*. Edited by Fredson Bowers. San Diego, CA: Harcourt, 1980.

Nemitz, Barbara, ed. *Pink: The Exposed Color in Contemporary Art and Culture*. Ostfildern, Germany: Hatje Cantz Verlag, 2006.

Núñez Puente, Sonia. "La novela rosa como mascarada de la muerte de lo social: Concha Linares Becerra y María Mercedes Ortoll." *Asparkia* 19 (2008): 105–22.

———. "The Romance Novel and Popular Culture during the Early Franco Regime in Spain: Towards the Construction of Other Discourses of Femininity." *Journal of Gender Studies* 17.3 (September 2008): 225–36.

O'Byrne, Patricia. *Post-War Spanish Women Novelists and the Recuperation of Historical Memory*. Woodbridge, UK: Tamesis, 2014.

O'Byrne, William R. *Naval Biographical Dictionary: Comprising the Life and Services of Every Living Officer in Her Majesty's Navy.* London: John Murray, 1849.

O'Rourke, Kevin H., and Jeffrey G. Williamson. *Globalization and History: The Evolution of a Nineteenth-Century Atlantic Economy.* Cambridge, MA: MIT Press, 1999.

Paoletti, Jo B. *Pink and Blue: Telling Boys from Girls in America.* Bloomington: Indiana University Press, 2012.

Porter, Dale H. *The Thames Embankment: Environment, Technology, and Society in Victorian London.* Akron, OH: University of Akron Press, 1997.

Price, Leah. *How to Do Things with Books in Victorian Britain.* Princeton, NJ: Princeton University Press, 2012.

Price, Warren E. *Paper-Covered Books: A Catalogue.* San Francisco: W. E. Price, 1894.

Rabinowitz, Paula. *American Pulp: How Paperbacks Brought Modernism to Main Street.* Princeton, NJ: Princeton University Press, 2014.

Radway, Janice A. *Reading the Romance: Women, Patriarchy, and Popular Literature.* Chapel Hill: University of North Carolina Press, 1984. Reprint, 1991.

Review of *Pride and Prejudice. Putnam's Monthly Magazine of American Literature Science and Art* 5 (May 1855): 554.

Rickett, Joel. "Jane Austen Dives between the Chick Lit Covers." *Telegraph* (London), January 14, 2006. Accessed online.

Rose, Jonathan. *The Intellectual Life of the British Working Classes.* 2nd ed. New Haven, CT: Yale University Press, 2010.

Royde-Smith, Naomi. Introduction to *Sense and Sensibility*, by Jane Austen. London: Williams & Norgate, 1949.

Sadlier, Michael. *XIX Century Fiction: A Bibliographical Record Based on His Own Collection.* 2 vols. London: Constable, 1951.

Schmidt, Suzanne Karr. *Interactive and Sculptural Printmaking in the Renaissance.* Leiden: Brill, 2017.

Schultheis, Emily. "Philadelphia and the Making of Jane Austen in the United States, 1816–1838." *Women's Writing* 25 special issue, "Bicentennial Essays on Jane Austen's Afterlives," edited by Annika Bautz and Sarah Wootton (October 2018): 454–67.

Southam, Brian. *Jane Austen: The Critical Heritage.* London: Routledge & Kegan Paul, 1969.

———. *Jane Austen: The Critical Heritage, Volume 2, 1870–1940.* London: Routledge & Kegan Paul, 1987.

———. *Jane Austen and the Navy.* London: Hambledon and London, 2000.

Spielmann, M. H., and Walter Jerrold. *Hugh Thomson: His Art, His Letters, and His Charm.* London: A. & C. Black, 1931.

Spiers, John. *Books for the Million: Popular Book Publishing in Late-Victorian and Edwardian Britain.* Brighton, UK: Edward Everett Root, 2018.

[Stead, W. T.]. "How to Get the Millions to Read: Why Not Penny Popular Novels?" *Review of Reviews* 12 (December 1895): 543–44.

———. "Our Penny Publications." *Review of Reviews* 14 (July–December 1896): 85–86.

———. "Wanted, A Reading Revival: Some Practical Suggestions for Reading Revivalists." *Review of Reviews* 13 (January–June 1896): 461–68.

———. "Where Britons Are Holding Their Own: The Story of Pears' Soap." *Review of Reviews* 24 (July–December 1901): 437–45.

Stokes, Simon. *Art and Copyright.* Oxford, UK: Hart, 2001.

Sullivan, Margaret. *Jane Austen Cover to Cover: 200 Years of Classic Covers.* Philadelphia: Quirk Books, 2014.

Sutherland, Kathryn. *Jane Austen's Textual Lives: From Aeschylus to Bollywood.* Oxford: Oxford University Press, 2005.

Tanselle, G. Thomas. *Book Jackets: Their History, Forms, and Use.* Charlottesville, VA: Bibliographical Society of the University of Virginia, 2011.

———. "A System of Color Identification for Bibliographical Description." *Studies in Bibliography* 20 (1967): 203–34.

Tennyson, Hallam Baron Tennyson. *Alfred Lord Tennyson: A Memoir by His Son.* New York: McMillan, 1905.

Thirkell, Angela. Introduction to *Persuasion*, by Jane Austen. London: Williams & Norgate, 1946.

Todd, William B., and Ann Bowden. *Tauchnitz International Editions in English 1841–1955: A Bibliographical History.* New York: Bibliographical Society of America, 1988.

Topp, Chester W. *Victorian Yellowbacks & Paperbacks, 1849–1905.* 9 vols. Denver: Hermitage Antiquarian Bookshop, 1995.

Troy, Michele K. *Strange Bird: The Albatross Press and the Third Reich.* New Haven, CT: Yale University Press, 2017.

Turner, John R. "Title-Pages Produced by the Walter Scott Publishing Co. Ltd." *Studies in Bibliography* 44 (1991): 323–31.

———. *The Walter Scott Publishing Company: A Bibliography.* Pittsburgh: University of Pittsburgh Press, 1997.

Watson, William Henry. *The Sunday School Union: Its History and Work.* London: Sunday School Union, 1869.

Wells, Juliet. *Everybody's Jane: Austen in the Popular Imagination.* London: Bloomsbury, 2011.

———. *Reading Austen in America.* London: Bloomsbury Academic, 2017.

Winship, Michael. "The American Book Trade and the Civil War." In *A History of American Civil War Literature*, edited by C. Hutchison, 17–32. Cambridge: Cambridge University Press, 2015.

———. "Manufacturing and Book Production." In *History of the Book in America*, vol. 3, *The Industrial Book, 1840–1880*, edited by Scott E. Casper, Jeffrey D. Groves, Stephen W. Nissenbaum, and Michael Winship, 40–69. Chapel Hill: University of North Carolina Press, 2007.

———. "Printing with Plates in the Nineteenth-Century United States." *Printing History* 5.2 (1983): 15–26.

———. "*Uncle Tom's Cabin:* History of the Book in the 19th-Century United States," 2007. University of Virginia multimedia archive, http://utc.iath.virginia.edu/interpret/exhibits/winship/winship.html.

Yaffe, Deborah. *Among the Janeites: A Journey through the World of Jane Austen Fandom.* Boston: Mariner Books, 2013.

Young, Alan R. *Steam-Driven Shakespeare.* New Castle, DE: Oak Knoll Press, 2017.

INDEX

Adult School Movement, 141

advertisements: in editions of Austen novels, 25–27, 39, 97, 104–6, 150; for soap competitions, 100–101; for soaps, 103–6

aesthetic movements (in book cover design): Art Deco, 150; Art Nouveaux 139, 236, 237, 239; Arts and Crafts, 148; Danish Modern, 119; Eastlake, 20, 21, 145, 167, 169, 170, 208, 209, 263n12; psychedelic, 229, 232

Airmont, 85

Airmont Classics, 228

Allen, George, *Pride and Prejudice* as published by, 61, 152–53

Allen, Sue, 258n5

American Library Association, 208

Ames, Mary Frances, 156–57

Appleby & Company, as publisher of University Classics, 77–79, 83

Armed Services Editions (US), 213

Armstrong, Eliza, 72–73

Armstrong, F. C., *Sunny South*, 99

Arts and Crafts movement, 148

association copy, 37

Attar, Karen, 14

Austen, Cassandra, ix, 143, 216

Austen, Charles, 89

Austen, Sir Francis, 89, 90

Austen, Henry, 219

Austen, James, 126

Austen, Jane: clergymen associated with, 126; devotees of, 126–27, 128; religious leanings of, 143–44; and women's rights, 131. *See also* reception and reputation of Austen over time

Austen, Jane, works of: advertisements in editions of, 25–27, 39, 97, 104–6, 150; Bentley's editions of, 9–11, 24, 49, 50, 129; bibliographies of, xii, 13–14, 16–17, 23, 27, 48–49, 66, 95, 131, 132; binge reading of, 155–57, 202; book wrappers as used for, 20, 132, 155, 163, 185, 207; cheap editions of, x–xv, 3, 5, 9–11, 14, 15–17, 19–21, 24, 27, 30, 44–45, 47–49; as "chick lit," 203, 204, 234–35; as collectible commodity, 148; for college students, 226–35; and commercial culture, 94–95, 106, 150–52; cover designs as influenced by movies, 186–91; dime novel editions

of, 44, 67–68, 179; as educational resource, 70–71, 74–79; first editions of, x, xiv, 9–10, 12, 197, 242; foreign editions of, 53, 189–91, 220–25; Henry James on, 11, 12, 29, 203, 235; for juvenile readers, 23–24, 205–7; and libraries' collecting practices, 241–44; Macauley on, 55; marketing of, xv, 12, 23–24, 46–47, 54–55, 80–81, 91–92, 187–91, 205–7, 226–35; mass-market serialization of, 44, 61–65; and men's role in recognizing Austen's literary merit, 202–3; modern editing of, 12–13, 250-51n23; modern rebinding of old editions of, 119–21, 123; as *novelas rosa*, 220–25; paintings used as covers for, 158–60, 162, 164, 192–94; pinking of, 231, 232–35; plates used for printing of, 112–18, 164–80, 265n36; postwar perspective on, 213–20; preservation and conservation of, 119–20; print runs of, 10, 15, 43–44, 56, 160, 170–73; as provided to soldiers, 203; as published in the United States, 12, 65–67, 76–79, 83–85, 158, 161–83, 226; religious dimension in marketing and presentation of, 125–28, 132, 135–36, 146–49, 150; as romances, 207; as school prizes, 113, 138, 139, 236, 237–39; sixpenny editions of, 44, 46, 47, 54, 55–61, 62, 80; and social improvement, 45, 69–74; as Sunday school book prizes, 127, 135–36, 167; threepenny editions of, 68–69; translations of, 53, 189–91, 220–25; Mark Twain on, 29–30; Virginia Woolf on, 36; working-class audiences for, ix, x, xiii, 11, 12, 19, 45, 69–71, 73, 93–94, 140–46, 241; yellowback editions of, 47–52. *See also* gender; paperback editions of Austen's novels; reception and reputation of Austen over time; *and titles of specific works by Austen*

Austen Memorial Trust, 106

Avon (publisher), 85

Baird, Captain Andrew, 202; edition of *Mansfield Park* owned by, 45, 86, 87–88, 89–90, 120; naval career of, 88–89

Balzac, Honoré de, 192

Bantam Classics: paintings used in cover designs for, 191–92

Bardot, Brigitte, 191

Barratt, Thomas, 106

Bautz, Annika, 12, 56

Bayntum, George, 243

Beard, Margaret, 121

Index

Index

Index

Index